anita brenner

anita brenner

A Mind of Her Own

by Susannah Joel Glusker

Foreword by Carlos Monsivais

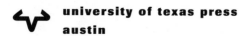

**university of texas press
austin**

Requests for permission to reproduce material from this
work should be sent to Permissions, University of Texas
Press, P.O. Box 7819, Austin, TX 78713-7819.

∞ The paper used in this publication meets the mini-
mum requirements of American National Standard for
Information Sciences—Permanence of Paper for Printed
Library Materials, ANSI Z39.48-1984.

Library of Congress Cataloging-in-Publication Data

Glusker, Susannah Joel.
Anita Brenner : a mind of her own / Susannah Joel
Glusker. —1st ed.
        p.   cm.
Includes numerous quoted passages from Anita Brenner's
diaries.
Includes bibliographical references and index.
ISBN 0-292-72810-7 (cloth : alk. paper)
1. Brenner, Anita, 1905–   . 2. Journalists—Mexico—
Biography. I. Brenner, Anita, 1905–   . II.Title.

PN4973.B74G5 1998
070' .092—dc21
[B]   97-48401

To and from my parents,
David and Anita,
in living and loving memory.

For the time to sow,
the time to reap.
The time to learn,
the time to teach,

From one generation to the other—
with love for David and Michael.

contents

foreword

Anita Brenner and the Mexican Renaissance
by Carlos Monsivais

IN 1923 Anita Brenner returned to Mexico, drawn by the revolutionary effervescence of the time and the echoes of cultural transformation. She was then a young woman of 18, having been born in Aguascalientes in 1905. Anita focused her energies on her studies, and essentially on proving to herself what she already knew: that she was not just another gringa, but a person responding to a rationally explainable deep fascination for a powerful and ancestral art, for a society that revolved around the balance between violence and the process of civilization—a process which endured and was contemplated by the crumbling of structures which had been rigid and constricting. Everything was chaotic, but the chaos was pristine. On the one hand the voracity for absolute power twisted and depressed; on the other hand national survival demanded a freer and more human order. Thus, the struggle to define key words was essential, and human was understood, from the perspective of a group of artists and intellectuals—more influential than they are now credited as having been—as the drive to get rid of traditionalism, to confront rampant racism, and to curb the myth that identified the revolution with machismo. Their agenda did not include much more, but this was of the utmost importance.

In 1923, Mexico was undergoing a merciless struggle between factions, a conflict between groups, regional parties, political bosses, and caudillos.

Yet in Mexico City there were those working on other projects who had drawn different conclusions from the experience. In 1974, Anita Brenner recalled life at that time:

> *It was a great moment in national life, a time when the world was beginning, we were making it in terms of "Here at last, something can be done, and we can do it." We believed that you could actually do something. Revolution was still real in the world.*

As the century comes to an end, we witness a worldwide relentless need to evaluate a hundred years of politics, culture, and society. This assessment or, better stated, this restructuring of canon, through which a nation judges itself, simultaneously becomes an inventory of goods and a revision of society's normative criteria. In the area of culture, this leads to a study of works, authors, and representative figures. Some of the most famous are ratified in the process. In other cases, the last suddenly become the first, and that which was postponed or invisible vigorously joins the mainstream.

Among the most important recoveries are the lives and work of women, forgotten, marginalized, or not even perceived during a century of patriarchal despotism. A very special group rescued is that of exceptional women, who were either born in Mexico or arrived there during the 1920s. The group includes the outstanding Frida Kahlo, Tina Modotti, Maria Izquierdo, Alma Reed, Antonieta Rivas Mercado, Nahui Olin, Lola Alvarez Bravo, Lupe Marin, and, thanks to Susannah Glusker, Anita Brenner.

What do these unique women have in common? First, they shared two spaces of freedom, minimal in terms of what was required, but extraordinary when compared to what had been available in the country until then. Mexico City, with its demographic volume and cultural environment, was the only "free territory" in the country where women, protected by shifting social morals and by the permissiveness afforded to artists, explored behaviors, aesthetic trends, and historic or literary creations. The second space of freedom was the Mexican Revolution itself, which I define not only as the armed uprising overthrowing the dictatorship of Porfirio Diaz (1876–1911) and the subsequent integration and disintegration during the prolonged war between factions, but also as the direct and indirect stimulus of previously inconceivable attitudes and behaviors. The Revolution legitimized those attitudes and behaviors, or at least tolerated them. The Mexican Revolution also generated a field of surprising energies which brought down the barriers of traditionalism. In an unequal fashion, amongst pressures and scandals, that which had been previously unthinkable for women in certain circles emerged: free love, independent criteria, creativity, flights of the imagination, political commitment, freedom of movement, and even bisexuality.

Almost without warning, a group—sector or form of alternative life— determined to distinguish itself, no matter what, from previous generations which had submitted to the strictest and most ridiculous notions of "respectability." In exchange for social ostracism, the women of this bourgeois bohemia were granted the entitlements offered by the political moment— anonymity, and the opportunities awarded by a great city. There was also the prestige of having demolished an artistic past and having experienced the expression of the modern spirit in motion pictures, music, architecture, as well as a glimpse of a sexuality more in tune with the demand for freedom. A new culture and a new set of social morality could be appreciated in apartments, houses, exhibits, concert halls, magazines, books, lectures, animated social gatherings, and squabbles.

In addition to the revolution and the city, these women shared other fortuitous environments:

1. Muralism, or the Mexican School of Painting, determined to be the artistic version of the revolutionary epic, the visual phenomenon that would educate the masses, and allow for a rewriting of history. The challenge of muralism was so monumental that it stimulated the formulation of other specific challenges during the process of setting new "rules of the game" in art: If art was suddenly so different, why wasn't everyday life?

The painter Diego Rivera, rotund, brilliant, and intractable, was at the center of muralism. In a period distinguished by its insolence, Diego is the insolent par excellence, the instigator, the eternal lover, the one who hungers for scandals, the provocateur of behaviors which under other circumstances would have been penalized by ostracism, at the very least. Even among those who despised or criticized him, the debt to Rivera was enormous. In many circles, his example impelled a discovery of the taste for transgression and for vital experimentation. He was especially good at instilling doubt and joy among women in the world of culture and politics. They loved him or they loathed him, but they recognized in him the audacity and courage to successfully thwart prejudice and hate campaigns.

2. The revolutionary nationalism of the twenties was far removed from the eccentricities of folkloric nationalism and chauvinism. This revolutionary nationalism claimed no superiority for Mexico, except that of being the country where the first revolution of the century was fought. (At that time an understandable reason for pride, which today becomes a fact for the Guinness Book of Records.) Nationalism in some forms squanders symbols, native faces, heroes, unforgettable images, and venerable sites. That is why it makes sense to underscore what is truly national, because it encourages the ability of the Mexicans and the pleasure that they take in the great tasks of culture. Ultimately, this nationalism is equivalent to a number of revelations concerning the originality and the value of the overlooked. What was overlooked was there all the time (folk art), or was emerging art. The message was clear: "Certain traditions, works, and authors should be taken into account, not because they are from Mexico, but because they were never taken seriously due to the prejudice against that which is 'made in Mexico.'"

3. Radicalism—that is, the certainty that the proletarian revolution and the struggle against fascism generated the first international mentality in history, the liberation of oppressed nations and sectors, among them women. Radicalism was roused by the rise of fascism throughout the world.

4. The break with traditional art and with the bourgeois view of the artist. Diego Rivera is the antonymous celebrity of this period: he becomes a friend of motion-picture stars and foreign notables, he challenges the right wing, and he is always an extremist because of his communism, his habits, his atheism, and his "promiscuity." And he does not stop producing great quality art which the academic world abhorred. That attitude is even sharper when it comes to women such as Frida Kahlo, Tina Modotti, and Maria Izquierdo.

Anita Brenner tagged the surging mood, the new concurrence of attitudes and works, as the Mexican Renascence, the Mexican Renaissance. The root of the name is obvious: it provides a luxurious comparison of events in a peripheral country with the great moment of Italian art and culture, as well as attributes to art the resurrection of the country. The Mexican Renaissance included both Mexicans and foreigners who came mainly from the United States, Italy, England, and France. Diverse media now looked with awe and admiration at the emerging copper masses within a country previously represented by the Europeanism of its elite. Thus painters, photographers, writers, designers, political organizers, engravers, sculptors, and musicians went to Mexico to discover Pre-Hispanic art (the strongest attraction). They were excited by the strength of muralism's outreach to the community; it communicated with the energy of a country which included a majority of indigenous peoples. In labor, although it was true that opportunities were scarce, stimuli abounded. Mexico, viewed from the perspective of the voyager, was a condensed utopia; some fled from racial intolerance; most took full advantage of the opportunities for adventure and the paradoxes offered by a convulsed and "magic" country—with the magic of the unexpected. They formed a small community in Mexico, presided over by Diego Rivera, and which also included other artists (Jose Clemente Orozco, David Alfaro Siqueiros, Roberto Montenegro, Xavier Guerrero), as well as writers, musicians, anthropologists, and historians.

Who were the foreign women? The Italian, Tina Modotti, tried her luck in Hollywood, became a member of artistic circles in San Francisco, and accompanied Edward Weston, from whom she learned the photographic skills she went on to dominate masterfully. Finally she became so radical as to destroy herself in Stalinism. The American, Alma Reed, arrived in Yucatan in 1921 to observe the revolution, and in Merida met the revolutionary governor Felipe Carrillo Puerto, who courted her; later, in New York, she became the tireless promoter of Jose Clemente Orozco. The Russian painter Angelina Beloff met Rivera in Paris, had a son by him, and, after they had separated, came to Mexico.

The Mexicans were extremely unique. There was Antonieta Rivas Mercado, daughter of an eminent bourgeois architect, Antonio Rivas Mercado. She wanted to live removed from the conventions of her social class; she produced theater; and she fell in love with a homosexual painter, Manuel Rodriguez Lozano. When he did not reciprocate her love, she became the lover of Jose Vasconcelos, the intellectual former secretary of public education and candidate for president of Mexico in 1929. Defeated by the official machine, Vasconcelos went into exile and Antonieta followed him to Paris, where, ill and disillusioned by the barbarian country, her family ties broken, she shot herself in the Cathedral of Notre Dame. Frida Kahlo, wife of Diego Rivera and victim of a traffic accident which would be a life-long source of torture, intuitively created unique work known worldwide, where she represented herself as a tender soul in pain, full of loving passion immersed in a sea of symbols. Maria Izquierdo, a painter, was determined to re-create a province of virgins, saints, children's games, circuses, and brightly colored architectural shapes of villages. Lola Alvarez Bravo, first wife of the great photographer Manuel Alvarez Bravo, worked tirelessly as a photographer, exacting, with a sense of irony, as well as a sense of composition and sensuality. Yet her work was not recognized until late in her life. Nahui Olin (Carmen Mondragon), daughter of a counter-revolutionary general, provoked conservatives, posed nude, and painted.

I dwell on these outstanding women of the period because Anita Brenner in Mexico takes full advantage of and benefits from the atmosphere of opening—defined by the struggle, almost always silent, determined, without much support, by women determined to lived in a different way. There is no doubt that before the explosion of temperaments and attitudes during the twenties, nothing that Frida Kahlo or Tina Modotti did would have been possible; it is also true that a journalist as serious and pugnacious as Anita Brenner would have been inconceivable.

Just as her daughter, Susannah Glusker, describes in this objective and very readable biography, Anita Brenner was part of at least three different communities: that of the Jewish diaspora, emigrants who arrived in Mexico and settled in Aguascalientes; that of the Mexican Revolution and the struggle for the development of civilization; and that of radicalism in the United States. She also participated in the birth of another tradition—that of modern art in Mexico. This ability to integrate cultural, idiomatic, and political legacies allowed her to accept from within and from without the complexity of what is Mexican, as well as the agonizing relationship between art and politics. Both of her classic books, *Idols behind Altars* and *The Wind That Swept Mexico*, reflect a deep understanding of the process of integrating historical periods, religious currents, opposite civilizations, cultures, and ideologies. The syncretism, the melting pot so magnificently described in *Idols behind Altars*, is a plausible way of uniting opposites in a country ruled by the most drastic authoritarianism and intolerance. What Anita observed and transmitted is the result of studying at Columbia University, living as a Jew in anti-Semitic environments, and having been part of the artistic vanguard in Mexico. What is most notable in *Idols behind Altars* is the determination not to accept predominant ideas or prejudices. Brenner limits herself to analyzing the course of artistic and creative currents.

The Revolution burst into the life of the Brenner family, landowners who ended up leaving Mexico for the United States. At school in Texas, Anita recovered, or, better yet, for the first time chose and purged her loyalties to traditions, histories, and behaviors. Citizen of the world, as they used to say, Anita chose her Jewish and Mexican identity. Her identity as a Jew was a very powerful living experience: the legacy of a racial community loyal to its past, with great ability to overcome the yoke of persecutions and victimizations. Her Mexican identity, introduced by her nanny, was acquired over time.

In 1923, Anita faced an astonishing panorama. Never before in the history of the country, or more specifically the city, had women aspired to a life of their own, not one controlled in every detail by a patriarchy. Even when they were still neglected within the public scenario, they were accepted and respected within the social and artistic world. Anita taught and came in contact with the cosmopolitan sector of the capital—the communists, the revolutionaries, the eccentrics. She believed she was in utopia. She wrote her friend Jerry Aron:

> Artists, sculptors, writers, socialists, musicians, poets—intelligentsia, but not the imitation of it that we have, Jerry. They are not a bit startling. That love is free is a matter so accepted that no one ever thinks to bother to state so. They all speak the same language, that is, all understand each other, whether they approve or not. . . . Of course I bask in it. . . . No snobbishness, prejudice, of any sort—racial, monetary, apparent. As to racial, there couldn't be. There are too many shades of skin and flag represented. As to monetary—well, practically all of them have their 'nombramientos' [contracts] which means an hour or two of work at the government schools, which means much politics and a haphazard chance of being paid. Everybody is always borrowing from everybody else which is quite comfortingly like home, you know. But it is so real, so easy, so unconstrained and not at all hectic, that I feel like lifting wings, putting my typewriter under my arm and going to heaven or to some quieter place to achieve a masterpiece.

For a young intelligent woman, repulsed by prejudice, with a sense of irony and a fair dose of frivolity (or the love for fashion), Mexico during the twenties offered a variety of things. The first was the phenomenon of a society with a vocation for rigidity facing the contradiction of introducing modernity in art, architecture, cosmopolitan living, and the initial testimonies of sexuality without guilt feelings. Anita met well-known people, affirmed her confident and critical position, participated in an outstanding support for new Jewish immigrants, expressed her vision of Mexico in publications in the United States, and, throughout it all, refrained from moralist judgments. Her activism had little place for ideological condemnations.

Anita was one of the main people to reveal the changes in a country marked by inequality, violence, the cult of authoritarianism, and the power of art. Like her teacher, Ernest Gruening, Anita wanted to dissolve the racist and paternalistic vision of Mexico and, on her own account, to contribute panoramic visions of art, culture, and history. When a revolutionary spirit decides to discover everything as if it were seen for the first time, there must also be a view of the whole that dissolves the burdens of anecdotes, apocalyptic versions, and racist slanders. Such was the origin of *Idols behind Altars* and *The Wind That Swept Mexico*: the drive to organize information about artistic processes and create a national history. The combination illustrates both the unity and the multiple interests of Anita Brenner: nothing primordial was foreign to her.

In the United States, Anita became part of the elite of radical thinking, and the liberal wing of the Jewish community. However, her radicalism was not an orthodox one; she had a profound dislike of Stalinism, way before the revelations of the Moscow trials. Anita's moral and political position was truly magnificent, ranging from denouncing Stalinist crimes in Spain during the Civil War to her ties with Carlo Tresca, the "pet hate" of the Stalinists. In Spain, Anita denounced the criminal purges of anarcho-syndicalists and Trotskyites. The Cheka intervened with its typical fury, and few protested from the left against the ominous persecution of the dissidents and the perverse lies of the communists. Anita supported the republicans without being a Stalinist accomplice.

In 1974, Anita Brenner died in Mexico in an automobile accident, ending a very full life. Strongly representative of the Mexican Renaissance, Anita was among the best women radicals of her time. Her daughter, Susannah Joel Glusker, pays her fair tribute in this book. On reading these pages, you will encounter a fascinating phase of history, a unique person, and the restless nature of the process of integrating women into the public life of a nation.

anita brenner

prologue

"VAMONOS! LET'S GO," my mother said in the midst of a torrential summer rainstorm.

"Do I have to?"

I knew the answer. My mother, my brother Peter, and I set off to cross Mexico City. Peter was fourteen years old and was going to boarding school in the United States. Before he left, my mother wanted Diego Rivera to paint our portraits together—tugging opposite ends of a rope. The sessions were long. My mother chatted and seemed amused. I hated the ordeal.

Diego Rivera was my mother's friend. He was a huge fat man; his eyes

Diego Rivera in his studio.
Photo by Lola Alvarez Bravo,
courtesy of *Mexico/This Month*
and Center for Creative
Photography, University of
Arizona.

bulged; he was unkempt. His studio was full of huge papier-mâché figures
in the form of skeletons. Pre-Spanish pottery was all over the place, along
with half-finished paintings and masks. It was a mess. I had to sit quietly
and keep my mouth shut while Rivera harassed my brother with verbal
abuse, knowing I would be next. Diego told Peter to keep still, and goaded
him, furious because he had refused to pose nude. When he moved, Diego got worse. I loved visiting Frida Kahlo, his wife, but kept out of the way
of the detestable fat man.

When my brother's side of the portrait was finished, he went off to school.

The chartreuse canvas—of a pale young man with blurry eyes dangling a rope—evoked unpleasant memories for me. I refused to pose, and my side of the portrait was never done. My mother accepted my decision.

Many children of famous people grow up in the shadow of their parents' world. My mother was well-known in Mexico and among New York intellectuals. She wasn't recognized on the street, but her name opened doors. I grew up labeled *"la hijita de Anita"* (Anita's little girl). I eventually accepted that in the eyes of some people I would always be an appendix, not a person in my own right. Fortunately some of my mother's friends accepted me as an independent person, among them Laura Bergquist, Lucienne Bloch, Leonora Carrington, John and Mary Elmendorf, Edmundo Flores, Mathias Goeritz, and Anne and Ben Stephansky. Those relationships made up for the others. I feel privileged to have inherited a wealth of wonderful people who became part of my extended family. The afternoon I spent having tea and walking with Henry Moore in his garden was unforgettable! I was there because I was "Anita's daughter."

The shadow of my mother's name followed me until I went to Israel and lived on a kibbutz. I integrated easily into an Israeli society where few recognized Anita Brenner's name. I was delighted to discover that Margaret Mead's daughter, Mary Catherine Bateson, described a similar experience in her book *With a Daughter's Eye*. It was especially meaningful because Anita Brenner and Margaret Mead were friends and colleagues at Columbia University in New York.

Once past stormy adolescence, I began to recognize the names of people who hung around my house and wondered what it was that my mother had done. What *were* those celebrities doing in our living room? Who *was* Anita Brenner, other than my mother?

It was hard to get her to talk about the past. I got bits and pieces, here and there, especially on long drives to the family farm in Aguascalientes. There was never enough time for stories. Some anecdotes she loved to repeat, such as how she earned a Ph.D. without a B.A. or a master's degree. This was her opportunity to tell the story about receiving her diploma in the mail. Deadpan, she would recite her letter to Columbia University, thanking them for sending the parchment and requesting "instructions for its use," which they had neglected to enclose. I knew she had published her first book, *Idols behind Altars*, when she was twenty-four, before completing her doctoral degree. I knew enough to know that I did not want to

Portrait of Peter Glusker by Diego Rivera. The original plan of a tug-of-war between Peter and Susannah fell apart when Susannah refused to pose. Photo by Michael Nye. With the permission of Dolores Olmedo.

compete. I wanted to be my own person and sought interests that I thought she never touched.

After graduating from Brandeis, where, by the way, I was "Anita Brenner's daughter," I taught Hebrew and Jewish history at an English-speaking conservative synagogue in Mexico City. It gave me my own identity. I was well-known among the parents of my bar mitzvah students. Once, while walking downtown with my mother, we ran into the mother of one of my students. She was a Cuban artist. Introducing us to her friend, she identified me as her son's teacher and Anita as my mother—*not* as Anita Brenner, but simply as my mother. My mother's reaction surprised and delighted me. She ranted and raved about being Anita Brenner, a writer, a well-known person, not just my mother, speeding up her pace as her fury increased. I felt an immense sense of pleasure and relief. I had achieved my goal: an identity of my own in her eyes.

My mother died in an automobile accident on her way to Aguascalientes. On the death certificate, local authorities recorded her vital statistics their way: "Woman of the Christian faith, merchant, who knew how to read and write." In contrast, the articles published by the Mexican and international press reported full details of her life and achievements. My curiosity about Anita Brenner increased as I read the obituaries—not everyone gets a full column in the *New York Times*. Then letters began to arrive asking for information about her and her colleagues from her archives. As I delved into files looking for answers, my interest grew. Her journals from the twenties made delightful reading, even though they were full of unfamiliar names. I decided to pursue my interest within the structure of a doctoral program in history at Union Institute, specifically, "The relationship among intellectuals and artists in Mexico and the United States between 1920 and 1940." That process gave me the context I needed to understand her work.

Anita Brenner, the woman and working journalist, was fascinating. The vast volume of material was overwhelming, but as I read, most of the pieces of the puzzle fell into place. I learned about my mother's life by reading what she wrote and by writing her story to share with others. I am deeply indebted to my grandfather, Isidore Brenner, for financing my project with an unsolicited, unconventional grant. (Income from the sale of family property paid for my degree.)

My quest began with Anita's journals and archives. I transcribed more than 900 pages of journals recorded from November 1925 to June 1930. I found periods without entries, and learned that she kept a journal in high school from an entry in October 1927. Unfortunately I never found those diaries. I did find, however, the manuscript of an autobiographical novel written in 1923. The five years documented in the diaries present a maturing young woman, defining her professional identity as a journalist and earning her Ph.D. in anthropology. The last entry in these journals, on June 29, 1930, was made the day before she married my father, David Glusker. I have quoted passages from the diaries as she recorded them, without correcting typographical errors.

Once the journals were in my computer, I began to read and pull quotes from letters and manuscripts. I drew up a list of people to interview by mail or in person. Their recollections corroborated data in the journals and manuscripts. The only activity that was not documented was Anita's work raising funds for Israel in the late forties. Many interviews could have gone on forever. Among them were those with Lucienne Bloch and Stephen Dimitroff, artists who worked with Diego Rivera. They provided facts and explained nuances that were extremely helpful in deciphering events. Ella Goldberg Wolfe (the Tass correspondent in Mexico in the twenties who is mentioned in the journals) sparkled with information that clarified my mother's political position. Elinor Rice, a novelist who was politically active in New York in the thirties, shared her memories of the New York radicals.

My endeavor has succeeded with the loving help and encouragement of friends, librarians, and scholars. I am especially indebted to Nancy Gurrola and Dan Lund for their supportive suggestions drawn from their reading and rereading of the text. Walter Bradbury, the first to encourage me, put me in contact with John Britton, then working on his book about Carleton Beals. Thomas Walsh helped me identify people mentioned in the journals who overlapped with his research on Katherine Anne Porter.

Cathy Henderson at the Harry Ransom Humanities Research Center provided assistance beyond the call of duty, as did Elena Danielson at the Hoover Institution for War and Peace at Stanford University. The staff at the National Archives in Washington, D.C., was most helpful.

I am also grateful to those who helped through their patience and encouragement, and through reading, fixing computer glitches, finding obscure facts, or delivering mail across the border. Alicia Azuela, Jose Cisneros, Enrique Daltabuit, Mary Elmendorf, Edmundo Flores, Nancy Gurrola, Sylvia Hill, Dan Lund, Cristina Montaño, Lloyd Rootes, John Solberg, Barbara Spring, and Tom Tate contributed as members of my doctoral committee. It was equally important to have the support of Michael and David Page, Sharon Aguilar, Bambi, Jose Bartoli, Herschel Bernard, Mary Katherine Boland, Joe Cantu, Teodoro Cessarman, Alfonso Cruz, Sharon Daltabuit, Betsy Dolard, Yolanda Fandiño, Jorge Franco, Patricia Gass, Alfred Glusker, Barbara Glusker, Peter Glusker, Mathias Goeritz, Teresa Grana, Sam and Gerta Katz, Renee Levine Packard, Janette Lever, Carolyn Lippert, Joanne Lopez, Marcela Medina, Juan Molina, Pedro Neuhaus, William and Pat Niven, Sylvia Pandolfi, Norma Raymond, Ben and Anne Stephansky, Monica Vickers, and Mary Margaret and Mary Jane Yonker. Theresa May encouraged me throughout the process. This book would not have been written without your help. Thank you!

Equally important are those who generously helped me complete the process of including illustrations to complement the text. I wish to acknowledge and thank Lucienne Bloch, the Center for Creative Photography, the Arizona Board of Regents, John Charlot, Zohmah Charlot, Armando Colina, Sita Dimitroff, Drows Studio, Hector Garcia, Jolinda Gomez, the Instituto Nacional de Bellas Artes, Jesus Mancilla, Ana Luna Merida, Michael Nye, Dolores Olmedo, Clemente Orozco, Adriana Siqueiros, and Smith's Studio in San Antonio. Last, but not least, I am grateful for the great job that Lorraine Atherton, Mandy Woods, and Jean Lee Cole did in making this book a reality.

an abbreviated chronology of anita brenner's life

1905   Born August 13 in Aguascalientes, Mexico. Registered as Hanna Brenner.

1910   Mexican Revolution.

1912   Brenner family leaves Aguascalientes for the first time.

1914   Brenner family leaves Aguascalientes a second time.

1916   Brenner family leaves Aguascalientes permanently to settle in San Antonio, Texas. Isidore Brenner and several members of the family returned to Aguascalientes to take care of business. Anita, Dorothy, and Leah lived in Mexico City at different times.

1922   Graduated from Main Avenue High School, San Antonio, in February. Attended Our Lady of the Lake College for one semester.

1923   Attended University of Texas at Austin. Returned to Mexico City in August and attended University of Mexico. Employed by the Presbyterian Mission School for Girls [*Escuela Normal de San Angel*] as an English teacher.

1925   Attended one semester at Columbia University in New York. Returned to Mexico City.

1927   Enrolled at Columbia University in New York in September.

1929   Met future husband, David Glusker. Published *Idols behind Altars.*

1930   Completed doctoral degree at Columbia University. Married David Glusker on June 30. Awarded Guggenheim grant to study Aztec art. Traveled with David to Europe on Guggenheim honeymoon.

1931   Honeymoon continued to Guerrero, Mexico, in January.

1932   Returned to New York City. Published *Your Mexican Holiday.*

1933   Made first trip to Spain.

1935   Traveled to Mexico, updated *Your Mexican Holiday.*

1936   Made second trip to Spain. Went to Mexico on assignment for *Fortune.*

1943   Published *The Wind That Swept Mexico.*

1944   Returned to Mexico with children.

1955   Established *Mexico/This Month.* Cited at the Caribbean Conference of the School of Inter-American Studies, by the University of Florida and the state of Florida for "distinguished services in the field of Inter-American friendship."

1961   Put family farm in Aguascalientes into production.

1974   Killed on December 1 in an automobile accident on her way to Aguascalientes.

introduction

Anita Brenner. Photo by Edward Weston, courtesy of Center for Creative Photography, University of Arizona.

ANITA BRENNER put down the phone and let out a whoop of indignant laughter: "Well, of all the nerve. Awarding an Aztec Eagle to a Mexican!" She was delighted, of course, to have been recognized for more than fifty years of writing about Mexico for an English-speaking audience. She was even more pleased to refuse the Aztec Eagle—the highest award granted by the Mexican government to foreigners—on the grounds that she was Mexican by birth.

Mexico and the United States have been interdependent for many years. The relationship between them exists on two levels: the formal one, involving governments, treaties, boundaries, and trade, and the personal one, between people who walk across the border. Some travel north to the "land of opportunity." Others travel south in search of fortune or simply adventure. People also cross the border, in both directions, to seek a haven from political persecution. They have been traveling back and forth, meeting, marrying, painting, and writing, for centuries. They compare lifestyles and document their reflections in a vast literature about U.S.-Mexico relations.

Anita Brenner's life (1905–1974) is a good example of a woman at home in both countries. She was born in Aguascalientes, Mexico, and educated in Texas and New York. She lived in Aguascalientes until the age of eleven, then in San Antonio, Texas, until the age of eighteen, when she returned to Mexico. After four years in Mexico City, she left for Columbia University in New York in 1927. She remained in New York for seventeen years, returning to Mexico City in 1944. She lived in Mexico until her death in 1974. Her familiarity with both sides of the border gave her the expertise to make Mexico known to an English-speaking public.

It was the Mexican Revolution of 1910 that sent Anita's family north from Aguascalientes to Texas three times, the last, in 1916, permanently. Moving back and forth had a major impact on her life, work, and way of thinking. Throughout her life she identified with the struggle of the Mexican people during the revolution. Born shortly before the revolution began, she witnessed the armed struggle, the dead and wounded, as well as efforts to reconcile differences. She had firsthand experience as a refugee and displaced person. Anita retold the story of that revolution in the two books for which she is best known: *Idols behind Altars* and *The Wind That Swept Mexico*. She included stories she heard from her nanny, Nana Serapia, in both books. *The Wind That Swept Mexico* was the first complete account of the Mexican Revolution in English. It has been reprinted for more than fifty years, and the University of Texas Press currently considers it among its best-sellers. In the following chapters, I have summarized the main issues and events of the revolution simply to provide readers with the context of Anita's life and work.

The Mexican Revolution is said to be among the best-documented conflicts in history. It was covered by independent journalists such as Lincoln Steffens, who sought interviews with powerful leaders who fascinated him on both sides of the border.[1] John Kenneth Turner's interviews were published as *Barbarous Mexico* and are still in print in Spanish.[2] John Reed joined the front lines of battle. William Randolph Hearst sent reporters, photographers, and filmmakers to record real battles.

Hearst also openly distorted information and published forged documents in an effort to rouse anti-Mexican feeling in the United States. He had his own agenda: get Congress to approve sending U.S. troops to Mexico to reinstate the Diaz government and revoke the new constitution. He was determined to retain the land he owned in Mexico at whatever cost.[3] The Hearst reports can be considered forerunners of the U.S. tendency to publish sensationalized negative news about Mexico, now commonly called "Mexico bashing."

Anita Brenner's work is the exact opposite. She presented Mexico in a positive light, stressing the Mexican point of view. She was one of two journalists who consistently depicted Mexico positively in the *New York Times*.[4] Her position was that of an independent liberal who defended workers, the disenfranchised, or those who were treated unjustly, no matter what their origin. She, like many Mexicans, was angered by U.S. attempts to interfere, and she felt that the Mexican people had a right to run their own revolution and country without foreign intervention. In her words: "Due to having been born in Mexico, I have tended to side with the underdog and be sympathetic to rebellion and revolution whose deepest psychological, economic and social roots have always intrigued me and into the research of which I have put much time."[5]

The key to unlocking Anita's life is the title of her column, "A Mind of One's Own," which closely defined her spirit. Anita pursued justice in the biblical sense of the prophet Isaiah, without wrapping herself in a robe of sanctity. She was very much a woman of her times. She could be a relentless, cocky personality with more projects on her desk than she could handle. She was also a charming hostess, with the gift of making irreverent remarks that stopped conversations.

That drive for an independent way of thinking is a major pattern throughout Anita's life. Her earliest published work defended Mexico as an appropriate place for Jewish immigration. She was a self-taught journalist who wrote about Mexico, its art, and its people. She joined radical intellectuals in New York involved in the Spanish Civil War and in issues of political freedom in the thirties. She organized and worked with groups focused on concrete goals, not ideologies. She read Marx but did not identify herself as a Marxist. She helped Trotsky come to Mexico without considering herself a Trotskyite. She shared activities with members of political parties without affiliating with any party herself. Some of her friends reported that the Communist Party would not have her, others that she would not have joined.[6]

Anita's professional life as a journalist was not limited to defending causes. She contributed regularly to the *Brooklyn Daily Eagle* as an art critic, wrote a column in *Mademoiselle* entitled "A Mind of One's Own," and wrote three books about Mexico: *Idols behind Altars, Your Mexican Holiday,* and *The Wind That Swept Mexico.* She also wrote five books for children: *I Want to Fly, The Boy Who Could Do Anything, Dumb Juan and the Bandits, A Hero by Mistake,* and *The Timid Ghost.* In later years she founded, edited, and published an English-language periodical, *Mexico/This Month* (1955–1972). The publication was popular among public-school libraries in the United States and subscribers. The Mexican government purchased a block subscription to send to its embassies and consulates all over the world.

The challenge of analyzing Anita Brenner's life and work called for following and understanding diversity. Her work is multidisciplinarian and multifaceted. Anthropologists see Anita primarily as the author of *Idols behind Altars.* Jewish intellectuals see the person who defended Mexico as a place for immigration and who fought anti-Semitism. Art historians credit her with making the artists of the Mexican Renaissance known in New York. Some Mexicanists see her through her articles in the *New York Times Sunday Magazine.* A few recall her work as an art critic for the *Brooklyn Daily Eagle, The Nation,* or the *New York Times Sunday Magazine.* Veterans of the Spanish Civil War remember her exposé of the underground police group known as Chekas. Mexicophiles remember the seventeen years of *Mexico/This Month.* Most of her work listed in the bibliography is related to Mexico. And yet, for some, Anita is remembered for growing first-rate asparagus.

My mission—to learn just who Anita Brenner was before I knew her as my mother—led me to embark on a long process of asking, reading, listening, and analyzing what I found. I sought to understand her within her context and time, through the issues and controversies in politics, art, and history. The chapters, therefore, are organized around those topics, rather than in strict chronological fashion. I chose to focus on her work from the early twenties through the mid-forties because it was the period when she wrote the most. My information and conclusions are based on personal experience, interviews, her journals, correspondence, and articles. (Her

Anita and Ambassador Hill show off the latest map at a staff celebration. Front, from left to right: Ambassador Hill, unidentified, unidentified, Toss Olson, Muriel Reger, Joanne Lopez Bermudez, Robert La Montagne. Courtesy of *Mexico/This Month*.

archives are a rich resource for future study, such as an analysis of her poetry, the influence of her work on U.S.-Mexican relations, or the contribution of *Mexico/This Month* in promoting Mexico.) Through her writings I came to know her as an intellectual who was affected by the great currents of her time and who contributed as an art communicator, as a critic, as a woman, and as a Jew. The experience was enriching beyond all my expectations.

Her lifestyle as a mother, wife, sister, and daughter is touched on briefly as pieces of the puzzle of her ideas and professional development. They could be subjects for a later book. I hesitated to define her family roles for two reasons: first, because the more I read, the more intrigued I became with her writings, with her ideas; and second, because my mission was to explore, not to define. The material I found indicated an overlap between her professional and personal life. Just as an anthropologist would see her differently from an art historian, I sense that each member of her family would have a different view of her life, work, and role. My goal was to understand her professional accomplishments. The Anita Brenner I knew, and the one I discovered through research, did not match any paradigms described in the literature about mother-daughter relationships.

Anita's passion for Mexico was engraved in her soul. It set a pattern in her writing that paralleled the struggles of the Revolution and of the underdogs she championed. She expressed it in the opening lines of *Your Mexican Holiday:* "Once the dust of Mexico has settled on your heart, you have no rest in any other land. So goes the proverb." Many years later, when she ran a contest in *Mexico/This Month* for the best translation of that proverb, she confessed that she had made it up. Anita carried that same passion into her writing about the Spanish Civil War, and it propelled her beyond writing into concrete action to change what she felt was wrong.

Anita was both a Mexican and American citizen during her lifetime, legally and figuratively. She was born a Mexican and died a Mexican. She contributed to making Mexico known to an English-speaking audience with information that remains timely, more than fifty years later. Unfortunately, the conditions that led to some of her writing have also persisted. Mexico is still largely misunderstood by many people in the United States, and the country is still very much locked in a struggle between the rich and the poor. The same players figure in the ongoing story: large landowners, powerful industrialists, the Church, and those struggling for their rights.

My research yielded an unexpected bonus: a multitude of similarities between Mexico in the twenties and thirties and Mexico today. Again and again, the timeliness, or timelessness, of Anita's writing struck me. This description, written in 1934, is still valid at the end of the century:

> *Today the entire cultural activity of Mexico is colored half by Marxist theory and half by an intense, Indianophile nationalism. [. . .] since a mind in conflict tends to express itself in skepticism, satire and acid laughter, the national temper is full of doubt and anguish overlaid by a certain kind of sardonic humor. Rarely will a Mexican, even talking casually with friends, reveal his real thoughts and feelings. Instead, he will make epigrams, witty caricatures, talk solemn absurdities, smiling a cryptic smile. In everything he says there will be an ample margin of fantastic laughter, directed especially at the grim, the painful and the horrible. [. . .] Deeper under these details of emotion, there is a real fear that Mexico will be swallowed up, peacefully but inevitably conquered, by American capital, and the treatment that he and his countrymen have generally received*

in the United States makes a nightmare of the American in his own land. [. . .] The worker and the peasant feel, with varying emphasis, much the same conflicting emotions.[7]

Anita expressed her concern in a letter to Ernest Gruening in 1961, advising him that she was coming to Washington. She was

interested in getting some close notion of what is happening, and in meeting some of the people who are key to the horrendous horizon in Latin America. I am torn between realizing that one relatively small voice can't do so very much, but on the other hand the scales are so delicately balanced at the moment that if only the wrong things aren't done a lot of danger could be averted, and it seems to me practically an obligation at least to do what I can.[8]

Anita was recognized for her work during her lifetime, and she enjoyed the positive feedback. The first major occasion came with the publication of *Idols behind Altars* (1929). At the same time, she was placed on the Jewish Honor Roll in the *New York Times* along with Waldo Frank, Walter Lippmann, and Ludwig Lewisohn.[9] She was pleased to receive a citation from the University of Florida at Gainesville for outstanding work in American studies in 1955. It gave her an opening to pursue a new edition of *The Wind That Swept Mexico*.[10] Some awards she enjoyed ironically, most notably her refusal of the Aztec Eagle. She did accept a citation as a distinguished tourism pioneer awarded by former president Miguel Aleman, who then headed a special committee to promote foreign tourism (1967).[11]

Sometimes recognition took the form of a generous speaker's fee. Anita kept a busy speaking schedule in the early thirties, promoted by the *Menorah Journal* Speakers Bureau. In Mexico, it was IBM that hired her to speak at several meetings honoring outstanding staff.[12]

Through it all runs her sense of humor. H. Allen Smith tells an illustrative story in *Pig in the Barber Shop*: Anita and David were invited by a wealthy member of the American colony in Mexico City to a "'silly party for people who are silly and we want you to dress up in silly clothes and come on over and do silly things. [. . .] Bring your silly guests with you.'

"So Anita, David, and their friends from New York schemed and decided to hold a picnic in the midst of the 'silly' party. They packed the baskets with meat to cook, flit guns [pesticide sprayers] for the flies and mosquitos, thermos jugs full of coffee and lemonade, and a charcoal brazier.

When they got there they spread out their *petates* (woven palm mats), laid out the food and equipment, built a fire, and kept up loud and jolly conversations. When the other guests approached, they did not respond, after all, they were only 'rude tourists'! Smoke permeated the entire house, and they departed, leaving eggshells, wads of crumpled wax paper, without a proper good-bye. 'The rich lady wanted it silly, she got it silly!'"[13]

Anita's irreverent, outrageous sense of humor often prevailed. In sharing this book with you now, I recognize that sometimes reality sounds silly, sometimes sad, and sometimes serious, but there is no doubt that Anita had "a mind of her own."

one

Nana Serapia

Luz by Diego Rivera. With the permission of Dolores Olmeda.

IT WAS AFTER MIDNIGHT when loud banging on the front door interrupted the Brenner family's sleep. What now? The Revolution brought troops. Aguascalientes changed hands frequently because it is about half-way between El Paso, Texas, and Mexico City. Every change meant issuing new money and requisitioning more goods. Doña Paula, a woman in her mid-thirties, mother of four children, the lady of the house, was wanted at the door.

The family gathered apprehensively in the background and listened. Anita, nine years old, peeked from behind Nana Serapia, her loving source of care and information. They heard soldiers politely requesting a cake. A cake! In the middle of the night in the midst of a revolution? Yes, the colonel was getting married and Doña Paula was the best cook in town. Impossible, Doña Paula replied. There were no eggs, butter, cream, or flour to be had anywhere. How could she produce a wedding cake?

The following night, the scene was repeated, and the soldiers solemnly delivered the ingredients. When the soldiers appeared on the third night, the Brenner family knew they were there to pick up the cake, but no one expected their return a few hours later—with a slice for the family.

When Halley's Comet appeared in 1910, Nana Serapia told Anita that terrible things would happen, and they did. Anita wondered, were these the men that Nana Serapia talked about? Had the farmhands who disap-

"It was a great cake, Doña Paula!" Courtesy of *Mexico/This Month.*

peared to join the Madero forces told them about her mother's cooking? Who were they? Which leader did they follow? Were they the ones who came through town a few weeks ago, leaving dead and wounded all over? Or were they the ones who fled, leaving their pink socks strung up on all the trees in town?

Isidore Brenner, Anita's father, arrived in Aguascalientes at the turn of the century. He had left Goldingen, a small town near Riga, Latvia, in the late 1880s at the age of fifteen. Anita recalled that

> he hated sweatshops, he was an adventurous outdoor guy, accustomed to country living. He didn't come from the usual poverty-stricken Russian village. He settled down in Iowa for a while, ran a store, fell in love and when he was engaged discovered that her parents had taken him for everything he owned, so he took off cross-country with his best friend peddling on bicycles, peddling whatever. They had a marvelous time and landed in El Paso, Texas, which was wild enough at the time. He prospered, he had a tendency to overextend, being optimistic, he took chances, until a depression or bad times hit him and wiped him out.[1]

When Anita was born, Isidore was in the process of making his second fortune of nine. He sought adventure rather than joining the community of Jewish immigrants from Goldingen who lived in Chicago. Isidore and his friend Joseph Fisher married two sisters from their hometown whom they met in Chicago, and set off for Aguascalientes. They were not concerned about getting a leg up from an established Jewish community; rather they wanted to take full advantage of a prosperous cosmopolitan town booming with foreign capital to make their fortunes.[2]

Aguascalientes was a railroad and mining center. American Smelting Company, owned by the Guggenheim brothers, had a major impact on the town. The company built railroads, established flour mills and foundries, and supported a community of foreign employees, including Scottish millers, British railroad experts, and French merchants. The climate was marvelous. "Americans and Germans had a very happy and gay life."[3]

Don Isidoro, as he was known, went to work as a waiter at the *Ojo Caliente* spa, and his wife, Paula, cooked at the restaurant. He went on to become manager, and as they prospered, she stopped working and stayed home with the children. He followed a typical pattern for an immigrant.

Family records show that Isidore bought and sold land, wheeling and dealing, until he owned a large spread, where he farmed, established a dairy, and cultivated orchards.

Isidore was proud to be an active member of the local community. He founded a Lions Club and a Rotarian group and sponsored a baseball team, *Los Tigres de Brenner* (Brenner's Tigers). He was known as a fair but tough man. People in Aguascalientes still tell the story of how he persuaded revolutionary leaders to cease fire for twenty-four hours so cattle killed in the crossfire could be butchered. He filed formal charges and fully expected Pancho Villa to reimburse him for damages.

Mexico was thriving economically and seething socially when Anita was born in 1905. General Porfirio Diaz had been in power for thirty years. He became president in 1877 after a long period of strife between liberals, who favored a U.S.-style republic, and Roman Catholic conservatives, who favored a European-type centralized government. Diaz was a *mestizo* liberal, a follower of Benito Juarez, the first and only full-blooded indigenous president of Mexico. Juarez had instituted the reform laws separating church and state, which were incorporated into the Constitution of 1857 and reaffirmed in the Constitution of 1917. The laws banned the Church from owning land and opened the doors to non–Roman Catholic immigration, allowing American Protestants and Jews, such as the Brenner family, to settle in Mexico. Immigration and foreign investment initiated under Juarez were encouraged by Diaz, who sought to emulate the conditions that had led to economic success in the United States. Groups of Southern Confederates unhappy with the outcome of the Civil War emigrated to Mexico. Other immigrants took advantage of Diaz's offer of awarding one-third of the land measured to the surveyor. Mexico had recently lost more than half of its territory to the United States, and Diaz wanted the sparsely populated northern part of Mexico surveyed and settled. Developers often purchased the remaining two-thirds at a relatively low cost.[4] Still other U.S. citizens went to Mexico within groups of settlers, who leased trains to move entire families and their belongings.

Private citizens such as William Randolph Hearst owned thousands of acres of land in the north of Mexico. British, Dutch, and American oil companies owned land rich in petroleum deposits on the Gulf Coast. Mining concerns invested in infrastructure to exploit Mexico's vast mineral deposits of oil, silver, gold, copper, lead, and mercury. Railroads were built linking Mexico City to the U.S. border.

British, French, and Italian investors joined Americans in business ventures, contributing to the economic boom. Diaz's greatest support came from the bourgeois nouveaux riches of Mexico and from foreigners. Reelected again and again in rigged elections, he gradually shifted his position away from that of his mentor, the liberal Juarez. This may be the root of the story that as time went by, Diaz's skin became lighter, physically with age, cosmetically with powder that streaked with tears, and figuratively with political positions favoring foreigners.

That was the world Anita Brenner was born into and the one she described in 1943 in *The Wind That Swept Mexico*:

> *But the process by which wealth was to sift down, reversing its ancient habits of traveling up, had not yet occurred. Instead, another process had been going on—a process of suction. Through it, the peasants—more than three-fourths of the population—had been stripped of land by laws which gave the* hacendados [large landowners] *more leeway for expansion, more water, more cheap labor. Many village and tribal holdings had been handed over, and most of the public lands, to great concessionaires, often with subsidies. Occupants who resisted being thus reduced to peonage were shanghaied into the army, or sold to work in the tropics, or sent to their graves.*[5]

The people of Mexico were ready for change. Francisco I. Madero, the son and grandson of wealthy landowners in the north, was an idealist, an ascetic, and, some say, a spiritualist. The Ouija board told him he would become president of Mexico, and he did. Madero ran as an opposition candidate in the presidential election of 1910. During the campaign Diaz had him arrested, in spite of the incumbent's protestations that Mexico would have democracy. Madero escaped, traveling disguised as a railroad brakeman to San Antonio, Texas, and began his revolt from there. Porfirio Diaz was elected to his eighth term as president on October 4, 1910. Underground guerrilla squads and spontaneous protests grew throughout Mexico. Madero forces took Ciudad Juarez on May 10, 1911. Diaz resigned and sailed for Europe on a German ship a few weeks later.

Anita was six years old when Madero headed for Mexico City. She remembered hearing about the earthquake that welcomed him to Mexico City. In *The Wind That Swept Mexico*, she recalled her nanny's reaction that the earthquake was a sign that a wicked era was over. Yet, for some, another had just begun.[6]

Powerful economic interests in the United States that had reaped profits under Diaz were alarmed. Henry Lane Wilson, the U.S. ambassador to Mexico, acted on their behalf by spreading rumors to enlist Washington's support for Diaz's forces. Ambassador Wilson supported the overthrow and murder of President Madero in 1913.[7] By then, however, President Taft had only two weeks left in office, and Ambassador Wilson was not able to maneuver U.S. recognition of General Victoriano Huerta, the leader of the pro-Diaz revolt. Ambassador Wilson instigated a full-scale publicity campaign, proclaiming that Mexicans were happy to have their former government restored; in fact, revolutionary leaders around the country were moving to take control. President Woodrow Wilson (no relation to the ambassador) sent his own emissary, Governor John Lind of Minnesota, who decided that if Huerta did not step down, the United States would have to take "less peaceful" measures to get him out. "There were no hurrahs for President Wilson among the revolutionaries. The only thing marked 'Made in the U.S.A.' they wanted was guns with which to do the job on Huerta themselves."[8]

Mexico was in the hands of several revolutionary leaders. One, Venustiano Carranza, a senator in the Diaz regime, controlled the northeast, including its oil fields, access to the U.S. border and weapons, and the railroad to Mexico City. A second, Pancho Villa, a former mule driver and cattle rustler, controlled the northwest, which included Hearst property. A third, Emiliano Zapata, a peasant leader, controlled the state of Morelos and environs southwest of Mexico City. Zapata focused on land distribution. His army took large holdings from wealthy absentee landowners and returned them to the peasants. The fourth leader, Alvaro Obregon, was a mechanic and farmer from Sonora who led Yaqui Indians to battle. Obregon was the only one who considered himself a socialist, planning his campaigns and political strategy with his followers and taking the needs of the labor sector into account for the future.[9]

The troops were identified with minimal uniforms: one group wore magenta socks, another bandannas, or purple shirts. They moved by rail with their families. The women foraged for food, cooked, tended the wounded, and picked up the dead soldiers' rifles to fight. *Tortillas* were made on the way, cooking on tin cans on the top of railroad cars.[10]

Huerta lost control of the country to the revolutionaries. He retained

Indian woman on petate. Photo by Edward Weston or Tina Modotti, courtesy of the Center for Creative Photography, University of Arizona.

Mexico City and a corridor to the port of Veracruz. When the same German ship that had taken Diaz to Europe was sighted on its way to Veracruz, loaded with arms and ammunition for Huerta, the U.S. Navy beat it to the port and occupied the city.[11] Many Mexican revolutionaries were undoubtedly pleased that they would receive weapons and ammunition meant for Huerta. Most, however, were insulted by the U.S. occupation.

> *Hate broke loose in riots everywhere. American flags were torn, stamped in gutters, consulates and business houses were stoned, all fair-skinned, foreign speaking people had to wear identifying lapel-flags—anything but the Stars and Stripes—or be hustled about by mobs. Trainloads of refugees fled to the ports or to the capital, intercepted often by gangs who did with the travelers as they saw fit. There was much distress and humiliation, surprisingly few deaths. But henceforth Americans, who had been the* civis romanus sum *in Diaz days, remained as barely tolerated aliens, each one's position as good only as his neighbor's opinion of him and his records with the people working with him.*[12]

The Brenner family left Aguascalientes three times during the armed struggle of the Mexican Revolution. The first was in 1912, when the U.S. consul warned all foreigners living in Aguascalientes that they were no longer safe in Mexico. Official orders recommended that people leave, and the Brenners left for a few months.

They left again two years later in 1914, when the U.S. Navy took Veracruz and revolutionary leaders gathered for a convention in Aguascalientes. In *The Wind That Swept Mexico*, Anita recalled watching leaders of the Revolution arrive to initiate the peace process: "Villa moved his troops up and turned the convention into a demonstration of strength. The town gaped as the powerful, thick-jawed man with the flicking animal eyes danced his horse up and down the reviewing lines. The famous Dorado cavalry galloped past, and the infantry kicked up the dust, and the Indians stalked solemnly by, and there was an airplane too, that sputtered and roared and circled miraculously in the sky."[13]

Nevertheless, Isidore Brenner brought the family back for another two years, until General Pershing led U.S. troops into Mexico in search of Pancho Villa, who had attacked Columbus, New Mexico. Anita recalled watching her father auction off all the family belongings to raise cash for the trip to the border the last time they left: her mother's dresses, the piano, everything.[14] After 1916, the Brenner family never returned to live in Aguascalientes.

Anita enjoyed telling the story of their dramatic departure. They drove through town to the railroad station waving a large German Imperial flag, which no one recognized. It served as a disguise, identifying the family as something other than U.S. citizens. No one questioned them. Their only luggage was a large picnic basket packed with delicacies, such as smoked ham and goose, bread, and jam. The border could be as far as two days away, under the circumstances.

The older children knew the routine—hit the floor when the shooting starts. If the train is stopped and troops come on board, say nothing; if necessary, speak only in Spanish or German, and hope for the best. They were stopped, but a passenger identified them as Germans and they were allowed to continue. Although they had left Mexico twice before, this time the danger was greater. They were on the train not because of a quiet warning, but because U.S. troops were on Mexican soil once again.

Anita told the story verbally and in writing. She described watching from her window as revolutionary factions struggled for control of the city of

Four of the Brenner children:
Anita, Leah, Milton, and Dorothy

Aguascalientes. She watched *soldaderas* (women who followed the troops) prepare food and nurse the wounded.[15] Anita got firsthand information from Nana Serapia, who knew which farmworkers had joined the revolutionary forces. The family wasn't a good source of information; the adults talked in whispers in order not to alarm the children. Anita bonded with Serapia, her loving nanny and a major influence on her life.

All it took for Anita to get going on childhood memories was one bite of fresh quince. She winced at the tart taste and described the smokehouse, gourmet delicacies, and adventures she and her older brother had trying to unravel the mystery of their identity. They searched and searched for clues, until they found books written in Hebrew and decided they were Hebrews. Anita recorded her fantasies of her people, a "race of princes," in a short story.[16]

The Brenners, like many Jews who emigrated to Mexico in the late nineteenth century, were not part of a community. They were isolated and not outspoken about their religion. They identified themselves simply as "not Roman Catholics."

When Anita was excused from religion class at the private Protestant mission school she attended in Aguascalientes, she knew she was different. She embroidered a complex fantasy about her Hebrew ancestors. She resisted Nana Serapia's invitation to come to mass but heeded her warnings about the devil popping out of the darkest corner in the room. One day, as she waited alone for the others to return from religion class, it happened, just as Nana Serapia said. The devil jumped out from the blackboard. Anita enjoyed embellishing the story, surrounding the blackboard and devil with flames. She would not experience Jewish traditions until the family settled in San Antonio.

Living on the farm in Aguascalientes gave Anita the freedom to roam and organize other children into complicated make-believe games. In an unfinished autobiographical novel, she described an attempt to act on her concern for poor children who wore only shirts. She went to her aunt and got clothes, then gave the bundle to the woman who was toasting peanuts while watching the children play. The woman thanked Anita, offered her some peanuts, and put the bundle aside, as if she had not received anything at all. The ritual had to be followed in order not to lose face; Nana Serapia explained that it wasn't polite to open the package.

Anita also enjoyed talking about riding her circus pony around town. It was great fun, because she never did figure out what the signal was for the pony to sit suddenly, letting her slide onto the ground. That was Aguascalientes.

In Texas, Anita lined up in the school courtyard ready to file into class. The teacher asked her, "What are you?" Anita was taken aback; she hesitated, and then answered proudly, "I am an Israelite." The repercussions were swift and devastating. Up to that point, she had been identified as "the little Mexican girl" and had one friend. She lost that friend as soon as she became "the little Jew girl."

Isidore Brenner was starting over, selling plants that Paula started in tin cans, selling candy and cigarettes, and shining shoes. His ventures would grow into a large nursery and the first major discount store in San Antonio.

Anita was sent to a synagogue, where she discovered that her people were just as foreign to her as those she met at public school. The race of princes she had constructed in Aguascalientes had nothing to do with the Jewish community in San Antonio. How could sparkling plates be unclean? Why did they talk so loudly?

Anita missed Aguascalientes, Nana Serapia, her playmates, and her circus pony. She took refuge in the public library. At Main Avenue High School, she wrote for the school paper and was a star on the debate team, ignor-

Ready for college at Our Lady of
the Lake in San Antonio, Texas.
Drows Studio, San Antonio, Texas.

ing remarks from her Jewish classmates about joining a "Gentile club." Her
unfinished novel records some of them: "I guess you don't know that the
Thessalonians are famous for blackballing all Jews. You're either a genius
or a hypocrite, because you're the first and only Jewish girl who has ever
entered their high and mighty roll-book."[17] Anita weathered the peer pressure and stayed on because she enjoyed the excitement. Her novel included
passages from her contribution to the championship debate, which she
identified as "the divine right of free speech and free press, granted us
by several fathers of our country." The debate was on Darwin's theory of
evolution and whether teachers should be fired for their beliefs or for teaching Darwin. She wrote about feeling alienated socially but respected intellectually; Anita felt like a social outcast. The debate team traveled to
Austin to compete at the state level, and when the others went to church,
Anita walked alone to a field where she cried her heart out. It was hard
not to belong.[18]

The first college Anita attended was Our Lady of the Lake College in
San Antonio, close to home. She treasured the porcelain tray and vase that
she painted while there and had given to her mother. Her memories of
that one semester included being called into the office and severely repri-

Isidore and Paula Brenner. Smith's Studio, San Antonio, Texas.

manded for plagiarism and the grueling experience of trying to prove herself innocent.

Anita stayed in touch with her professor Sister Angelique and passed along the sister's advice: "When you know what you want to say, the story writes itself." Both of Anita's younger sisters (Dorothy and Leah) followed her to Our Lady of the Lake and transmitted regards from Sister Angelique in their letters. When *Idols behind Altars* was published seven years later, in 1929, Anita sent the nun a copy.

Anita left Our Lady of the Lake College for the University of Texas in Austin. She pursued her interest in writing in an English seminar taught by J. Frank Dobie, who felt that her group was unusually talented; everyone went on to publish. Anita corresponded with Dobie until she died. He kept her up to date with news about the others in the group.

Anita was active at the university, working on the school paper, *The Texan,* in addition to her classes. In her autobiographical fiction, she described feeling awkward socially, and she confirmed her mood a few years later in New York (after she had met David, the love of her life) with the following journal entry: "In the daytime entertained Sophie—friend of my youth. She sighed and gurgled when I told her of my status quo. I felt very sheepish because I was always a kind of wall-flower when I knew her, although she says it isn't so. Anyhow I felt like one."[19] The autobiographical novel includes long passages about moving from one rooming house to another when her landlady discovered she was Jewish; Jews were not welcome. At the house that accepted Jews, the girls threw loud parties where Anita again felt like a social misfit.

The novel also includes a mystical experience at a seance on the edge of town in Austin. Anita arrived alone, waited, and joined others communicating with spirits. A voice identified her pain and said, "You do not believe, and your pain is greater because you have no faith. Your heart is rebellious, and you set your own spirit as the only reality." The voice continued, and Anita "took a pencil and wrote 'Today life is terrible for you, you are a rebel in futility. But you shall go to a strange land, and there many men will want you, and you shall see many things that only lofty spirits know. You will reach truth if you have faith, and men will shrink from blood-thirsting giants to amusing giants, and then will be the time for compassion . . . Through your hand you will tell to the world many radiant things, for you have the gift and need only your faith . . . Peace be with you.'"[20] Anita walked out, went home, paid her rent, emptied her bookcase, and packed to leave Austin after attending the University of Texas for only one year.

two

Mexico Welcomes Anita

Diego Rivera by Tina Modotti.

IN THE SUMMER OF 1923 Anita returned to San Antonio and persuaded her father to let her go to school in Mexico City. Isidore Brenner consulted Rabbi Ephraim Frisch, who reassured him that she would be safe. Dr. J. L. Weinberger, who headed the B'nai B'rith office in Mexico City, kept in touch and did not report any problems. The armed struggle between the revolutionary leaders was over. Alvaro Obregon was president. The others—Carranza, Villa, and Zapata—were dead. The University of Mexico was in session.

Anita arrived in Mexico City in September 1923. She was eighteen years old. She would spend the following four years going to school, working to support herself, and launching a career. Her first job was teaching English at the Escuela Normal de San Angel, a Presbyterian mission school. Her wages included room and board. Many patterns for the future were set at this time. Her social life shifted dramatically. She moved from feeling out of place to feeling proud to be part of an exceptional group of people, some of whom would later be considered Mexico's most important artists and intellectuals.

It all came together quickly. Rabbi Frisch's letter of introduction to Weinberger gave Anita her entrée to the world of writers, artists, and intellectuals. Weinberger was married to Frances Toor (also known as Paca, or Panchita), a member of the group of intellectuals.[1]

Visiting with Panchita was great fun, in contrast to the solemn life at the mission school. Frances lived in an apartment overlooking a shared courtyard, and her neighbors were friends and colleagues, including Carleton Beals and Bertram and Ella Wolfe. Frances took Anita to the YMHA (Young Men's Hebrew Association) for tea. Carleton took her dancing to the Salon Mexico, and they all went to Sanborns (the House of Tiles), "the only place where one could get decent coffee" and where people went to rendezvous. Anita bubbled with excitement in a long letter to her friend Jerry Aron in Austin.

> It is quite fashionable, particularly tea-time. But at breakfast it is different. You lounge through your meal, and interesting people whom you know—or ought to know, drop along and talk—oh, books and politics and the theatre and gossip—over the cigarettes and the coffee. There is Goopta, a Hindu revolutionist, who teaches Sanskrit in the University and also teaches in the public schools, who is famous and intriguing and delightful. There are the Wolfes, com-

munists, avid readers, satisfying and quite charming, particularly the lady. There are lots of others—everybody who has any sort of claim to intellectual—ism (?) is sort of loosely bound into it. Artists, sculptors, writers, socialists, musicians, poets—intelligentzia, but not the imitation of it that we have, Jerry. They are not a bit startling. That love is free is a matter so accepted that no one ever thinks to bother to state so. They all speak the same language, that is, all understand each other, whether they approve or not. . . . Of course I bask in it. . . . No snobbishness, prejudice, of any sort— racial, monetary, apparent. As to racial, there couldn't be. There are too many shades of skin and flag represented. As to monetary—well, practically all of them have their "nombramientos" [contracts] which means an hour or two of work at the government schools, which means much politics and a haphazard chance of being paid. Everybody is always borrowing from everybody else which is quite comfortingly like home, you know. But it is so real, so easy, so unconstrained and not at all hectic, that I feel like lifting wings, putting my typewriter under my arm and going to heaven or to some quieter place to achieve a masterpiece.[2]

Anita was swept up into a world of people and ideas. She resigned from her job at the mission school to protest the firing of an American teacher for dating a Mexican; she later fictionalized the event in a short story.[3] The job she found next, with Weinberger at B'nai B'rith, included meeting boats bringing Jewish immigrants to Veracruz; keeping records on the number, occupations, and needs of people who arrived; writing reports; and helping to settle the immigrants into a new culture.[4]

Anita began to write for publication. The earliest articles established her lifelong pattern: writing positively about Mexico. Her first article, "The Jew in Mexico" in *The Nation* in 1924, was a response to U.S. criticism of Mexico as an inappropriate place for Jews to settle. Maurice Hexter, head of the American Jewish Committee, felt that Mexico was not safe, even if the armed conflict of the 1910 Revolution was over. He considered Mexico too culturally dissimilar from European culture. Jews needed to leave Europe, and the United States had closed its doors to new immigration. Anita felt that Mexico *was* appropriate. She wrote a series of articles for the *Jewish Morning Journal*, sent numerous dispatches to the *Jewish Telegraphic Agency*, and sent fiction to the *Menorah Journal*. In them all, she presented

Anita Brenner by Jean Charlot. Photo by Bob Schalkwijk. With the permission of Dorothy Zohmah Charlot.

Mexico enthusiastically, describing the lifestyle of European Jews and the community's social and cultural events as well as economic activities, effectively countering the bad press Mexico had received in the States.[5] Anita identified as a Jew. She did not practice her religion within an orthodox tradition, nor did she join a Zionist movement, but she was committed, as an independent journalist, to helping Jews escape pogroms in Europe and to defending Mexico.

Mexico City bustled with activity in 1923. The revolution was over, but the country was far from settled. The armed struggle was limited to occa-

sional guerrilla skirmishes. Obregon's government was working on imple-
menting the Constitution of 1917. *Agraristas* (federal armed forces) broke
up large landholdings and distributed land to peasants.

Jose Vasconcelos, the first to occupy the newly created Ministry of Education, sent out cadres of teachers to remote rural areas to educate people.
European values were out, pre-Spanish traditions were revalued, and gradually the skin color of leaders shifted to darker Indian shades. Mexican and
foreign intellectuals and artists plunged into the process. Easel art for private enjoyment was out; murals in public buildings for everyone to see were
the order of the day. Vasconcelos commissioned murals and paid artists by
the square meter, matching masons' wages. Free *Aire Libre* (open-air) art
schools were established to introduce children, young people, and adults
to the world of the arts. Enterprising teachers created self-supporting cooperative "miracle schools" where students lived and worked.[6] The atmosphere was optimistic.

The forces of change attracted foreign intellectuals and artists to participate in rebuilding Mexico. They believed in building a society that
valued indigenous peoples and provided a better life for the poor. Ernest
Gruening, a journalist who would become Alaska's first governor and senator, contributed by writing favorable articles and facilitating contacts.[7]
Carleton Beals taught English and wrote about Mexico from a radical point
of view.[8] Their articles and lectures in the United States made Mexico's
revolutionary reality available to English-speaking intellectuals. The information was part of the complex diplomatic relationship between Mexico
and the United States. Beals, for example, created a major stir when he
presented documentation showing that Ambassador Wilson had received
a regular check from the dictator Porfirio Diaz at a Carnegie conference
in Washington, D.C.

Gruening, Beals, and other independent liberal journalists, such as
Herbert Croly, wrote about the social changes taking place in Mexico.[9] Anita
joined them in writing about the cultural upheaval of the time, later termed
the Mexican Renaissance. She developed as a professional journalist among
friends and colleagues focused on common goals. In 1974 she reminisced:
"It was a great moment in national life [. . .] a time when the world was
beginning [. . .] we were making it in terms of 'Here at last, something
can be done, and we can do it.' [. . .] you believed that you could actually
do something. Revolution was still real in the world."[10]

The Mexican Revolution of 1910 brought about profound changes in

Senator Ernest Gruening visits Mexico in the late 1950s. From left to right, front: Joe Glazer, Anita Brenner, Dorothy and Ernest Gruening. Courtesy of *Mexico/This Month.*

the way Mexicans looked at themselves. After forty years of being ruled by Porfirio Diaz, Mexicans turned to revalue their own people, their indigenous roots, art, and customs. One of the most important people in this endeavor was Manuel Gamio, a self-educated anthropologist.[11] With Zelia Nuttal's recommendation, he studied under Franz Boas at Columbia University in New York. He returned to Mexico to make major contributions to the *indigenista* effort, studying and revaluing the indigenous peoples of Mexico. Anita worked with Gamio as a translator and editor. She was deeply influenced by him and helped him disseminate his ideas.

The artistic aspect of the Mexican Renaissance was an integral part of *indigenismo.* In 1928 Anita wrote:

> *Mexico, so long camouflaged in bandits, oil, and revolution, emerges*
> *with an art which is not only a significant expression of itself, but*
> *a rebirth of genuine American art, representative ultimately, not only*
> *of the purple-mountained home of artists south of the Rio Grande,*
> *but of the entire Western Continent. [. . .] long before the Chris-*
> *tian Era, nowhere as in Mexico is art so intimately linked with daily*

> *life. To paint, to carve, to make some thing of color and form—this is a Mexican need. Thinking and feeling in color and form, it is only through the things that Mexico makes that she can be clearly seen.* [12]

Anita agreed fully with the view that art is for everyone, not solely for the wealthy few who can afford to purchase it. Another issue at the time was whether art was valuable for its own sake or whether art should be part of the Revolution, from the people and for the people. Anita emphasized the argument in many of the articles she wrote about art. In 1936 she linked Lucienne Bloch's art in New York with the Mexican Renaissance:

> *It is the first crystallization, in our idiom, of a new approach to painting that stems from the Mexican revolutionary muralists. Article one of this philosophy is that the artist is a creature of social responsibilities. Article two says that, since the artist is as a rule economically one of the masses, his work should be directed toward their enjoyment, instruction, and benefit. This implies a repudiation of the intellectual and social snobbery that determines much of the appearance and character of "modernist" work. In fact it requires a complete revision of the function of the artist that it brings about a new school and new style [sic]: as also new forms, and even new instruments and new techniques and materials. One of the first results of this revolution in attitude was the revival of mural painting. As the Mexicans argued, the decoration of public buildings is one obvious way to make art for the benefit and enjoyment of the masses.* [13]

Anita and her friends focused on a revolution that would change the lives of people, meaning indigenous peasants, farmers, and workers—in short, the underdog. Anita was aware that under the new agrarian law, her father, as an absentee landowner, was vulnerable to losing his land. Although Anita's letters and journals did not mention discussing the issue with her father, she probably knew about the measures he took to protect his property. [14]

Not all large landowners accepted land reform. The landed gentry lived in Mexico City alongside the officials administering the reforms. They visited socially. Anita was friendly with Rica Suttor, a woman married to a large landowner. She visited their hacienda and recorded a detailed account of their situation in her journal. She took them to see and buy artists' work to help artists survive. The tone of her comments about the Suttors was nonjudgmental; she listened and learned, expressing a desire to incorporate their story into a novel at a future date.

Anita was aware of the murder of Rosalie Evans, an American woman who came to Mexico to claim and work her land.[15] Although the events were widely covered by the press, Anita did not record the story in her journals. Edward Weston, who kept a journal at the same time, does not mention it either. Neither Anita nor Weston used their journals as a historical chronicle of the period. Both report events en passant, as if there had been a heavy rainstorm, but they had not gotten wet. Anita's diaries provide more information about episodes in the love life of artists and intellectuals than about dramatic political events, unless members of her group were involved.[16]

The contradiction of a young woman contributing to building a new society while her family faced the possibility of losing their land did not seem to concern Anita. Many artists and intellectuals (such as Diego Rivera, Jose Clemente Orozco, David Alfaro Siqueiros, Antonieta Rivas Mercado, and the Marin and Asunsulo families) were in a similar situation. They too belonged to educated upper- and middle-class families. Anita knew of the problems of the wealthy, but that did not temper her enthusiasm for creating a new society. At the same time, she never took an antagonistic attitude toward her family and other landowners. Political affiliations of individual artists and writers are also not mentioned by Anita or Edward Weston in their diaries. Tina Modotti, who lived with Weston at the time, was a communist sympathizer and later a party member. Bertram Wolfe was busy organizing the Mexican Communist Party. Ella Wolfe was the correspondent for Tass. Anita was, however, aware, critical, and open to the situation. The critical Anita recorded: "Mrs. Goldschmidt had an automobile accident—went to see her today—a too comfortable environment for people so flaming with love of the masses—How can they love what they do not know? And if they know, how can they prefer the bourgeois setting with lace covers and rose bedroom lights and overdressed people in to tea?"[17] The open young woman wrote:

> Last night Diego [Rivera] came over to get an article typed—"Art of the Revolution" and derived therefrom a long and thrilling conversation, in the course of which I became actively a revolutionist, puesto que [since] you are either for or against and passivity

is negation. . . . Incidentally, perspective of Diego as a really great man. Painting for ideological repercussion. Playing admittedly with several different hands, because "revolution" is now only a skirmish, or guerrilla warfare, and you use guerrilla tactics. At midnight I was exalted and felt converted, Diego taking it for granted—conversationally, at least—that I had been so long ago. The value of the conversion for me is that it gives reason to work. Otherwise, work— for what? Personal gain? It vanishes with existing. Good of humanity? A silly sort of vanity. But for the sake of nothing at all and only because it means functioning this is a road that is possible.[18]

She was willing to explore and was open to ideas without seeming to need a partisan identification. Her focus was on the struggle to improve the living conditions of the poor, an interest that had been a part of her life since her childhood in Aguascalientes.

Two of Anita's most important role models were Carleton Beals and Ernest Gruening. Beals was the first writer to read her work and help her publish. Gruening became her mentor while she worked for him as a research assistant. She did the legwork for him in Mexico during all of 1926 and the first part of 1927. She clipped newspapers, read, scouted political information from records at the Department of Interior, took him to meet

"Panchita and me on the Tepozteco, after a four-hour climb. We are standing where the blood and the *mole* used to flow and we can see all over Mexico . . ."

"For my
roommate . . ."

key figures in the artistic world, wrote up the information, and found answers to questions he sent from New York. Throughout her journals of this
period, she was busy with Gruening's work, which paid well and gave her
a chance to learn about Mexico under the supervision of a seasoned liberal journalist. When Gruening was in Mexico, she took him to see idols
in churches or to listen to the revolutionary ballads of Concha Michel.
Sometimes she enjoyed the work; other times she felt uncomfortable, as
if she was intruding on people's privacy during interviews.

Gruening also gave Anita her introduction to left-wing intellectuals from
the United States. Although it was a time of witch hunts in the States, Anita
did not mention the persona-non-grata labels, nor was she reticent about
meeting so-called Bolsheviks, followers of the Russian Revolution, socialists, union organizers, and pacifists. Dinner parties at Gruening's home in
Mexico where she met John Dos Passos and Charles Erwin, among others, were highlights in her journals. Her entries record talk about the "good
old socialist" days, and although she seemed out of her depth, she soaked
up the flavor of New York radicals.

Anita did not focus her life exclusively on work and intellectual pursuits during this period (1923 to 1927). She bloomed as a woman as well as a professional, recording her social life and feelings with great gusto. In her journal, Anita noted the mood that Jean Charlot (1898–1979) captured after a farewell party for Tina Modotti's sister in 1925. Charlot, an important member of the group, was a French painter of Mexican ancestry who came to Mexico in 1920. He is credited with reviving the fresco mural technique as well as the art of woodcuts.

> Charlot remarks that we "the familia" had become so accustomed to certain things and certain attitudes—simplicity and naivete, a certain infantile directness, that we can hardly conceive of how strange we must look to outsiders. We even have our own language and certainly an etiquette that is original and unmatched. One does what one wants but who wants to promenade in fashion? Etc. etc. Scorn for sentimentals, humanitarians, reformers, moralists, and authorities & or not exactly scorn but surprise at their stupidity. It is indeed comfortable in spite of the undeniable family atmosphere.[19]

Anita recorded parties, flirtations, conquests, and disappointments in search of her "Prince Charming." Jean Charlot was one of several suitors who pursued her at the time. The men in Anita's life included colleagues, friends, and employers. She charmed employers, sometimes noting the difficulty of keeping them at arm's length. She was seductive and flirtatious with boyfriends. She shared thoughts and ideas with colleagues, such as Beals, listening to him read his work and vice versa. Friends were companions for movies and dances. Anecdotes about a new man on the horizon were woven into a narrative about progress on her book, alongside her amused reactions to the paternal protectiveness some men displayed. On one occasion Salvador Novo told her politely that her petticoat was showing.[20] Another time, Frank Tannenbaum took her aside "seriously and said 'I wish you wouldn't use rouge. Not that it is very much, but I don't like it on you. You don't need it. You are a beautiful girl without it and it makes you ugly.' So I said I wouldn't."[21]

Anita began exercising a talent for hosting wonderful parties at this time.[22] Part of her secret was the guest list. One friend remarked that she seemed to "set a stage, and let things happen." She had such a good time that it was contagious. She didn't limit her entertaining to intellectuals and artists. While I was growing up, and especially during my high school years, our house was known as the great party place. The food was good and plentiful, the punch spiked, the music loud, and my mother would step in, teach us how to Charleston, and then discreetly disappear.

The journals often describe a full day of work, topped off by a large bash. Weston recorded menus in his journal; Anita recorded people and anecdotes. The first party Anita mentioned took place in April 1926 and included many members of the *"familia"*:

> *our first semi-pretentious affair. Wild success. House full of notables, smoking and talking. All elements, from art to Charleston. Diego, sitting in one corner and explaining Mexico to admiring gringos, [. . .] Frank Tannenbaum in one corner, paternally blessing our heads; [. . .] Salvador Novo examining books and offering awkward gallantries. I think he is reforming his preferences and now has more use for females, among them Lupe* [Marin], *beautiful in electric blue with her dark skin and large deep gray eyes and black close cropped hair. [. . .] Carlos Merida & Mrs., Carleton* [Beals], *Frances* [Toor], *[. . .] Edward* [Weston], *[. . .] Tatanacho, . . . Tamayo, lean, sensual, shy; many others, some of whom I don't know and many whom I don't remember."*[23]

Anita related to different people within the group in different ways, establishing her personal identity as a prominent individual within this odd extended family.

three

A *Family of Artists and Intellectuals*

Orozco, *Horrores*. A "Horror of the Revolution" for the "apocryphal foreign buyer."
Photo by Michael Nye. Courtesy of Fundación José Clemente Orozco.

THE NAMES of the people in Anita's extended family read like a biographical dictionary of intellectuals and artists active in Mexico in the twenties. The nature of the group comes through clearly in the journals: they were friends who helped one another, clashed occasionally over politics or relationships, collaborated and competed while struggling to survive economically. Conflicts did not usually last long. For instance, Diego Rivera went after anyone with talent who might steal a bit of his limelight. He was intensely jealous and protective about walls for murals and was particularly competitive with Jose Clemente Orozco. In 1925 Anita noted that "after sneering at each other so publicly and so constantly [they] are now inseparable."[1]

The diaries record conflicts, incidents, feelings, moods and introspection, as well as philosophical issues. The entries from the early period (1925–1927) depict a woman maturing intellectually, earning a living, concerned with her future, with boyfriends, clothes, and her family in Texas. The people she saw most frequently were artists, especially Jean Charlot, with whom she established a close relationship. He was the person mentioned most often in her journals, until 1929, when she met David Glusker. Diego Rivera, Jose Clemente Orozco, and Francisco Goitia followed in terms of the number of references. Today, Rivera, Orozco, and Siqueiros are recognized as the three most important muralists of the Mexican Renaissance. Anita considered Francisco Goitia (1882–1960) one of the best artists of the period. He survived his hermit-like existence with a salary from the Ministry of Education and was not part of the *"familia."*

There are patterns in the way Anita recorded seeing people. Paul O'Higgins, Abel Plenn, and someone named Miguel usually visited her together. O'Higgins (1904–1983) was an American artist who worked with Diego Rivera on his murals at that time. He remained in Mexico, became a Mexican citizen, and changed his name from "Paul" to "Pablo." Abel Plenn was Anita's first cousin, son of Isidore Brenner's sister, Dora. He lived and worked in Mexico City and later in Spain, where he wrote *Wind in the Olive Trees*. Miguel may have been Miguel Fonserrada, an artist who later moved to Tijuana. Siqueiros and Roberto Reyes Perez, who lived in Guadalajara and worked on murals together, mentioned each other in their letters. Carlos Merida (1901–1984), a Guatemalan artist who settled in Mexico, always called alone, as did Goitia, Orozco, and Rufino Tamayo. Tamayo (1899–1991) was younger than most of the others in the group of Mexican artists. He was independent because he did not believe in the revolutionary-art philosophy espoused by Rivera and others. He was an "art for art's sake" artist.

The best-known minor figures included Nahui Olin (1893–1978), a painter and poet who lived with Dr. Atl during this period and whose real name was Carmen Mondragon; Xavier Guerrero (1896–1973), a painter and a militant member of the Communist Party, who lived with Tina Modotti before he left for Moscow in the late twenties; and Maximo Pacheco, a young assistant to Diego Rivera, who grew in the arts and was given his own walls for murals.

The character and quality of her relationships varied, yet the role Anita played with each one was similar. She was highly supportive of their work, wrote about them, defended them when they were attacked unfairly, and promoted their work. She brought clients and bought work for "clients" she invented when she knew the artist was broke and would not have sold her their work. Anita was especially protective of Goitia, who lived a secluded life in Xochimilco. Some of the people she took to see him were possible clients; others, such as Edward Weston and Tina Modotti, photographed his work. When Anita discovered that he had been left out of an art exhibition planned for New York, she lobbied for him until he was included. Clearly, she was not a mere young girl following the masters; she conducted herself as a full-fledged member of the family. In 1927 she felt privileged and impressed with herself for belonging: "I am so proud when I think that the best of Mexico is my closest friends . . . Orozco, Charlot, Goitia."[2]

There is no indication that she was pursuing a personal agenda or remuneration. On the contrary, she borrowed money to help those in need. She typed articles for Rivera, wrote with Charlot, encouraged Orozco to paint for foreign buyers she had invented, and collected money to deliver to Goitia.

The community was small, and not all the people mentioned in the journals became well known. They socialized regularly and, thanks to the manageable size of Mexico City at that time, bumped into one another on the street, at Sanborns, or at the movies. Anita belonged to the gang but did not join any of the formal organizations, such as the Syndicate of Painters and Sculptors or the Communist Party.[3]

The journals from the days of Anita's first meetings with Rivera, Orozco, and Charlot are lost. Diego Rivera was undoubtedly the best known and most controversial of the group. Seemingly oblivious to his comings and goings with the Communist Party, Anita wrote about him, partied with him, planned to write a ballet with him, fought with him when he lifted Orozco's ideas, borrowed his coat for a street costume party, and ate regularly at his home. Diego was sensitive to her writing and jealous of her attention. An ongoing point of contention between them was Anita's protection of artists that Diego would have liked to annihilate, such as Charlot, Orozco, and Goitia. Although she thought highly of Rivera's work, her journals reflect her aversion to his deviousness and pursuit of publicity. The entry from April 10, 1926, reflects her position:

Carlos Merida in this morning. Tells me Diego proposed to remove frescos [by] *Charlot and Amado* [de la Cueva] *from Secretaria. He can't now, I don't think, though he might. Carlos says Diego said he'd offer them six hundred pesos,* por cuenta de la Secretaria [to be paid by the Ministry of Education], *and if they accepted the frescos would be removed, and if they didn't they would be removed also. Diego wants the whole thing to himself, of course, but wants the removal with publicity of approval, in order to establish a precedent and thereby safeguard his own stuff. He is a magnificent* sin-verguenza [scoundrel]. *Siq*[ueiros] *says he has changed a lot. In Paris, under the auspices of Angelina Beloff he was "todo un maestro"* [a grand master]. *Love of art and also principles. Amado said, tho, that under Lupe* [Marin, Rivera's current wife] *he has changed completely. Influence of the woman being one favorite theme of his. This money making stunt that sometimes seems the pivot of Diego's actions* [is] *due* [to] *Lupe. But Diego told me once that he didn't want to leave Mexico for the States or anywhere else. Says he has only at the most ten years left in which to paint and wants to paint what he knows and what he is, not go out and multiply hats for Lupe. It seems to me, however, that he has descended since the Preparatoria* [murals at the preparatory school]. *From the splendor of geometry to the sentiment of the picturesque Cubism to Gauguin.*[4]

Anita respected and admired Rivera's work but did not hesitate to exercise her own critical thinking, combined with a healthy sense of humor. For example, around the same time in 1926 she wrote:

paid a visit to the Universal and got for my pains "Orteguita's" book of interviews with contemporaries. Diego, Atl (who has a vacilada [humorous irreverent statement or event] *in today's papers about a* compañia planificadora [planning company], *which "con muchos millones de pesos"* [with many millions of pesos] *will entirely remake Mexico City). If Orteguita had only followed Diego's interview up with another one also* [with] *Diego, of entirely contrary opinions and pronouncements, the portrait would have been admirable, instead of only excellent.*[5]

The running commentary in the journals included observations of the similarities between Rivera's work and that of other artists. She drew a parallel between Pieter Brueghel's *Autumn* and Diego's *Chapingo*, which "has several leaves taken out of the same book."[6] The most amusing anecdotes describe Diego's outrageous behavior, and scandalous events he concocted to attract publicity, such as chasing Nacho Asunsulo all over town and reporting him to the police, and shooting bullets into the air to clear traffic jams in Coyoacan. He was a popular tourist attraction for admiring American women, who liked to watch him work. Lupe generated her own scandals on a regular basis, either with loud fights with Diego or by verbally attacking women when she felt that they were getting too close to him. Anita recorded the time when Diego beat Concha Michel, who just happened to be visiting when Diego and Lupe had one of their spectacular rows.[7] Nonetheless, the period recorded in the journals was the beginning of a lifelong friendship between Anita, Diego, and Lupe.

Jose Clemente Orozco was a highly sensitive, volatile person. His relationship with Anita, as well as others, was a stormy one. He was most angry when he decided that Anita *too* had fallen under Diego's influence. She noted that Orozco usually overreacted whenever Diego was written about in the press.

Anita learned about Mexico from Orozco, wrote about him, and planned a book of the cartoons he published in *L'A.B.C.*[8] Unlike Rivera, Orozco did not know how to promote himself. He was not good at pursuing contracts or clients. He needed help, which Anita and others provided discreetly because of his sensitivity. That intervention was decisive at particularly difficult periods for Orozco. The first time seems to have been when Orozco's contract with the Ministry of Education was canceled, even though Rivera and others were still working.[9] Orozco's reaction was predictable: rage and depression. Anita and Carleton Beals went to work with a letter campaign. She visited key people, insisting that Orozco be reinstated.

To get him working again, she fabricated an absent foreign client interested in buying Orozco's scenes from the Revolution. Early in September 1926, she "saw Orozco. He says that he is all mixed up and does not know what's what in painting. He has been quite ill. He suffers a great deal. But he is doing beautiful work. I am going to get him to do a group of 'revolution' drawings. Pretext of customer—he wouldn't sell them to me."[10] Orozco came by regularly to bring Anita work for the "client." The series, known as *Los Horrores* [the horrors], is now considered to be among his best work. In 1928 he repeated the series in New York as lithographs to generate badly

Jose Clemente Orozco on the scaffold at the National Preparatory School.
Photo by Tina Modotti.

needed income. "In the afternoon Clemente came, and we talked and had
dinner. He has a beautifully sound eventual solution (mass production, wide
distribution) via lithograph and engravings, but in the meantime his problem is serious. This evening F. Paine came over and I made this clear and
set the burden (or attempted to) on her shoulders, since she is incorporated to 'foment Mexican art' (Rockefeller, 15,000 [dollars])."[11]

The journals also convey Orozco's off-center sense of humor. Orozco
teased Anita about her Jewishness, usually by slipping anti-Semitic cartoons

Portrait of my ancestors. Photo by Leonardo Singer. Published in *Mexico/This Month*. Courtesy of Clemente Orozco Foundation.

under her door. She understood that this was his way of telling her that he was angry but wanted to make peace. She laughed, identified the Jews in the cartoon as her "great-grandfather," and hung them on the wall.

Orozco went to New York in 1927, shortly after Anita enrolled at Columbia University. For the first few months he had a hard time adapting and earning a living. Anita showed his work to many people, among them Alma Reed, John Reed's sister.[12] At that time, Alma Reed was prominent in a salon sponsored by Madame Siquilianos, a wealthy patron of the arts. The group met regularly to listen to Kahlil Gibran read his poetry or to study Greek and Hindu philosophy.

Alma adopted Orozco, promoted his work, and negotiated several mural contracts for him in the United States. She wrote books about him and established the Delphic Studios art gallery, to sell his work. Anita described his reaction to success:

> *Clemente is acting very funnily these triumphing days. He's written up in every art page and always gets a very respectful break from the critics, and is altogether "made." The first result was to make*

him "delirio de grandeza" [delusions of grandeur] *with money; (like me) and to make him a fairly frequent guest at parties; and to take away his sense of* vacilada *in all the neo-Greek and Buddha business at Alma's; and to make him proclaim that now he was never going to be shown in a group with Mexicans again. There was a show planned at Harvard, which I was asked to help arrange; and also I wanted to put out a special edition of my book with an Orozco lith; on both these points we had a very insane interview. We got all tangled up in each other's emotions and now he doesn't speak to me and magnificently send me* "regalos" [gifts] *of drawings and such things (through Alma). [. . .] he is ill, afraid, angry, and feeling persecuted. He is getting the money he needs from Weyhe* [Gallery], *for lithographs; but he fears I don't know what . . . everything[, . . .] that they will assassinate him and steal his children, for example, on account of some drawings, or because of such a thing as the caption of a fresco in* Folkways—Malinche and Cortes, y el indio debajo sus pies [and the Indian under their feet]—*which he and A.R.* [Alma Reed] *impute to the machinations of Diego* [Rivera]. *But it is on record that Clemente himself gave that explanation or name of the panel; and anyhow the panel is obviously that.*[13]

Orozco resented being "identified with the movement," when he considered it Diego Rivera's invention. Throughout the journals, Anita recorded his attempts to counter Rivera's activity. When Diego was interviewed by the press and presented his biography, Orozco wrote a parody of his own autobiography, full of exaggerations and lies, snickering at Rivera. Orozco's attitude toward publicity was mixed; he recognized that he needed exposure but hated to admit that he would stoop to Rivera's methods to sell his work. Ever protective, admiring, and despairing, Anita cherished Orozco and his work and dealt with his mood swings with a great sense of humor. Their relationship wound through a rocky road with ups and downs, but survived.[14]

Anita's relationship with David Alfaro Siqueiros was less intense. She met him in 1926 in Guadalajara, where he lived. Siqueiros wavered between working as an artist and organizing labor unions. Anita saw him less frequently and mentioned him in her journals when they met or when she received a letter from him. They met when Anita visited Guadalajara and went to see the murals that he and Amado de la Cueva did there. In her journal, she praised the style of the murals as artistically and ideologically unique and unified and noted her first impressions of Siqueiros:

> *His eyes are green. He has an almost over-sensual face and talks too well to record. Far more educated and informed than I had imagined, and far less picturesque. I revise the theory (that all geniuses are insane). He has an amazing quality of youth, and a bicycle. [. . .] He is an artist of strength and I think, genius. But he is absorbed in this business of the social struggle. He can't remain out of it, he says, to be an amusement maker for the rich. He can't devote himself to it and also paint—there is too much to do and too few people to do it. He stresses the economic end of revolution and holds from the political, a sweet, amiable, curly sort of youth.[15]*

She embroidered on her description in a separate entry on the same date:

> *Siqueiros, I met for the first time. He has a sensitive, strange face, glittering eyes, clear, greenish blue, or hazel, hard and weird. Fine nose, small sensual mouth. Black, dark brown hair, slight cushion under chin, beautiful queer hands* [sketch in journal], *and great charm. He is much interested in the social end of the question. Organized the house and sign painters into a syndicate, writes articles, & so forth. He has flashes of real genius. Strong, and seemingly— this contrary to legend—quite balanced.*
>
> *All the work being done here is interesting & within the thing made by him & Amado. Intellectually, that is, plastical intellect, Amado is not to be* despreciated [mixture of English and Spanish, meaning "not to be disregarded"].

The journals describe several amusing adventures of his. Once, he decided to hoist a red flag on the church steeple and was caught. Brazenly he brought the flag down, masquerading as the hero who removed the flag. Another time he confronted a priest who caught him stealing ex-votos [small artistic panels offered to a Virgin or a saint in appreciation of a miracle]. The priest pulled a gun, and Siqueiros was saved by the authorities.[16]

Anita met with Siqueiros when he came through New York. She helped him sell his work when he needed money and mentioned borrowing to help him. She and Charlot also located a plate so he could etch a lithograph and raise funds to return to Mexico. She broke with him in the late

Three from Guadalajara:
David Alfaro Siqueiros,
Amado de la Cueva, and
Carlos Orozco Romero.

thirties after he participated in the machine-gunning of Leon Trotsky's house in Mexico City. She found his actions intolerable, especially since Trotsky's five-year-old grandson was wounded.

Jean Charlot, a French artist of Mexican ancestry, arrived in Mexico in 1921 with his widowed mother and was instrumental in Anita's shift from feeling like a wallflower to being impressed with herself as a member of the group. After serving with the French Army in World War I, he worked with woodcuts and graphics in Europe before coming to Mexico and joining the revolutionary artists' group. He had known Diego Rivera in Paris, and they reconnected in Mexico. Charlot made major contributions to the community of artists, expressing their revolutionary ideals. By combining information from a mason who knew the fresco murals at the pyramids of Teotihuacan outside Mexico City with information from chemistry and art history textbooks, he discovered the secret of fresco murals. He was the first to try the technique, on his mural *La Conquista de Tenochtitlan* [The Conquest of Tenochtitlan] at the National Preparatory School in 1922. He was also responsible for reviving woodcut and lithograph techniques in Mexico. His work in Europe translated easily to Mexico, where Jose Guadalupe Posada, an engraver who published penny sheets before and during the Revolution, was a master of the art. The methods allowed artists to illustrate the poster wall journals such as *El Machete* by lowering production costs.

Charlot began writing about Mexican art in the early twenties. His articles and books made a significant contribution to the field of Mexican art history. He can be considered a participant-observer who described the Mexican Renaissance and its major figures.[17]

Charlot was a loving, jealous friend and Anita's constant companion in Mexico City. Their relationship existed within a complicated aura of conflicting tenderness, sexual frustration, and professional cooperation. They wrote articles together; in one publication she would take credit, in another he did.[18] They collaborated, and she wrote with him, about him, and for him. Anita translated and edited his work. He helped her revise hers. They worked together on a book about Jose Guadalupe Posada which they did not finish. Hovering over their stormy relationship was the large nebulous cloud of religion. The conflict stirred in Anita the need to define her identity as a Jew in contrast to Charlot's Catholicism. In 1928 she observed him kneeling in front of a confessional in "thorough, complete submission and absorption."[19] When he mentioned the possibility of joining a religious order, she noted the moment in her journal.[20] The clearest expression of the conflict is a poem that she wrote and rewrote over a period of years. One version of it marked a radical change in their relationship, in 1929, when Anita met and decided to marry her Prince Charming, David Glusker. She sent it in a letter to David to soothe his jealousy toward Charlot.

> *Jean has been tutor and guardian and teacher and keeper, and chaperon and father confessor and collaborator and companion, [. . .] I wrote a rather incoherent poem that describes it.*

ALEPH BETH
For Hart Crane, after reading *The Bridge*.

*My father's cows were branded with a twisted mark
An Aleph Beth.*

I knew as little as the cows
The meaning of that brand.
And now I know as much.

For branded on my brow and flank
God's mark, with numb and mighty thongs
Bound me from sagging pleasantly among
The postures of complacent songs,
Bound me from flight to the bright
Deserts of achievement, where rot the renegades.
Come to Communion, my foster-mother said
A brown mysterious woman, smelling of smoke and maize.
Her skin as taut as a flushed plum
Her body like a tree
Her head a lava flow with inset turquoise eyes
Her breath a whistling water-reed
Her heart a complex pendulum of drums at night
And Death the inner palm of her right hand.
You shall have, she said,
Breakfast: chocolate and fruit and bread,
A new dress, and a veil upon your head.
The sunlit prairies of belonging

Stretched for my Yiddish feet
And I, who hardly knew how to link word to word,
Let my soul speak. I think,
My mother would not like it,
I heard it say.
And God's mark tingles underneath
My grey and meager skirt.
Then one day, one year, and
Many hundred miles away,
I heard something again.
. . . .

There was a man who loved me
And he was not a Jew
but this was nineteen hundred and twenty four
Not fourteen ninety two.
Come to Communion, this lover said

Your soul will find a place.
but the Aleph Beth on my flank and brow
Sniggered in my face.
My feet they have no resting place
My head it has no home
My house is bare of family trees
And no roots bind my bones.
My breasts are full of bitter milk
And wordless is my tongue
My flanks are wide and my belly full
Of the circumcised in my womb.
Daughter of two countries, citizen of none
A Zion star your only firmament
Get to your Synagogue.[21]

Charlot married Zohmah Day in 1933. He and Anita continued to collaborate and correspond until her death in 1974.

four

Sisters, Foes, and Role Models

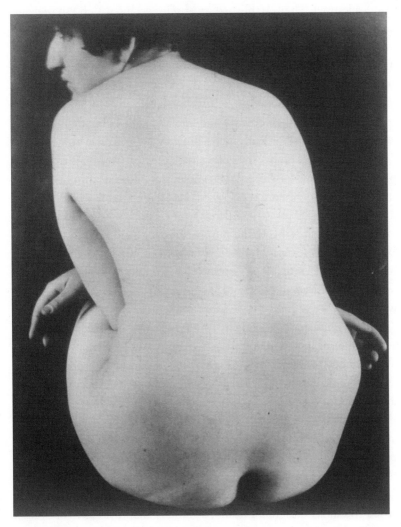

Anita Brenner nude. Photo by Edward Weston. Courtesy of Center for
Creative Photography, University of Arizona.

THE WOMEN of the informal extended family whom Anita mentioned most in her journals were her roommate Lucy Perry Knox, Lupe Marin, Nahui Olin, Concha Michel, Tina Modotti, Frances Toor, and Ella Goldberg.[1] They were Anita's contemporaries and friends during the early twenties in Mexico City. Frida Kahlo was the exception because Anita was living in New York when Frida and Diego married. Anita met her after she stopped keeping a journal. They established a warm friendship which I shared and that is documented by letters and interviews. This community of women shared concerns and interests similar to those expressed by women in the sixties and the nineties. Their style, however, was different. Anita and her sisters were de facto feminists. They didn't form or join feminist organizations, nor did they demonstrate with suffragettes active in Mexico. Most were independent in their creative and intellectual lives but highly dependent in their relationships with men.

The bibliography on the lives of women artists in Mexico is expanding rapidly as consciousness of women's issues grows and the outstanding women of the twenties are recognized. Hayden Herrera's book on Frida Kahlo was among the first to popularize women artists in Mexico. The most popular women, in terms of the number of books, are Frida Kahlo, Tina Modotti, Antonieta Rivas Mercado, and Nahui Olin. Frida and Tina are full-blown legends, mysterious, controversial, wild. More than twenty books have been published on Frida and at least seven on Tina. Nahui is on her way, with two books and a movie script in the works.

Tina was photographed nude by Edward Weston, her lover at the time. The daughter of Italian anarchists, she had worked as a movie actress in Hollywood before coming to Mexico to bury her husband, Robo. Arriving in San Francisco at the age of sixteen, she worked in a department store until she married and left for Los Angeles. She met Edward Weston in California, while she was still married. After her husband died, she persuaded Weston to follow her to Mexico. They lived together, and Tina learned the art of photography from Weston.

Nahui Olin, whose real name was Carmen Mondragon, was the daughter of a famous general in Porfirio Diaz's army, part of the aristocracy. She married Manuel Rodriguez Lozano, a military man who later became a painter, and went to live in Europe. The marriage ended in 1922 when, driven by passion, she scandalized society in Mexico City by living with Gerardo Murillo, a painter and volcanologist. He had taken the name "Dr. Atl," which in Nahuatl means "Water is the source of all life," and renamed her "Nahui Olin," which means "renovating movement of the heavens in the cosmos." Both artists were known by their adopted names. She painted, wrote poetry, and frequently modeled for photographers and painters.

Concha Michel, a singer who wrote her own ballads about the revolution and surrounding events, held a special attraction for Anita, although Anita never mentioned working with her, just visiting and sharing views. Concha was proud of her trip to seventeen countries on $17. She scandalized the Communist Party, which called for her expulsion when she accepted an invitation to sing for John D. Rockefeller at his home in New York.[2] Lola Alvarez Bravo (1907–1993), a Mexican woman of the thirties, became a photographer while married to Manuel Alvarez Bravo. After they separated she worked on her own quite successfully.[3]

There were no rules. Most of the women married at least once. Some divorced their first husbands and married a second time. A minority—including Lola Alvarez Bravo, Frances Toor, and Anita—did not remarry or establish a long-term intimate relationship. Lupe Marin married Jorge Cuesta after her divorce from Diego Rivera.[4] Nahui Olin lived with Dr. Atl and others after separating from Manuel Rodriguez Lozano. Tina Modotti was widowed from her first husband, Robo (Roubaix de l'Abrie Richey), and lived with Edward Weston, Xavier Guerrero, Julio Mella, and Victor Vidalli.

Four prominent members of the group posed nude. Tina Modotti posed for Edward Weston while living with him. Rivera painted Tina and his wife Lupe nude in his murals at the chapel of the Chapingo agriculture school. Nahui Olin exhibited and published her own nude portraits in a major daily in Mexico City, scandalizing her family and prominent members of the prerevolution establishment.[5] Anita's pear-shaped posterior, a well-known Weston image, hangs in the Museum of Modern Art in New York without an identification of the model.[6]

Nonetheless, Anita seems to have been more conservative in her sexuality than some of her sisters. Although other women of her time were openly breaking with their mothers' traditions, Anita did not. At the age of 20, she was concerned with sexuality: "It is too bad to get the habit of craving mental stimulus—and I can't work unless I am constantly in touch with working people. I lose the stimulus. It becomes pointless to expend energy. So [is] it a vice, an organic necessity, or a sentimental delusion with me? But I do get close to things and balanced and a thrill out of it— without it I should be always perceptibly restless—Essentially a sexual thing,

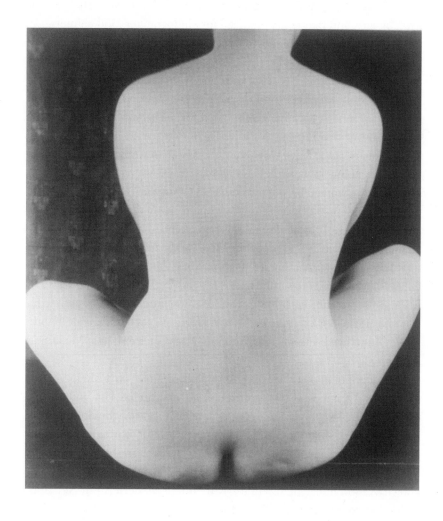

Photos by Edward Weston. Courtesy of Center for Creative Photography,
University of Arizona.

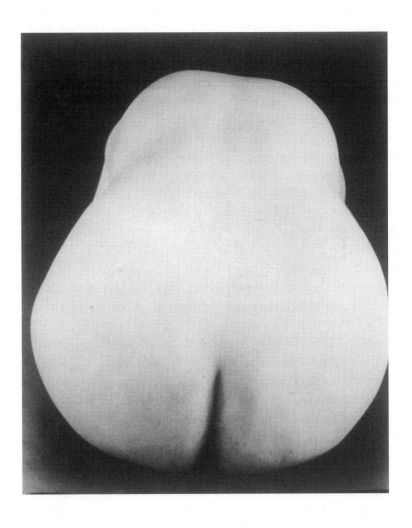

I imagine—would marriage blot me—creatively speaking?"[7] The subject came up again a few weeks later, after exploring the issues with Nahui Olin. "Nahui was here all afternoon. Spoke of many things. Most especially of Atl, & painted her relations with him as such a dark diabolical thing that it made my spine shiver and gave me an idea for the 'Sihuatl' story I based on her."[8] Ultimately, Anita recorded moods and feelings but not details of her intimacy. She did not share living quarters before marriage and yet was not judgmental about women who did.

On the other hand, Anita was not at all conservative in her intellectual and professional activities. She came from a family of working women. Paula Brenner, her mother, worked as a seamstress in the sweatshops of Chicago.[9] Anita did not question working to earn a living or to build a professional career. In contrast to the experience of many women of my generation, I was encouraged by my mother to follow my interests. It was not a question of studying while I looked for a husband, but neither was marriage denigrated; it was assumed to parallel the pursuit of a career.

There don't seem to be maternity patterns in the lives of women of the twenties and thirties. Frida Kahlo was obsessed with having Diego's child. For Tina Modotti it was not an issue; it is said she could not have children. Nahui Olin lost an infant that some say was smothered, others that it was heaved down from a loft.[10] Before she married, Anita was afraid of the overwhelming responsibility of having children and questioned motherhood, but ultimately changed her mind.[11]

Anita's biting sense of humor bloomed when she wrote about the women of the group. Patterns of relationships, roles, and shared interests emerge from the journals, including conflicts with Tina and a vague competitive battle with Frances Toor.

Anita plotted, shared, and quarreled with Lucy Knox, her roommate. Lucy came from Texas and worked for *Revista de Revistas,* a publication in Mexico City. They traveled together to Yucatan to visit Jean Charlot and Lowell Houser.[12] Both women earned doctoral degrees in anthropology at Columbia University in New York at the same time. Anita sent Lucy Knox a copy of *Idols behind Altars* when it was published, but the journals do not mention her after Anita graduated from Columbia.[13] There is little information in the correspondence: one letter mentions Lucy's leaving Hawaii to go to Peking, another her recovery from tuberculosis. Before that, they shared adventures, threw parties, squabbled on occasion, and schemed like sisters. The following entry is a good example of the tone. It was written in early 1926.

> *At seven o'clock Lucy kicked the chair.*
> *At ten o'clock Lucy kicked the chair.*
> *At one o'clock Lucy kicked the chair.*
> *At three o'clock Lucy kicked the chair.*
> *At five o'clock Lucy kicked the chair.*
> *At seven o'clock Lucy kicked the chair.*
> *At nine o'clock Lucy kicked the chair.*
>
>   *I don't complain but it's getting monotonous, as Mark Twain says.*
> *She is writing her cock-eyed* Revista *Section:* Lenguage familiar [fam-
> ily language]. *My helpful suggestions are not received cordially. But*
> *what could be more "familiar" than:* "Yo soy su padre, hijo de la
> tiznada" [I am your father, you son of a so and so] *and* "chingue
> su madre, sobrino del diablo" [screw your mother, nephew of the
> devil] *etc? However, I always go unappreciated.* [. . .] *Lucy and I*
> *agree that the irregular life is much more pleasant—We like nerves.*
> *Determined to die at the age of 55, at the latest—And double the*
> *whistles and bells right now.*[14]

Lupe Marin came from a large family in Guadalajara. Her sisters (Carmen, Maria, Victoria, Isabel) and brother (Federico) were part of the gang. Lupe, then married to Diego Rivera, was known for her explosive fits of jealous temper, which often resulted in diatribal letters to women she felt were getting too close to Diego. She was also known for her talent as a first-rate seamstress; she made Diego's clothes until he died. Anita experienced both sides of Lupe. Tina, Anita, and Nahui each got one of the famous "insulting notes" telling the recipient never to darken her door. Before the letter and later, once the incident blew over, Anita would go to Diego and Lupe's house to sew and stay for a bite to eat.

Anita was sensitive and careful about her appearance, her image, and the impression she made on others. The story of a young woman exploring her femininity unfolds on the pages of her journal in 1925.

> *Dress is a big part of satisfaction with me, for I think purely aes-*
> *thetic and sexual—not social—reasons. Social gestures and their*
> *mimicry embarrass me. My foot, unable to be shod properly* [she

had a broken ankle], *and the sudden change in mode without a corresponding change in pocket, depress me.* [. . .] *Austerity and sobriety I find beautiful, but after all I am twenty and feminine, and I like dainty buckles and perfumes and exaggerated effects and the feel of silk and many mirrors and powders wherewith to dress—* [. . . .] *Above all, flowers when I want them and tea with expensive cigarettes—Fripperies and frivolities—details that add much to one's self respect and sharpen, I think already too keen sensibility—Oh well. Vegetables and carfare are quite within reach.*[15]

Anita's interest in clothes and her appearance lasted throughout her life. She made some of her own clothes in the twenties and years later, occasionally, for me. There are numerous entries about errands to dressmakers and delight with packages her mother sent from home, for instance, "Another important incident of the day was the arrival of two pairs of shoes and some hose from home. One pair is of soft kid, of almost rose-color or peach—the shoes. They are lovely. The other is black. I have a nice mamma."[16] A friend in New York remembered fondly the hours they enjoyed shopping together for the right outfit for a presentation or lecture.[17]

Although the journals present a very full life, Anita made time for breaks, as she noted in 1927 while doing research at the dusty archives of the Ministry of Interior.

Really the day is not long enough for me! [. . .] *I took a half hour off to have my nails manicured because at lunch time I saw some hard faced females and they were so masculine that I became uneasy—what with my haircut and my black velvet jacket and my mannish shirt and black bow tie and soft felt hat—yet Lucy assures me that no matter what, I never look anything but feminine, and what with my changed ideas about boyishness I am glad. A boyish silhouette is all right, but if it stops at silhouette; mannerisms and spirit are another thing. Anyway, American women haven't a hint of coquetry. It is either clothes rack stuff or the intellect or another very crude thing way beyond coquetry.*[18]

Anita took mischievous pleasure in posing as a mysterious woman. She was smooth as she combined political awareness with charm to dodge unwanted advances. She was also subtle, using womanly wiles to evoke mystique and proceed as an independent woman. She called it the technique of "Mexi-

In a velvet blazer. Photo by Tina Modotti.

canisms," which meant evasions, changes of subject, and claims of igno-
rance. She associated her way of dressing with her success in invoking
mystery to achieve her goals. She was researching the politics of Mexico
at the Ministry of Interior, and through some fluke in the bureaucracy, she
ended up among the confidential files. She had read about half of the states
of Mexico when she was caught:

I was called up before the head of the Gobernacion [Ministry of Interior] *secret service and he very kindly but firmly announced that it was all a mistake and I couldn't use the records of his dep.* [department] *any more.* [. . .] *he called me in and said: "We don't want you to have any politics in what you publish.." I pointed out to him that I was doing the political history of the states and could scarcely be expected to do that without having any politics in it, to which he replied: "Well, those things are there for the government to base its policy on. But we don't want it known that when a man is elected legally and legitimately, we put in another one because the first one may not be 'conveniente'* [convenient] *to us."* [. . .] *I replied that it was more to the central gov. credit that it did do so, and he said, "Yes, but they will say that we have no democracy! You know all foreigners are our enemies . . ." He asked me what I was, and I replied that I was born in Mexico. He then said: "Well, do you know I thought you were French. You walk like a French woman, and you have the 'gracia'* [charm] *of those women.." To which I replied that we should not take anything away from the Mexican women to give it to the French, and he was proceeding to more personal and paternal investigation, such as did I live alone and independent and did my parents approve and I replied that the reason I loved Mexico was because many things exist in common and that one was that we both had to struggle for our independence . . . etc. etc. I then asked him just what he did not want put in, and he said, "Well you know the idea. We don't want anything that will* denigrar [denigrate] *Mexico published. Bring me a copy of what you do." To which I replied that since it was all incoherent notes,* [could] *I bring him a resume, and he said no, he wanted to see what I was going to publish, to which I returned vague Mexicanisms and the conversation returned to the secular note so I made an exit. I feel watched and expect the house to be searched for what I have, any minute, which is very exciting but not entirely probable.*[19]

Anita did not limit her identity as a woman to appearances and wiles. She identified and bonded politically with and was sympathetic to her sisters. She explored political and feminist issues with Concha Michel in 1926, shortly after interviewing her for Ernest Gruening. After a long conversa-

Concha Michel. Photo by Tina Modotti.

tion with Concha, Anita tagged her "a very noble person."[20] "Lunch here with Concha Michel and the Lopez family. We have the same philosophy, which recognizes sex as the key to things, and the plane upon which woman's position is placed—and should be. Since it is creative energy, it is for her to direct it. To be able to do so, she herself must be physically pure. Therefore vegetarianism. This, not suffrage, woman's right."[21] A few days later, Anita referred to a conversation with Concha Michel and Elena Torres, cofounder of the Feminist Party in Mexico (1921) and a member of the Communist Party who worked with Felipe Carrillo Puerto, about the importance of the home as the key to reform. Anita reported in the journal that "Concha said they [the conversation] came to nothing, however, because Elena with the 'right' theory has no conception of practice."[22]

Anita's relationship with Tina Modotti was professional and social. They met regularly because they were part of the same group. Tina is first mentioned in the journals shortly after Anita and Edward Weston signed a book contract with the National University. The content of the entry refers to work, but the tone reflects animosity: "Finished and sent my 'Investigation is Being Conducted' to the *Dial,* I like that story for the *vacilada* [humor] of it, and for its bizarre parentage. [. . .] Only reason I'd like it accepted would be to hear T.M.'s [Tina Modotti's] comment—She deems my work 'perfect publicity'—and me a vulgar scheming adventuress. Feel important, having an enemy."[23] Anita alludes to the possible sources of the problem in other entries. First, Tina was reported to have said that Anita "was nothing" but that Jean Charlot had created an idealized version. Anita confessed in 1927 that she "never bothered to talk to Tina seriously" or take an interest in her, which could have influenced their relationship.[24]

Tina is mentioned frequently throughout the period when Anita and Weston worked on the book. Tina traveled with Weston and his son and collaborated with Weston on the project. Weston returned to California shortly after they finished. Tina moved in with the artist Xavier Guerrero and worked as a professional photographer. Anita turned to Tina when she needed photographs. The two women worked together, with and without animosity. In February 1927 Anita wrote:

> It is now eleven o'clock and I have just finished the newspaper clipping. I suspect G. [Gruening] will overwork me for a while but I don't mind in the least. I want to justify my existence, curiously enough, and wonder which of us all has the right way of doing so. Would a life like Tina's diffusing much joy by numerous cohabitations, and also by fine prints, weigh with Goitia's chastity, and Michael Angelo's? Or am I off in supposing that there is any connection?[25]

Anita recorded incidents when Tina was pleasant to her or produced a great photograph. She was aware of conflicted and complicated relationships, and a few days later she wrote out an analytical table identifying people who were "Actively Friends; Actively Enemies; and Actively Both." Tina was in the last column. There were more friends than foes, so Anita drew her conclusions on the bottom line: "Satisfactory—So what the devil do I care?"[26]

One concern was that Tina seemed to question her capability. It struck Anita like a sharp point. In May 1927 she wrote:

> *In certain intellectual—high powered circles it is said that Jean* [Charlot] *does my writing for me. Also that this is obvious since I don't know anything about painting. This can be directly traced to* el *Gran Don* [Great Lord] *Diego* [Rivera]. *Madame Charlot* [Jean's mother] *may have had something to do with it, since she believes it. Diego is of course deliberate about it. Tina is his little megaphone, I scarcely doubt.*[27]

Anita recognized the "undercurrents of hostility" when she owed Tina money, "and she probably needs it."[28] She also seethed with anger and felt betrayed when Tina sold photographs that Anita had commissioned for future articles. The images were published in *Studio* magazine, and in October 1927 Anita reacted with: "They are unethical, some of these 'comrades.'"[29]

Anita's acid tongue and sense of humor put their ambivalent feelings into perspective. While in New York, Anita recorded an amusing Tina anecdote in January 1929:

> *I find in the Mexican papers the murder of the young Cuban student leader and communist, Julio Antonio Mella (real name Nicanor McPartland, illegitimate child) love of Tina, murdered apparently and most probably by agents of Cuba government for being too noisy about social revolution. Tina's private life dragged through the press; Diego* [Rivera] *to her defense; all the labor organizations protest; Mex. president shifts chief of police to try to better find murderer (as former chief was trying to tangle Tina up and make it look crimen passionnel); and since Tina had just broken with Xavier, to turn to Mella, what of her now? The logical thing would next be Atl, then psychoanalysis, then spiritualism, then the Church penance and absolution; or the attitude would be logical not for her sins but because of her temperament.*[30]

Anita was supportive of Tina in her predicament. "Tina behaved with great poise and dignity throughout [. . .] One answer to the innumerable and stupid questions is Tina in a coup . . . Asked if she loved Xavier, or if she had loved him greatly, she said: 'Sí, en su época' [Yes, at the time]."[31]

Tina remained "a friend and an enemy." She took beautiful photographs of Anita's mother and sisters and sent the negatives of the photographs Anita

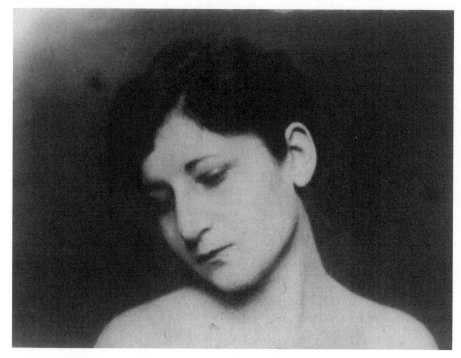

Dorothy Brenner, Anita's sister. Photo by Tina Modotti.

ordered. They were in contact and corresponded occasionally. Anita sent her a copy of *Idols behind Altars* and visited with her in Germany in 1930.

Frances Toor, an American Jewish woman, came to Mexico in 1922 with her husband, Dr. Weinberger. She was known as *Paca* or *Panchita*, the diminutive of "Francisca," her name in Spanish. Paca taught foreigners at the National University's summer school. She founded and edited *Mexican Folkways* (1924–1933), a bilingual magazine about Mexican culture supported by grants from the Ministry of Education.

Frances and Anita were close when Anita first arrived in Mexico. Anita wrote for *Mexican Folkways* in 1924 and 1925 and praised the publication in her own writings. She said the magazine "is noted for its charm, its accuracy, its simplicity, sincerity and beauty. [. . . It] helps to make Mexico, always tragically in need of explanation, sympathetically clear."[32] There are few clues in Anita's archive that explain the development and later deterioration of the relationship between the two women. Anita was initially enthusiastic about writing for *Mexican Folkways*. She often met with Frances for lunch or tea to plan future issues. The first indication of trouble is a

Paula Brenner, Anita's mother. Photo by Tina Modotti.

change of tone in the journal, when Paca is referred to as Frances and not Panchita. The problem seems to concern a special issue of *Mexican Folkways* that Jean Charlot was preparing about the engraver Jose Guadalupe Posada. Anita discussed working on a book about the artist with Jean, and they visited the Vanegas Arroyo family to locate the *clichés* (printing blocks) that Posada used for his cartoons. Anita, however, was not included in the Posada project for *Mexican Folkways*. After Jean went to Yucatan with Sylvanus Morley, an American archaeologist working in Yucatan in the twenties, Anita was responsible for recovering the Posada material. In October 1926, Anita acknowledged the conflict clearly in this journal entry describing a meeting with Frances on the street: "and as usual, [Frances] acted like a venomous female and would not let me have the cliche which cost Jean and me so much 'work.' Considers herself our victim. Done her the wrong to help her. Oh, well. Pobre de Frances, as Gamio says."[33] The relationship degenerated over the Posada printing block. Rumors circulated and accusations flew. Anita became critical of *Mexican Folkways* and placed Frances within the "Actively Enemy" column on her relationship balance sheet.[34] The last mention of Frances in the journal is on Saturday, August 26, 1927. Anita was on her way to New York, tired and nervous but confident about her accomplishments. She and Jean had just finished working on her book. "Jean tells me that in the music number of the Folkways Frances has written an article with whole sentences swiped from my 'Mexican Ballads'[. . . .] But I don't mind. After all it shows it made an impression. And I am beginning to believe in collective art. Goitia does not sign his pictures. If people remember it is not the name."[35]

Anita came in contact with an impressive roster of women: socialists, communists, poets, some of whom were also wives. Rose Rolland, Miguel Covarrubias's American wife, appeared sporadically at parties. Mona Sala, the wife of the painter Rafael Sala, loved to tell about recommending Anita for the job with Gruening. The journal mentions dropping in at Antonieta Rivas Mercado's salon. Anita met the poet Idulla Prunell in Guadalajara, where Idulla lived and published a small poetry magazine. Occasionally Anita would visit Diego Rivera's sister, a folk healer who cleansed evil spirits in times of distress for Anita and other members of the group.

One of the most unusual of these women was Rica Suttor, the wife of a wealthy landowner. Their rapport was strictly personal. Journal entries do not address the contrast between their lives or bring up Anita's idealism about revolution in art. The relationship with Suttor gave Anita a close view of life on the Suttor family's hacienda named *La Llave* [the key] and the opportunity to witness negotiations between them and the *agrarista* leader redistributing land. Anita was totally nonjudgmental; her entries in her journal do not mention her own background as the daughter of a landowner in Aguascalientes or Rosalie Evans's fruitless struggle.[36]

Anita listened to Suttor's marital problems, went horseback riding, and met for tea. She took the Suttors to see Goitia, and they bought one of his paintings. Sometimes there were other members of the landed gentry present. Amelita Martinez del Rio, Dolores del Rio's sister-in-law, was among them. She opened a chic tearoom, where guests included President Calles's secretary, Cholita. Anita's description of meeting Amelita at Rica Suttor's, in May 1927, reeks with distilled disdain. "Amelia Martinez del Rio, daughter of the aristocracy, and so much aware of her money and position that she accentuates it by taking liberties with it, such as having a flair for art and archaeology, and the freaks that she comes into contact therewith. She is little, emaciated almost, and corn-colored. Silky and feverish. Talks a lot, somewhat affected, somewhat intelligent, not very educated."[37]

The contrast between the political positions of Rica Suttor and people such as Tina Modotti did not seem to concern Anita. She focused on Rica as a character in a novel late in August 1927: "I am very anxious to write the La Llave episode into something good . . . All the elements are there . . . The landowner, the peasants, the legend, even the *patron* [owner-boss]— *el Divino Redentor* [the Divine Redeemer]—the good man on the wrong side and the bad men on the right side, and the liberal trying to make a compromise and bewildered by his lack of success. [. . .] Revolution and the rest of it[. . . .] Also Rica. It's wonderful just as it stands."[38]

Anita managed to visit with other women occasionally, such as Mrs. Goldschmidt, the wife of the German socialist who taught economics at the university. She met Charlot's mother regularly for lunch and French lessons. She described dropping in on Lola Cueto, who rented apartments to several members of the gang, including Diego Rivera. Anita admired her embroidered panels. "They are very lovely, like tapestries, and quite individual and discreet, also very Mexican."[39]

One of Anita's most interesting acquaintances was Maria Sandoval de Zarco, the only practicing woman lawyer in Mexico, whom Anita interviewed for Gruening in May 1927. She "has been practicing for thirty years, and she looks it. Her office is a combination of musty Diaz-days lawyer and old maid. Big desk and also cushions with lace covers over pale blue china silk. She says Mexican women have all kinds of rights but won't take them. She gave me her picture, in a folder on one side of which there is the chromo of a bunch of violets, with 'Maria' in one corner, in gilt."[40]

The journals provide a glimpse of a wide spectrum of the world of women in Mexico in the twenties. Anita's experience with that wide variety of women was part of the process of growing up. The journals indicate that she listened, learned, and shared with many women. She did not adopt anyone in particular as a role model. Rather, she created her own way with a guiding hand from many sisters.

five

Moving On

Anita. Photo by Edward Weston. Courtesy of Center for Creative Photography, University of Arizona.

ANITA ACQUIRED a broad education during those four years in Mexico. She grew from a young student into a full-fledged professional journalist. The people and ideas she encountered cemented her sense of identity as a Mexican intellectual and as a believer in the principles of the Mexican Revolution.

During those years Anita was published in *Mexican Folkways*, *The Nation*, *The Arts*, *The Jewish Morning Journal*, and *The Menorah Journal*. She was also the Mexico correspondent for the *Jewish Telegraphic Agency*, which gave her wide exposure in the Jewish press in the United States. She became an authority on Jewish immigration to Mexico, and articles about Jewish issues were a main source of income for her from 1924 to 1927. Concurrently, her articles on many Mexican themes, especially its art and artists, were published.

By 1927, it was time to move on. The situation in Mexico was shifting. The utopian challenge of building a new society gave way to a government determined to throttle the process. President Calles grappled with power struggles and rebellions, such as the Cristero movement, supported in part by the Roman Catholic Church. The Cristeros fought to reinstate Church control of education and social services. Labor leaders had been co-opted by the postrevolutionary political process. Neglected workers renewed their struggle on their own, staging frequent strikes. Calles stepped down in 1928, and Obregon was selected to occupy the presidency a second time. The plan was upset when the president-elect was shot by a religious fanatic. Some said the assassin was independent. Others felt that he was part of the movement opposed to reelection. Still others believed that Obregon's murder was part of a conspiracy to keep Calles in power as the strongman behind the throne. The country, then and now, grappled with the corruption of power. In Gruening's words, "Mexico has never enjoyed democracy. [. . .] Change of office was always wrought by force never by constitutional methods. [. . .] *jefes politicos* [political leaders] were appointed, as were Senators, Deputies and Judges, although the farce of an election form was generally complied with. [. . .] nullification of democratic procedure has rested not so much with the largely illiterate electorate as with the supposedly educated legislators."[1]

Government funding for public murals dried up. The community of artists scattered. Political repression drove the Syndicate of Painters and Sculptors underground. Anita made plans to go to New York and enroll at Columbia University, adding organizing a Mexican art exhibit to her agenda. The summer before her departure, Anita carried an impressive workload. She completed Gruening's research, wrote a series of dance descriptions for Letty Carroll, translated Gamio's "Preliminary Report on Mexican immigration to the United States, undertaken for the Social Science Research Council," and produced two manuscripts, later combined and published as *Idols behind Altars* in 1929.[2] She also worked on the art exhibit, visiting artists, gathering their work, securing letters of authorization, and processing permits to take the art to New York. She recorded her inner conflict between her educational goals and her work as a journalist, yet she never mentioned enrolling at Columbia University until she was in New York. There are no letters of application or other clues, perhaps because admission procedures at that time were less formal than they are today; students simply appeared at the Office of Admissions and enrolled.

A grueling schedule was typical for Anita. She often had as many as three projects going (not counting her own writing), to generate income to survive without having to turn to her authoritarian father for support. On her way to New York, she stopped in San Antonio to visit the family. Her description of a wonderful tub full of hot water in a large tiled bathroom in the family home inspired a journal entry that crystallized the many layers of unresolved issues and conflicts in life-styles. On the one hand, she was terribly hurt that her mother was not there when she arrived. Both her parents were at the new beach house in Rockport. Anita's brothers, a sister, and a cousin were "hardly aware of her existence." On September 8, 1927, she wrote,

> *I also resent still the fact that I was made to go through the pinchbeck summer grinding at this and that and economizing like the very devil, when the gasoline bill of one of the cars would have meant freedom and sweetness and light and all the rest of it, to me . . . There is so much money here, a little of it, without strings, would make me so happy, and it is not making anybody particularly happy as it is. Oh well. My comfort is that soon I will leave. It seems that I cannot find my place here at all. I always come home in all good faith and wanting [to] like everybody and somehow the whole thing gets on my nerves horribly, I have to make an effort at sanity and control.*

The Brenner family lost everything during the Revolution except their lives and their land. I. Brenner, as he was known to the family, was proud that

Negotiating
with Papa.

he had been able to get back on his feet financially. Anita was proud to
have achieved economic independence during the four years she spent in
Mexico. She identified on a personal level with the Mexican Revolution's
struggle for independence from wealthy foreign landowners. Anita chose
to follow her heart rather than stay at home under her father's control.
I. Brenner's style was to lay down the law. He granted and withdrew support in fruitless efforts to control her life, challenging Anita to survive on
her own. She earned his respect with de facto defiance and with success.

There is a rough analogy between the attitude of foreign interests toward the new government in Mexico and that of Isidore Brenner toward
his daughter. Anita and Mexico were out of control. Powerful entrepreneurs, such as William Randolph Hearst and oil company executives, lobbied the U.S. government to pressure Mexico to annul the laws that limited land ownership and confirmed that minerals in the subsoil were the
nation's property.[3] Anita's father also owned far too many acres to be within
the law. I. Brenner pressured Anita to return to San Antonio, where he could
retain his paternal authority. Anita took an occasional swipe at her father
for not helping her. On December 4, 1925, she wrote in her journal, "Job.
Helping Gruening. Research work. Reading, making notes, etc. To begin
in January. Solves my problem beautifully and without chains! [. . .] Papa

writes [. . .] he will be here in January. Wants to take me home. Getting bored with that sort of thing."

Anita did not elaborate on her relationship with her father in her journals. Her writings and correspondence complement my impression that more than anything else in the world, Anita wanted her father's respect and approval. She knew him well enough to know that she could achieve her goal through independence. She dedicated her first book, *Idols behind Altars*, to him.

Anita's mother didn't emit opinions: she sent clothes and money to help Anita out in times of need. Anita mentioned her mother in the journals when money was tight or when news arrived. Most of the time, she was too involved with her own life to harp on the issue. She recorded the following on August 10, 1926, when Abel Plenn, a first cousin, returned from San Antonio: "Abe came back with news about Mamma, Papa, Henry, Dorothy—all of them mixed up with themselves and suffering. I guess also that the U.S. hasn't much spiritual rope left, and soon it will hang itself. They are sick, sick—Too much money and growing weaker and weaker, and blind. Revolution means making the true values recognized—not distributing the money equally."[4] References to the family were not always negative. "On board train to Mexico City," in January 1927, she recorded:

> Left San Antonio the morning of Jan. 9, and shall arrive in Mexico tomorrow early, just in time to see a few days of Jean [Charlot. . . .] Gruening insistent about my waiting for him, but Papa came to the rescue (not liking the idea of me traveling with G.) and said rescue much appreciated. Left the family with Dorothy home over the weekend, for the first time in a good while, [. . .] Papa feeling good over the purchase of a summer place in Rockport. House and 14 acres of land and 10 of oyster ground from which we sampled some 350, Papa finding twelve small pearls in one single oyster while he was eating it. He is also beginning to work on the remodelling of the Continental Hotel building, a block of city property he just bought. Oh, yes, much prosperity. Curiously, however, he is very sweet about it and in general reasonable and magnanimous and also pathetic because he is so lonely. We all—himself included— wear good armor.[5]

Anita became an informal go-between for her father and her younger sisters. Both of her sisters wrote long letters explaining their problems and asking her to "talk to Papa." Sometimes he reprimanded Anita for advising them; at other times, she reproached herself for intervening, because her sisters didn't keep their side of the agreement. The role of "confidant and adviser" took on added importance during periods of family crisis.

A dramatic Brenner family crisis occurred in the early thirties. I. Brenner, the successful entrepreneur, indulged occasionally in escapades to the "West side Mexican" neighborhood of San Antonio to enjoy the dance halls with store employees. Once, he was caught by both his sons, who confronted him in his office. The discussion culminated in blows. Milton, who had returned from horseback riding, whipped his father and the female "assistant" with fists and a switch. I. Brenner had his sons arrested and fired them. Anita was called on to help. The most pressing issue was dealing with her mother's complicated position. One suggestion was that Paula Brenner and the youngest daughter, Leah, go to New York until the situation blew over. Like many family skeletons, the outcome was not clearly documented. Local press clippings and letters provide some of the information, yet when Isidore died in 1952, both his sons worked with him at the family store.

Anita left the family behind and took the train to New York, indulging in a manicure on the train. She took to New York like a duck to water. She had been there for the spring semester in 1925, and other than finding a place to live and building bookcases with her roommate, Lucy Knox, the transition seems to have been so smooth that it did not merit comment. There is no mention of culture shock or difficulty in adapting to a new scene. She promptly got in touch with friends from Mexico, such as the artist Max Gorelik, who helped her get settled. The life she described was similar to the one she led in Mexico; even though New York City was much larger, she ran into friends on the street and at restaurants.

six

Harvesting Mexican Efforts

Goitia took Anita Brenner and Edward Weston to visit this patio where women washed in Xochimilco; she took his work to New York. Photo by Edward Weston. Courtesy of Center for Creative Photography, University of Arizona.

ANITA HAD several goals in New York: promoting Mexican art, getting her book published, earning a living as a journalist, and attending Columbia University. She tackled them all, seemingly at once. The first mission was to trace and retrieve the art she had shipped from Mexico that had been lost in transit. Arturo Calles, the president's brother, was the Mexican consul in New York. Charles Erwin, a labor leader Anita had met at dinner with Ernest Gruening, worked at the consulate. Calles and Erwin were mobilized and rescued the art.

The community of Mexican artists and intellectuals in New York welcomed Anita into their circle. She contacted Rufino Tamayo, the poet Octavio Barreda (married to Carmen Marin, Lupe Rivera's sister), Carlos Chavez, and Miguel Covarrubias.[1] The *Mexicanada*, as Anita called the group, got together regularly, at parties and at each other's artistic events. She had known most of them in Mexico and fit in without any problem. It was Tamayo who, in mid-1928, insisted that Anita meet Frances Flynn Paine, who managed a fund of 15,000 dollars of Rockefeller money to sponsor Mexican artists.

John D. Rockefeller II was a major stockholder in oil companies in Mexico. It was to his advantage to foster stability in the country. His strategy included sponsoring the arts, giving left-wing artists work to keep them happy, funding murals in Mexico, and supporting exhibits and concerts in the United States, primarily in New York City. Frances Paine was in charge of the effort, which included theater productions, Carlos Chavez concerts, and art exhibits. Anita declined Paine's invitation to work as her employee and chose to collaborate instead. Anita's participation meant that Frances did not have to travel to Mexico to contact artists and get their work for exhibits. It also facilitated Anita's search for spaces (galleries and museums) in New York in which to exhibit Mexican artists' work. They complemented each other. Anita had the artists' work in New York and Frances had the contacts with the museum and gallery world.

The combination of the Mexican consulate's help in importing the art, Frances Paine's contact with the "Art Center," and Anita's selection of artists yielded the desired results. The first exhibit opened at the Art Center in 1928, and it included work by, among others, Jean Charlot, Jose Clemente Orozco, Maximo Pacheco, Diego Rivera, and Francisco Goitia.

After it closed Anita brought a stream of people to her apartment to see it. Among those who came was Alma Reed, who at that time hosted a salon. The relationship between Alma Reed and Jose Clemente Orozco is

Orozco cartoon. "And the Revolution made them dance." Photo by Tina Modotti. Courtesy of Instituto Nacional de Bellas Artes y Literatura/Museo de Arte Alvar y Carmen T. de Carrillo Gil.

well documented, although the fact that it was Anita who introduced them is seldom mentioned. Alma arranged exhibits and eventually opened her own gallery, Delphic Studios, to exhibit and promote Orozco and other Mexican artists. She was a key factor in the promotion of his work, negotiating contracts for murals at Dartmouth College and Pomona College (in California) and publishing a book about him, which Anita reviewed in *New Masses*.[2]

Anita embarked on a personal crusade for recognition of Mexico's art with her earliest writings. In New York, she continued to write about Mexico and Mexican art in prestigious journals such as *The Arts*, *Creative Arts*, and *The Nation*. She proudly showed the paintings and drawings and sought opportunities for exhibits and sales. Anita also visited galleries and arranged exhibits for Jean Charlot. Her promotion of Mexican art continued until the day she died.

Anita's career as a journalist continued. She landed in New York in the fall of 1927 and played the "famous New York sport" of making contacts.[3] She called Freda Kirchwey at *The Nation*, Forbes Watson at *The Arts*, and checked in with Elliot Cohen, managing editor of the *Menorah Journal*.

Carlos Merida's work on Anita's
agenda. Photo by Michael Nye.
Courtesy of Ana Luna Mérida.

All three had published her work and expressed interest in further contributions.

Her introduction to *The Nation* was probably made by Carleton Beals, who wrote for the publication from Mexico. Anita and Beals met often; she mentioned listening to him read his work more often than reading her work to him. Although Anita did not explicitly identify Beals as a mentor or adviser, what Mexicans call "a godfather," his letters express satisfaction with her progress and hope for further success. In the fall of 1927 Beals wrote, "Congratulations on all your activities [. . . .] 'Creative Art' piece was very good, also *Menorah Journal*. We expect much from you. Keep it up."[4]

The Nation published a second article by Anita, "Idols behind Altars," in 1926.[5] By then Anita was seasoned enough to record that she received a check for $25, while the *Jewish Morning Journal* paid $50.[6] Her expertise was Mexico, Mexican artists, and the ongoing artistic revolutionary process known as the Mexican Renaissance. The number of articles published increased as her competence grew.

Ernest Gruening may also have contributed to Anita's success at *The Nation*, since he was there as the managing editor in the late twenties and

"We expect much
from you—keep it up."
Photo of Carleton Beals
by Tina Modotti.

again in the mid-thirties.[7] Anita had already worked for Gruening in Mexico for almost a year when *The Nation* published "Idols behind Altars" in 1926. When she arrived in New York, Gruening had left *The Nation* and was in Portland, Maine. He was supportive of her efforts to publish her book and wrote several letters of introduction to help her.[8]

The Nation published Anita's review of the Mexican art exhibit that she and Frances Paine organized, as well as book reviews and editorials about news from Mexico.[9] Anita also worked with the material Carleton Beals sent from Nicaragua when he interviewed Cesar Augusto Sandino, who was leading the resistance to U.S. occupation. She accepted the position of Latin American editor, which meant establishing reciprocal publication rights with Spanish-language periodicals throughout the American continent.

After a few years at that pace, Anita collapsed from nervous exhaustion and quit as Latin American editor for *The Nation*. Her contributions to *The Nation* dwindled to occasional articles and book reviews, until the mid-thirties, when Gruening returned as an editor and she began reporting from Spain on the Spanish Civil War.

Anita's professional relationship with the *Menorah Journal* was very different. She sent short fiction from Mexico, the first published in August 1927. After she arrived in New York, Elliot Cohen, the managing editor, invited her to drop by for a visit. Anita enjoyed meeting other contributors, such as Herbert Solow and Louis Berg; they were stimulating and easygoing people. When Orozco was starving, Anita borrowed from the *Menorah Journal* against future work and used the loan to buy some of his work, feigning to be a third party. Although her journals don't comment on it, the use of Jewish financing to bail out the man who teased her with anti-Semitic cartoons must have appealed enormously to her sense of humor. That flexibility characterized her relationship with the *Menorah Journal*. She could drop by and borrow or reciprocate by turning out translations on short notice. In contrast, the correspondence from *The Nation* was about outstanding debts of small amounts: $11.63.[10]

The *Menorah Journal* is the only publication that printed Anita's fiction. Her first story, "Yankele's Kaleh" (1927), is about a young Jew who immigrated to Mexico from Palestine. Yankele, a newlywed with a pregnant wife, fled to Mexico after killing an Arab during a clash when his house was burned down. He cut sugarcane to raise the money for his wife's fare to Mexico. The work was hard and the pay was low; however, he dreamed of his unborn son. The boat that brought Yankele's wife docked in Veracruz a day before schedule. His wife followed the advice of other passengers and identified herself as Yankele's sister, not his wife. She did not know that Mexico did not allow single women to immigrate. In spite of her pleas, she was put back on the boat, which sailed to Cuba. Yankele was devastated when he came to meet her, and put in many more hours cutting sugarcane, enduring dizzying high fevers, to earn passage for his wife from Cuba. In his misery, he fantasized that his new son would say *kaddish* (a memorial prayer for the dead) for him. When he was finally reunited with his bride, he received a daughter, not a son. Yankele swiftly shifted his *kaddish* fantasy to dreams about the beautiful *kaleh* (wife, in Yiddish) his daughter would become. The story probably includes elements of real events. The twist of turning an anticipated son into a future bride was the first published expression of Anita's dry sense of humor and irreverence, which she exercised and enjoyed verbally throughout her life.

The second story, "Afternoons of a Patriarch" (1928), is a narrative about an old man cared for by two aging servants. He lived surrounded by books and documents about Jews in Mexico. He was meticulous about his library and circumspect about who he allowed in to read or to view the documents he kept in an old wooden armoire. The old man loved to tell stories about his ancestors and their escape from Spain to the New World. There were also tales about his students at the university, and he was proud of the roster of important figures who had attended his classes. There was a mystery, though. Every afternoon the old man disappeared at the same time. No one knew where he went. The neighborhood wasn't affluent, by any means, and there was a teahouse of doubtful repute nearby. The narrator met a young woman from the teahouse and listened to her story about an old man who came every afternoon to regale the girls with wonderful tales. He spoke French and English! So, one afternoon, the narrator followed the patriarch through narrow streets, carefully keeping out of sight. His destination was indeed the teahouse where the young woman worked. There he was, surrounded by attractive young women, telling stories, delighted and delighting the girls, who listened in awe.

The patriarch clearly fits the description of Francisco Rivas Puigcerver, a Jewish teacher and scholar known for his library, documents, and stories about his students. Rivas claimed to be a descendant of the Spanish poet Judah Leon Abrabanel, who left Spain in 1492 when the Jews were expelled. The poet settled in Campeche, changed his name, and transmitted the family's secret Jewish origin to his descendents on his deathbed. The Inquisition in Mexico was long over, and therefore Rivas returned to practice his ancestors' faith: Judaism.[11] Anita irreverently combined the figure of the old patriarch with material she had found for Gruening about prostitution in Mexico City. On May 4, 1926, she recorded in her journal a visit to the Ministry of Health's inspection center, describing soldiers and policemen "dragging around" after the women and doctors, who were "Dickens villain types." "On the way out, one of the military guards tried to detain me, for I had no card of health!"

seven

An Art Critic's Career Unfolds

Edward Weston. Photo by Tina Modotti.

ANITA'S FOCUS on Mexican art and artists was not that of an academic art historian but more that of an anthropologist. She observed, learned, and reported to a general public. Art, for Anita, was the key to understanding Mexico, its people, customs, and frivolities. It was the door that opened the eyes of foreign readers to a view of the country without prejudice. When she reviewed an exhibit, she did not compare schools or styles at different periods. On the contrary, she shunned the use of "isms."

Anita mentioned her interest in anthropology in her journals and in letters as early as 1925.[1] She expressed her love for Mexico through art and anthropology. The first articles she published that were not about Jewish issues were about Mexican culture.

The connection between art, anthropology, and Mexico is apparent in her article about Manuel Gamio published in 1925, in which she presented basic elements of Gamio's work with the people of Teotihuacan.[2] Through descriptions of Aztec dances in churches and plays performed on holidays, Anita focused on the philosophy of recognizing and re-valuing Mexican indigenous values. Gamio wanted people to dance in the theater as well as in the church courtyard; his goal was to build the self-confidence of indigenous people by creating opportunities for them to appreciate their own culture. Anita defined it as "building a nation upon folk-lore. Or rather, of letting it rebuild itself."[3] Like many artists and intellectuals of the time, she was a firm believer in the *indigenista* philosophy. Her work was a vehicle to deliver the values of the Mexican Revolution. She identified with Gamio's work, and in the same article wrote,

> *Tragic, indeed, is the story of Tlahuicole, but more tragic is the subsequent story of his race and of all other native Mexican races, who lost everything to the conquerors and gained only a religion unintelligible to them, and the Christian privilege of long and most humble service. Romantic, also, is the story of Crown of Cotton. But more romantic is the realism of the plan for the regeneration of these people, to be surpassed only, as in the theatre which is an illustration of it, by the reality of accomplishment.*[4]

Anita began writing about individual artists while working for Ernest Gruening. She wrote biographical sketches about people who were part of the community, many of whom were her friends. Some were published in Spanish in *Forma* (although it is unlikely that she received any payment for them), and others were in English.[5] In the profile of Carlos Merida published by *International Studio* in 1926, Anita defined his work as "almost a religion of color, recalling the Maya and Aztec artists, who never conceived of form without color."[6]

It was at this time that Anita began formulating her passion for art and artists into plans for two books. One would present a catalogue of Mexican decorative arts. The second would focus on the story of the role of art in the Mexican Revolution. She worked closely on both with Jean Charlot. Together, they tackled a description of the role of art in the Revolution. They discussed and outlined, then she wrote and he edited, or vice versa; together they developed the final text of several articles. She wrote and published it in English; Charlot translated it into French.[7] The idea of "Mexican Renaissance in the sense of constant rebirth" came in 1925 while they were working on "Mexican Decorative Arts." Anita wrote, "It makes my mouth water but it is hard to keep to the idea — modern, living, major and result of tradition."[8] They may have been the first to use the widely accepted term "Mexican Renascence" to describe the role of art and artists in the postrevolution period. They intentionally chose the "renascence" spelling for an article they wrote together because it reaffirmed the identification of Mexico as a place of religion and revolutions with the concept of rebirth, as if it were a messianic endeavor to undergo rebirth.

A few months later, once the decorative-arts book was outlined, Anita developed the list of illustrations, selecting and identifying the samples of different art forms to illustrate the catalogue as well as the images that would transmit the story of Mexican art. She made a list for Weston of the things to be photographed in Mexico City.[9] She drafted the outline of the Mexican Renaissance book while negotiating a contract with the National University of Mexico to finance photographs by Edward Weston for the catalogue of Mexican decorative arts. She would write the text, Weston would take the photographs, and the University of Mexico would hold the rights, in exchange for advancing funds.

Anita knew Weston socially and admired his work. She reviewed his 1925 exhibit, identifying him as an artist who displayed great talent for natural and subtle emotional expression.[10] She felt that his role as the photographer was crucial for the success of the project, because it would be the images of Mexican art that would make the catalogue of Mexican decorative arts. The work for Anita's book required Weston to travel to specific sites that Anita had spotted during earlier travels: stone carvings on buildings in Queretaro; unique murals in a church in Tupataro, near Patzcuaro,

Michoacan; and the Guadalupe Zuno collection in Guadalajara. The contract specified 400 images. Both Anita and Weston recorded in their journals the excitement of seeing the progress of their project every time Weston returned to Mexico City to develop the shots he had taken. He and Tina Modotti made several trips to shoot the images that Anita requested or others that Edward and Tina found en route. There were ups and downs: heavy rains made it difficult to travel during the summer, and obtaining extra railroad passes so Edward's son and Tina could both travel for free was complicated. The National University agreed to provide two passes, but Weston needed three: for himself, his son, and Tina Modotti.[11] Anita continued her research work for Gruening and others, but described her passion for her own project. The images that Weston and Modotti captured were magnificent. Anita conceded that Frances Toor was right: the photographs would make the book, no matter what the text said.[12]

When Anita arrived in New York she searched for publishers for both books. The University of Mexico wanted them published abroad for prestige and wider distribution. She wrote descriptions and proposals, and went to interviews, all to no avail. There were two main reasons for the rejections: first, books about Mexico were not considered commercial; second, the cost of reproducing photographs was high. Thus, Anita was forced to combine her manuscripts on "Mexican Decorative Arts" and the "Mexican Renaissance" into *Idols behind Altars*, cutting text and photographs. Nonetheless, the Mexican Renaissance remained one of Anita's favorite themes. During the process of looking for a publisher, Anita published several chapters of *Idols* as independent articles, bringing in income and promoting Mexican art.

The Mexican Renaissance material falls into three categories, corresponding to a historical sequence. The first period deals with popular religious sculpture, pre-Hispanic idols, and later versions crafted after the Spanish Conquest and the imposition of Catholicism. Popular art is the second major theme: Indian crafts and art evolving as Mexicans continued their artistic activities in spite of the Conquest. The last period involves modern Mexican artists and their attempt to retain and revive Mexican traditions such as murals. All three, but especially the last, transmitted the political realities of the country. Anita was not satisfied with descriptive narratives that did not carry a political message. Artists and intellectuals active at that time felt they were engaged in a revolutionary process, identifying the development of Mexico's history and its art as one.

Photo by Edward Weston
or Tina Modotti. Courtesy
of Center for Creative
Photography, University
of Arizona.

Idols behind Altars was originally titled "The Mexican Renascence." The early period, that of the pre-Spanish cultures, was covered in an article, "The Living Art of the Mexican Primitives," that appeared in *L'Art Vivant* in 1926. Anita described the process by which indigenous Mexicans produced Christian images with the same dedication they devoted to idols. It did not interfere with the ongoing production of idols, which were placed discreetly on altars built by Christian conquerors at the sites of pyramids. "The idols, though melted back from priestly plastic formulae into the elasticity of the primitive, are the passive resistance of an old faith."[13]

The second period includes chapters about ex-votos and *pulqueria* murals. An ex-voto, also known as a *retablo* or *milagro*, is a small portrait of an actual event, a miracle, "the thing seen as it is, that is, a true portrait, not a copy, nor an imitation."[14] Victims and survivors hired a *milagro* painter to portray an accident, medical problem, or assault so that they could place it in the church in honor of the saint who saved them. "The spirit of Mexican painting is the sober, profound recognition of reality, [. . .] a sensitiveness to truth that makes miracles of daily happenings."[15]

Anita mixed her descriptions of particular genres with comments about Mexican society and politics. She compared a collection of ex-votos to a visual narrative of Mexican history that included aspects of life not often mentioned, documenting sociological and anthropological information. For example:

> The profound social differences between city and country, and the relationship between them, is apparent in the roles given in each place to the man who wears dark clothing and shoes, and to the man who wears white cotton and a big sombrero. Then, the changes of occupation, clothing, and attitude from period to period, against the same background; the intensifications of certain kinds of miracles at certain periods; the new miracles of each period. [. . .] The peasant who retained his land, painted the miracle of it.[16]

Mexicans transposed pre-Conquest practices smoothly to new images brought by Spaniards. But Spanish missionaries were not prepared for the abundance of miracles. The Mexicans

> were so pleased with the new style that immediately many more miracles occurred, than the friars were prepared to admit. If they were all authentic, they concluded, then heaven must be making special dispensations to the converts, to make real Christians of them. [. . .] But the Indian, who could converse with God daily, did not see why he should believe it only once a century or so. His standpoint makes the miracle into a normal thing, so tangible that it can be painted.[17]

Anita was not promoting folk art or describing trinkets that tourists could buy. Her text described a social phenomenon that grew out of Mexico's historical development. She focused on the reaction of the Spanish missionaries and the opportunity for freedom of artistic expression. Miracles were not for sale.

Anita presented the material with the same subtle, irreverent sense of humor that she used in her fiction. It was important to her to get Mexican reality and the *indigenista* philosophy across in such a way that readers would not just understand but also become sympathetic to the cause of the Mexican Revolution, which for Anita was part of the "Mexican Renascence."

In the article "Street Murals in Mexico" (1929), Anita described the transformation of the ritual of drinking *pulque* from the pre-Conquest to the Colonial period of Mexican history. *Pulque* is a juice drawn from the heart of the Mexican agave cactus. It is fermented, sometimes with other fruit to add flavor. Originally it was a part of sacred ritual practices, used by priests and people in power to mark special occasions. However,

> Pulque, *the religious institution and conscientiously administered native possession, was affected by the conquest because it became a source of gold and a means of double-exploitation of the peasants.* [. . .] *Fortunes out of* pulque *bought aristocracy for many immigrants. The drink was soon* [. . .] *vulgarized. The quantity each man might drink was made unlimited, if his pocket and his stomach corresponded.* "Peons are machines that run on pulque," *the* hacendados *often have said; contemptuously, but not regretfully.*[18]

Anita described scenic panels that decorate the outside and inside of places where *pulque* was sold. Such places weren't bars, since they served only *pulque*. Women were not allowed in, and there was a small window for carry-out orders. Anita focused on the social aspect of the murals, in defense of the indigenous people of Mexico.

An ongoing theme is the Mexican need for visual expression, whether through pottery, blankets, palm toys, or masks. That same need is evident today in the production of new forms of popular art for local and foreign buyers. There is always a new expression of popular art available at public markets or peddled by vendors in the street.

Another favorite subject was contemporary artists. Whether in profiles of individuals or events, or later in weekly reviews for the *Brooklyn Daily Eagle* in the thirties, Anita brought up and repeated the central issues of the Mexican Revolution in her material. She discussed the narrative quality in the work of modern Mexican artists, who "arise out of a long chain of revolutions." She compared them to the artists of Europe's Renaissance, mentioned their need to overthrow foreign influence in Mexico, and quoted Diego Rivera, confirming the identification of artists as workers: "I am not an artist. I am a worker with paints."[19]

> *The modern Mexican painters, of which this group is salient, do not pose as cultural messiahs. For they recognize that they cannot resurrect what never died, and Mexico, in spite of all her suffering, indeed, because of it, has never lost the impulse to express herself, nor the power to do it beautifully. Yet they really resemble very much the artists of the Renaissance.* [. . .] *Like the artist of the renais-*

sance, they are illogical above logic, irrational beyond reason. They appear fantastic, weird, insane. [. . .] "Art for art's sake," says Rivera, "is an aesthetic fallacy: art for the people is a piece of inconsistent sentimentalism. Art is a thing of the people."[20]

Anita repeated some of the major concepts in her review of the Mexican art exhibit that she organized with Frances Paine in 1928. She accepted the bloody reality of the Mexican Revolution and did not sweep it under the rug. She led with: "Mexico, so long camouflaged in bandits, oil, and revolution, emerges with an art which is not only a significant expression of itself, but a rebirth of genuine American art, representative ultimately, not only of the purple-mountained home of artists south of the Rio Grande, but of the entire Western Continent." She went back to the pre-Christian

Woman Thinking by Diego Rivera. With the permission of Dolores Olmedo.

Photo by Edward Weston or Tina Modotti. Courtesy of Center for Creative
Photography, University of Arizona.

era to describe Mexicans' relationship to art, discussing the need "To paint, to carve, to make some thing of color and form." The Mexican people create in spite of anachronisms and contradictions. Centuries roll past in brief sentences, from the stone age to the feudal age to the machine age. She stressed the continuous stream of Mexican creation through revolutions: "Revolution takes on a new meaning, for as in all times, great tragedy here gives birth to great art. The tragedy is four hundred years old, for since the conquest of Mexico by the Spaniards, it has been a land divided against itself, endlessly struggling to unite. The Indian layer, majority of the population, passively resisting European culture, imperceptibly proving it out of place, and surging, slowly, upward to assert itself, physically in revolution, spiritually in art." Once she had set the stage and readers knew about Mexico's struggle for freedom, she moved on to the contemporary exhibit she was reviewing: "In quantity alone, their achievement is astounding. Mexico cannot send its walls, though that would be the greatest courtesy; but it sends enough to give somewhat an index to the quality of the work. [. . .] Ultimately, the work of the Mexican artists belongs to all the world, but intimately, it belongs to all America, in the north creator of sky scrapers, in the south of pyramids; coming together in painting that partakes of the spirit of both."[21]

Many of the articles that were published in the late twenties were written in Mexico. Anita moved from writing about Jewish immigration to writing about art easily with Charlot's help, Gruening's research, and translations for Diego Rivera. Her expertise evolved as she made regular contributions as an art critic. Art, whether Mexican, French, or American, gave her a scenario within which she could focus on politics from an anthropologist's perspective. Anita's three cultures—American, Jewish, and Mexican—came together in New York in the thirties.

eight

Idols behind Altars

Woodcut by Jean Charlot. With the permission of Dorothy Zohmah Charlot.

ANITA was twenty-four years old when *Idols behind Altars* was published in 1929. Her journals tell of painful efforts to publish both manuscripts, "Mexican Decorative Arts" and "The Mexican Renascence," as separate books, as well as the difficult process of rewriting the two into one book. Although she had been at Columbia University for two years by the time *Idols* was published, her style was not academic. She quoted amply and identified her sources, yet did not footnote. Unlike her later book *The Wind That Swept Mexico, Idols* did not include an introductory statement that it was not intended to be academic. The hypothesis was woven into the text without identifying any methodology. The book was a product of her journalistic activity, as opposed to her concurrent academic world of anthropology.

The focus of *Idols behind Altars* is the Mexican Revolution. Anita identified with artists and intellectuals in the twenties for whom art was part of the revolution. Once the armed conflict was over, intellectuals went to work helping to rebuild the country.

Anita presented the visual context first: for instance, the geography, images of volcanoes, and their similarity in shape to pyramids. Then she described the background of the person or historical period that she was writing about. The third step was to provide an intellectual context, the history of ideas related to her subject. Finally she discussed specific artists or groups of artists.

Idols was written for foreign readers. Anita presented Mexico, its customs, traditions, peoples, and politics with a personal touch. The information in the book overlaps with journal entries, although Anita did not identify any material from personal experience. She combined anecdotes with quotations from historical sources and ballads to get her message across.

There is a constant interplay between past and present, with the past emphasizing traditions that survived for more than 400 years and the present focusing on 1926, when she wrote the first draft. Today, in the nineties, it might be considered a multidisciplinarian approach to Mexican art, anthropology, history, and sociology.

Her introduction to the revolution describes the ousting of foreign influence and control, landowners, business, religion, and schools of art. The vehicle for education and communication was art, the people's expression of their own religion and way of life. Anita emphasized the grafting of pre-Reformation Catholicism onto an indigenous stem of beliefs. The Mexican people did not replace their religious and social concepts; they simply added the new onto the old. They modified rituals and practices in the presence of Spaniards.

Revolution meant casting off the inner degradation brought by alien rulers. It meant releasing creative energy to give birth to a new people. The process contributed to a developing sense of pride and self-confidence, an assurance that Mexicans could solve their own problems. Anita compared it to the "dawn of selfhood" in adolescence, when one realizes that one can be one's own person, respecting and accepting oneself and others.

That revolutionary process paralleled Anita's personal experience. She arrived in Mexico at the age of eighteen in the midst of her own dawn of selfhood. Two years later she was a working journalist with the same sense of self-respect that she said the Mexican people had garnered from the revolution. The book's subtitle, *The Story of the Mexican Spirit*, alludes to the wide scope of material included; however, it can also be seen as a symbolic coming of age for Anita's spirit. Anita, the underdog, must struggle for independence from the foreign landowner—her father.

Idols behind Altars follows a chronological sequence. It opens with an in-depth description of Aztec, Maya, and other indigenous Mexicans, presenting a return to Mexican roots and spirit. The description includes the communal nature of land tenure, deeply rooted principles against ostentation of power and wealth, and the system of transmitting codes of behavior and ethics from generation to generation. She did not gloss over or deny the practice of human sacrifice; rather, she reported, as a journalist, the origins and beliefs that led to the bloody practice.

A key factor in her presentation was the continued prevalence of ancient beliefs in 1926; they remained part of the historical reality of events such as the appearance of Halley's Comet during the early phases of the revolution. The personal experience of being held up by her nanny, Serapia, to see the comet and learning that it meant destruction, death, and trouble was included. Anita wrote as a participant-observer about the revolution's background and the people's beliefs.

Early chapters dealing with pre-Spanish cultures focus on three major themes: land, art, and religion, along with the relationships among them and their place in a global structure of beliefs. The indigenous peoples of Mexico were part of the land. They blended with the color of the extracted clay used to create religious images and artistic bowls for everyday living. The complex communal land tenure patterns that Aztecs practiced were illustrated and simplified with a line from a poem by Netzahualcoyotl, one of their last rulers: "The land belongs to him who works it with his hands."[1]

Many Mexicans to this day feel an ancestral mystical bond with the land where they were born. People drop everything, put jobs and careers on hold, to go back to their *tierra* to participate in traditional festivities. Migrant workers living in the United States travel thousands of miles to be home at that special time. There is no staying away, although union contracts have still not written this reality into contracts as a fringe benefit.

The Constitution of 1917 reaffirmed Netzahualcoyotl's policy. The land a single person could own was limited. Communal land tenure systems (*ejidos*) were established or, one might say, reestablished. Large absentee landowners, especially foreigners such as Hearst, objected to what for them were new laws, but the Mexican people had gone to war to reclaim their dignity with the cry "Tierra y Libertad" (land and freedom).

The Aztec philosophy also calls for doing your job well, no matter what your occupation. Working the land was vital. Religious beliefs and practices centered on agricultural cycles, water, and crops. Major deities included the Goddess of Corn and the Lord of the Water, as well as local miraculous beings. The primeval indigenous philosophy may have been ingrained in Anita by her nanny, Serapia. Anita identified with Aguascalientes, the land of her birth, and returned there to work the family farm years later. It was important to do it right. Yet Anita did not invoke Aztec deities to work the farm; she turned to experts from the United States Department of Agriculture, Rockefeller Foundation, and Israel for information and guidance.

Art was part of the Aztec religion. Artisans and artists were organized into guilds and produced idols, images, and objects for daily use without signing their work. Francisco Goitia, one of the artists who merited a full chapter in *Idols behind Altars*, followed that tradition by refusing to sign his work. The idols that Mexicans placed on altars came from the same molds they had used for centuries, even before the Spaniards' arrival. Although many collectors believe their figures are authentic in some sense, it is widely accepted that there is no accurate way to date an idol—it could have been made yesterday or hundreds of years ago.

The indigenous peoples of Mexico transmitted their history through murals and codices. The Spaniards destroyed many codices, but the murals remain. The people who created them are not identified. Jean Charlot revived their fresco technique through experimentation with the help of an artisan from Teotihuacan in the early twenties. Anita described such artistic activity as a release of creative energy that gives birth to a new people or rebirth to the ways of earlier peoples.

The first part of *Idols behind Altars* closes with a historical analysis of the Spanish Conquest and draws parallels between Spanish rule and Porfirio Diaz's dictatorship. Diaz repeated the degradation and humiliation of the Conquest four hundred years later. Preparations for celebrating the centennial of Mexico's independence included rounding up Indians and putting them in corrals. Diaz considered them offensive to the image presented to foreign dignitaries.

The second part of *Idols* analyzes the fusion of indigenous and Spanish art, following the main themes of land, art, and religion. Anita identified key elements of pre-Spanish culture found in street murals and *retablos*. She then analyzed the blending of Christian and pre-Spanish art, using the styles of crosses, crucifixes, and saints as examples.

Spanish missionaries initiated the process of transforming Mexico with Catholicism (they considered it civilizing) by placing churches on sites where pyramids and temples stood. The clearest example of the fusion is the Virgin of Guadalupe, commonly known as *La Virgen Morena*, or the "dark madonna," now patron saint of Mexico. The shrine to Guadalupe is on the site where Our Mother Tonantzin was worshiped. Guadalupe is honored on December 12, close to the date when indigenous people of Mexico paid homage to Our Mother.

Another example is the Mexican celebration of the Day of the Dead. Anita described in great detail taking picnic spreads to cemeteries to feed the dead (and the living) their favorite foods and beverages. Halloween treats in Mexico are candy skulls with names on them, chocolate coffins, complete with skeletons, and Dead Man's Day bread. She identified Jose Guadalupe Posada, the artist known for popularizing skeletons, as the Prophet. Posada's profile includes his development from illustrator to full-fledged revolutionary artist, mocking authorities with cartoons. Here again Anita integrated a childhood experience—reading wall newspapers aloud on the streets of Aguascalientes for the illiterate—into her work.

Anita herself incorporated the belief in comets and earthquakes as omens, not isolated natural phenomena. Nana Serapia had initiated her into the world of spirits and ghosts. Although she considered herself a Jew, she, like many Mexicans, accepted the existence of spiritual beings that are not human. Her files include the transcription of a conversation with Manuel Hernandez Galvan—after he was murdered. Her side of the conversation

Manuel Hernandez Galvan.
Photo by Edward Weston.
Courtesy of Center for
Creative Photography,
University of Arizona.

is written clearly. Where his spirit guides her hand, the writing is scribbled and interrupted by frequent requests for him to clarify what she didn't understand. Anita mentioned hearing noises, wanting to know what the spirit wanted, and going to see Diego Rivera's sister, a white witch, to achieve a more peaceful existence. She also recorded the experience of the head of Mexico's Department of Anthropology, who had a conversation with a person in his office and yet, when he went to look for him a few days later, discovered he had been dead for two years.

Transcriptions of conversations with spirits are not the only indication of Anita's interest in ghosts. In 1966 she published a children's story about a Mexican ghost who needed to find the right person to show where large quantities of gold could be found.[2] The candidate had to be satisfied with a modest life. People whose responses revealed greed and a desire to accumulate wealth were disqualified, in keeping with Aztec etiquette. Anita enjoyed defining Mexican ghosts as friendly beings who have unfinished business or just want to look around.

Her relationship to ghosts was not limited to written material. In the early sixties, farming in Aguascalientes, she talked about a woman ghost who pulled at her elbow to show her the treasure hidden on the farm. She took it seriously, and for years she believed that she would find the gold. Family and friends were drafted, metal detectors and all, to dig for the treasure. Holidays were spent discussing logistics and out-guessing the priest who had hidden the gold.[3] The people of Aguascalientes have not forgotten. Twenty years after Anita's death, a friend cautiously shared a story broadcast by a local television station. Anita had been seen (about three feet off the ground) playing with children at the low-income housing project built on the farm's orchards. Anita, the eyewitnesses reported, wore black; her long *blonde* hair floated behind her as she instructed the children to plant trees, to love and respect the earth. It was highly amusing to hear that my mother, who had pitch-black curly hair, was portrayed as a blonde foreigner. I took the opportunity to caution people to treat me properly or to expect my mother's return. They didn't laugh.

The last part of *Idols behind Altars* opens with an overview of Mexican artists and their philosophical positions. Anita covered the historical background and discussed the debates over art for art's sake among artists in the twenties. Five individuals are presented: David Alfaro Siqueiros, Jose Clemente Orozco, Diego Rivera, Francisco Goitia, and Jean Charlot. The closing chapter includes writers and musicians who participated in the rebuilding of Mexico, especially Mariano Azuela and Carlos Chavez.

Anita's journals are a rich counterpoint to her published writings, with *Idols behind Altars* as a recurring point of reference. She did not record the process of writing in detail but mentioned key information briefly with a few words. She began visiting publishers in New York in September 1927. In spite of Miguel Covarrubias and Gruening's introductions, she was turned down by at least three publishers before getting a definite commitment in August 1928. "Payson-Clark definitely accepts the book—making it a five-dollar popular opus, NOT an art book. And since they are such darn nice people and do get the point, I submit, and cut."[4] The manuscript was due in January. She delivered in June, six months late. Anita recorded feeling a letdown, which Charlot attributed to finishing the book, but it didn't last. There were proofs to be read and the excitement of details such as choosing the binding. Anita recorded pleasure, surprise, and awe with her accomplishment. She was in love with David Glusker, and on her birthday, she pondered her situation. "I even mentioned the matter of twenty-four years being completed, to David[. . . .] But it promises to be a full year. A book, a doctorate, and a husband! I have to take it all placidly or it would seem much too unreal. Is this me, anyhow?"[5]

Once the book was out, Anita exercised her irreverent sense of humor with the remark that "It looks very pretty but a little hypo-thyroid, due to unusually heavy paper for such a long book."[6] She reported events to promote the book, interviews, speaking engagements, amid the myriad of activities as a student, full-time work at *The Nation*, and, of course, David. Sometimes her concern focused on "what to wear!"

> *In the afternoon, dragged myself deeply into debt at Wanamaker's over a green Patou dress and a green-beige Agnés turban, and a black velvet dress; but I'll be swank in the limelight though I'll shweat with the midnight oil. It's sheer vanity partly excused this time by the fact that for the first time in my life, due to the peculiar mode of the moment, I achieve a certain elegance. My lusty breasts and other curves fit right into the "shaped" dresses and even the saleslady seemed sincere about her admiration. I paraded for Jean [Charlot] and he very grudgingly said he wants to look at magazines to keep from looking at me; so he snatched up an old* Creative Art *and some sardonic fiend turned it to the abstract* nalgas [rear end] *Edward* [Weston] *did of me.*[7]

Anita's delight with success is greater than her sense of self-importance. Her humor helped override stress and emotion until she collapsed with nervous exhaustion, a pattern she would repeat throughout her life. There wasn't time to pause; the concern was the next presentation, a last fitting of a green tweed, and buying a

> *dinner dress in which to eat and speak at the American Woman's Association, a monstrous big thing which is eating regularly devoting each time to one country. Mexico is the first menu, and me a dish, perhaps ominously* the piece de resistance. *The lady who called on me wanted to feature women, and so if I had to be featured, or in case I had to be featured, I shall be featured in a gorgeous deep blue velvet, of which papa bears the brunt—I sincerely hope.*[8]

Idols behind Altars was well received by reviewers, intellectuals, collaborators, and the press, notwithstanding the fact that the book was released in October 1929, when the stock market crashed. There are more than sixty clippings of reviews in the files, not including syndicated columns. Twenty are long descriptions that quote the book. An equal number are short mentions. Anita expressed concern about George Vaillant's review in *The Na-*

Photo by Tina Modotti.

tion, and after reading it, she wrote, "Lunched with George V. on Saturday, and read his review of Idols, which for George contains unusual praises; he never commits himself, even in matters of scientific fact, and he actually goes so far as to say that Idols is an accurate interpretation of the *pais* [country] that is so dear to us both."[9]

Anita did not comment about other reviews, such as those by Carleton Beals, Ernest Gruening, or Ernestine Evans. Gruening praised *Idols be-*

hind Altars as an "important supplement to the existing literature and knowledge of Mexico" and discussed the photographs and the artistic renaissance. His only reservation was the complexity of the book, difficult for amateurs and the "not specially informed reader." He closed with the opinion that the book "fills a gap impressively and establishes for the first time the importance and significance of Mexican art in the modern world."[10]

Beals praised Anita as the "Vasari of [the] modern Mexican school," adding, "No pedantic art criticisms here, but precious vignettes of the local scene."[11] However, he considered Anita's treatment of Diego Rivera inadequate compared with the number of pages dedicated to Charlot and Goitia. There was a subtle contradiction in his approach vis-à-vis Rivera. He was critical of Anita's "design" and discussed the future of Mexican art, asserting that "The Czardom of Diego Rivera will have to sink into historical perspective[, . . .] and Mexico [. . .] will have to rise up against the foreign invasion and rediscover its soul."

Ernestine Evans, who worked for one of the publishers that turned the book down, reviewed *Idols behind Altars* in *Creative Art*. She added something of her own agenda to the review in promoting *The Frescoes of Diego Rivera*, a book that included an introduction written by her.[12] Her connection with Anita began in 1927 in Mexico City when Evans demanded Anita's help. The review exposed Evans' festering resentment that Anita was "too young" to have so much information about Mexico. Anita noted the fact in her journals.

The journals of 1927 report a scene that Evans created in the presence of several others at the National Preparatory School, where Diego Rivera was working on his mural. Anita's sin was going to a dance instead of meeting with Evans. "You have been very fortunate," Evans remarked, according to the journal, "in having been placed in such circumstances that you have happened to get this material but you are doing it because you have lived here so long and it is not really journalism. You could have saved me a lot of time. And you are young and inexperienced and I could help you to get assignments. She said: [. . .] I invited you to dinner and you broke the engagement. [. . .] And you have all the material. [. . .] Why, I don't see why you should be angry! I say it for your own benefit!"[13] The next episode took place in New York. Tina Modotti had given Ernestine Evans photographs of works by Jose Clemente Orozco and Francisco Goitia, taken for Anita. The photographs were published in London, and Jean Charlot wrote to Anita asking whether she had released the material. The original photographs, which appeared in *Idols behind Altars* two years later, had been published without Anita's knowledge or permission. Anita was furious. Frances Paine offered to help and sought the advice of a lawyer, but there was nothing to be done.[14] In spite of everything, Anita considered publishing "Mexican Decorative Arts" and "Mexican Renaissance" with Ernestine.

Evans continued to offer Anita further work, such as other books and articles, throughout 1927 and 1928. Anita was interested. Ernestine, however, still expressed resentment that Anita should have access to so much information. Anita, determined to publish her book, seemed unmoved.

> *In the morning, saw Ernestine Evans. Nothing definite decided yet. She read part of my book. Likes it all right, but too presumptuous. Why that tone of authority? Unbecoming in a person my age, says she. Implied that I was the megaphone of other authorities. It was a criticism that on the one hand made me wonder if I am too flat-footed about how I write, and in another way it pleased me because it shows that she swallowed the material. She did not question ideas and most of all they went over, so the construction is all right. If they're good enough for her to think they're Diego's given her idea of Diego, why, hurray.[15]*

The project fell through because the publisher wanted a subsidy from New York University to cover the cost of including all the photographs. Ernestine seemed "hysterical" at the idea that Anita would try someplace else if it fell through.[16] A few days later the publisher rejected Anita's book.

Evans's review transmitted her disappointment: "If it has faults, it is that it is too rich." The quality and amount of material that Anita included would require "companion volumes" to supplement the information.[17]

The only other reviewer who seemed concerned with Anita's age was J. W. Rogers, who praised her: "for an author of 24, her volume reveals precocious erudition both about Mexico in particular and the field of art in general." Rogers went further, recognizing that Anita would prefer for her book to be judged on its own merit, "regardless of the age of its author, and she has justification, for her book is an achievement to her credit at any age."[18]

Anita sent the book to more than fifty people. Most were in Mexico. They included artists mentioned in the book, government officials, and her sponsors at Mexico's National University. Others were people she had

Anita beckons the spirit to visit the orchards. Photo by Hector Garcia.

known either in Mexico or New York, such as Gruening and Beals, her bridges to New York intellectual circles. The list reflects Anita's circle of friends at that time: Mexicans, Columbia University students and professors, and *Menorah Journal* colleagues. Edward Weston and Tina Modotti, who took the photographs, both received books, and both wrote glowing letters. Weston said, "It is a privilege to have your book and to feel that I had a small part in the making. I like what you say and the way you say it. The most interesting book on Mexico I have read. Clear thinking, sympathetic without sentimentality. And how well printed! My congratulations to you and to the publishers. [. . .] I am talking and boasting everywhere! Affectionately, Edward."[19] Tina wrote before reading the book. Her letter was less formal, with more information about her own life. She was feeling the need to move on, to "test myself anew, reaffirm myself [. . .] a spiritual need." At the same time, she described the bond with Mexico: "I almost dare say snake like attraction that pulls one back." She included the news that Diego Rivera was out of the Communist Party. Carleton Beals was about to return; Mexico was not the same; the issues were turning from race to class.[20]

One feature of the book mentioned most often by reviewers was the "photographs never seen before," making it clear why Anita had been upset with Tina for selling some of those photographs to others. Once the book was out, however, that earlier betrayal was no longer an issue. Tina identified with Anita: "I feel vicariously the satisfaction you must experience at having given birth to your first brain child!"[21]

Anita enjoyed the exposure but also reacted with a need to withdraw, "an urge to look, or dress, insignificant. Like a midinette, or just any student, preferably of the East side. This, of course, particularly when seeing pretentious or very rich people. It's a Mexican way to protest. Also Jewish."[22] The excitement of being a successful young author with the telephone ringing wore off.[23] Entries in the journals from this period reflect Anita's satisfaction and need to develop a new long-range project. The list of things she wanted to write included books she did write, such as the stories for children, a guidebook to Mexico, and the story of the Mexican Revolution.[24] Others never got beyond the idea stage, such as the novel about Rica Sutter's hacienda and the biography of Leon Toral, the man who murdered Alvaro Obregon.[25] Her life was full and complex. She savored success:

> My total reaction to fame—if clippings and new respect from acquaintances (surprised respect usually) could be called fame—is this: I am more than ever impatient of things second rate, people second rate, books second rate, ideas muddled or hypocritical . . and I am looping the loop back to my old rather savage and rude contempt of the great majority of people I meet . . intellectuals, usually. That may be the explanation. But the fact is, and this I swear is not vanity, that I can usually run circles around most of them, and usually I find them poor in spirit. Perhaps bourgeois is the word. One would think I would mellow [. . .][26]

The frenzied pace of activities, emotions, and demands caught up with Anita a few months later when she collapsed from nervous exhaustion. She was under the pressure of her final year at Columbia, with papers and a dissertation due. Further, her desk was piled high with articles and translations. David was in Rochester finishing medical school, and she missed him. Anita needed to stop and be nurtured and pampered. She resigned from *The Nation* and went to Rochester for some pampering, although she made sure she could use his typewriter to keep working.

After a few days of rest Anita was back in the saddle in New York, re-solved to focus on finishing her degree. Her intentions were good, yet she was distracted by the need to complete her application for a Guggenheim grant and to enjoy her fan mail:

> Life consists now of anthropology, and it will be that way until I take my examinations in May. Then I shall be free! Today I had an interview with the Guggenheim people. It seems settled that I shall have a fellowship, to study Aztec art. Idols has been success-ful enough to bring me letters from illustrious people; I particularly prize two: Unamuno and Richard Hughes, who flatters me by say-ing that our styles are alike . . I now seem to be a "successful young author," and strangers often know me. Which is gratifying.[27]

It took her two months to answer the letter from Miguel de Unamuno. She continued to enjoy the notoriety that *Idols behind Altars* brought, and she kept up her hectic pace, which included writing a short dissertation and organizing a wedding.

nine

An Atypical Student

Flor de Manita by Tina Modotti.

ANITA ENROLLED at Columbia University in the fall of 1927 and received her Ph.D. in the summer of 1930. She met the requirements without earning a bachelor's or a master's degree. Accreditation for previously completed work and life experience seems to have been easier at that time. Franz Boas, head of the Department of Anthropology, was the determining factor in getting Anita through the hoops.[1]

Boas attracted students who went on to excel, among them Margaret Mead, Ruth Benedict, Elsie Clews Parsons, George Dorsey, and P. E. Goddard. They were Anita's contemporaries, both students and professors. Melville J. Herskovits considers the widely used "Boas school" a misnomer because Boas did not impose methodology or theoretical orientation. On the contrary, he stressed academic freedom. Students were expected to act independently. He was concerned not with the way students proceeded but with their results and that they should take full responsibility for their work. Boas did not impose topics for dissertations to fit his own interests; he encouraged independent thinking.[2]

Boas encouraged Anita to pursue a doctoral degree. He did not recoil from confrontation with bureaucratic regulations. In fact, he was known for his struggles with administrative policies. When Anita registered as a graduate student, she recorded: "Today I also went up and got caught in the academic machinery again—Boas is an old darling. He has a sense of humor and lots of *buena voluntad* [good will] and something may come of it yet."[3] She had not intended to enter a Ph.D. program when she first enrolled at Columbia. Her sense of humor was with her every step of the way as she jumped administrative hurdles:

> *It invariably makes administrators and clerks angry to have to handle my record. Foxy "Papa Franz" is trying to accumulate me enough undergrad credits for me to get graduate standing immediately.* "Con ese motivo" [for that reason] *I had an informal exam from the Spanish department. That is, a talk with Onis, at the written request of Boas, and Onis pronounced me as knowing the undergraduate work and whatever they teach of Spanish and Pan-American literature. It was very simple, I just gave him my opinions of the poets and passed judgment lackadaisically on Prieto, Gutierrez Najera, etc. etc. Also said I preferred Unamuno and Ortega y Gasset to Spanish modern poets . . . and voila, the exam was over. Oh, facade, facade, how New Yorkese you are!*[4]

Boas may have been motivated to encourage Anita because he respected her achievements. He had spent time in Mexico doing fieldwork and establishing the International School of American Archaeology and Ethnology. Anita had worked for Manuel Gamio in the early twenties, after Gamio returned from studying with Boas.[5] She was exactly the type of person that Boas encouraged.[6] She had a track record in Mexico and shared Mexican and American friends with Boas.

Anita's circle of friends in Mexico overlapped with intellectual circles in New York. One of the best examples is George Vaillant, an archaeologist who visited Mexico in July 1926.[7] Charlot introduced them, and they saw each other often, enjoyed each other's company, and shared an interest in art and the indigenous peoples of Mexico. When Anita and her roommate, Lucy, looked Vaillant up in New York, he introduced them to members of Columbia University's faculty. They met Vaillant for dinner, Anita went by his office to chat, and he dropped in at their apartment and brought others. Anita recorded conversations with Vaillant and his friends about Mexican art as well as gossip about mutual friends. Vaillant was instrumental in moving Anita and Lucy into the inner circle of professionals.

Anita also shared the Columbia experience with others she had known in Mexico. Frank Tannenbaum, who did his undergraduate work at Columbia, had been in Mexico doing research and teaching at the National University's summer school program. Anita learned about land distribution and foreign holdings from him.[8] He visited, attended parties at Anita's, and tried to enlist her help with his research.[9] While in Mexico City Tannenbaum and John Dewey had been particularly interested in the worker cooperative school known as "La Bolsa." The "miracle school" (a primary and junior high) was a live-in cooperative where the students supported themselves and at the same time handled an informal community outreach literacy campaign. Anita introduced Gruening to the school as part of Mexico's reality.

Anita would later share political struggles with other Columbia alumni, such as Joseph Freeman, Sidney Hook, and Lionel Trilling. She did not refer to them as part of the Columbia group, perhaps because her relationship with Hook and Trilling came through the *Menorah Journal*.[10] Anita, Freeman, and Hook described different Columbia experiences in their journals and memoirs. Freeman was an undergraduate who was not associated with a particular professor. Hook reported his relationship to Dewey as "unusual." Anita met Dewey when he taught in Mexico at the National

University's summer school, but she didn't mention following up the relationship until the thirties. Hook wrote, "During those years at Columbia, we graduate students never socialized with our professors. What we got to know about them was largely hearsay or inferred from public prints, reviews, association meetings, sometimes news stories."[11] Anita recorded a completely different atmosphere:

> *Friday evening at Dr. Boas', with students and anthro notables dripping brains all over the place. Most animated and fantastic gathering, with hours of talk about science. Boas took me apart and gave me a biblio. on art. That's the newest kink in anthro, apparently. He is having a book out on it soon. I shall be therefore a "disciple" of said kink. [. . .] Mrs. Boas very nice. The whole thing very "students-in-old-Heidelberg-ish." Tail end of the good old days, we take it. Boas is really an amazing and remarkable man.*[12]

Photo by Edward Weston or Tina Modotti. Courtesy of Center for Creative Photography, University of Arizona.

From time to time Anita mentioned attending weekly luncheons, taking great pride in being accepted and respected for her expertise. The image she projects is definitely not one of a meek admiring graduate student. The only scholar she followed as a mentor was Boas. The luncheons were opportunities to record irreverent comments.

> *Went to the regular Thursday anthropologische luncheon. G. Reich-ard had a new hat. Acted feminine. Question: was it the hen or the egg first in her case? (Goddard is very pleased and with the spring makes more raw remarks than ever.) In ribald moments L. [Lucy] and I describe him as "a disreputable old goat." That's his charm. At the luncheon met Erich Schmidt, a cute little man who started on Arizona and is now in Turkey. His description of a "human headed bird" pot he found in Arizona got me all excited (for reasons which have their roots in this bee in my bonnet about Tarascan and George Lothrop-Hay. "Q culture.") Anyway I got a picture of the thing and took it to Hay and demanded what it was and he promptly said "tarascan." So I plumed. Schmidt talked to me a long time. I was very much impressed by the way he reflects or expresses the Boas attitude (i.e. relationships) in method of archeology. Such beautiful vcharts![13]*

Anita was on track, concerned with contemporary questions and issues that she claimed as her own. She was pleased and fully involved when she recorded:

> *Things keep on happening. Classes as usual and seminar, at which Boas made the leading question one I asked him in conference— Do you go out and get everything in sight or is there a definite prob-lem in your mind? He was quite genial and in full bloom of his "grand old man" manner. He is a grand-old man, magnificent lec-ture, at which George [Vaillant] introduced Lucy [Knox] et moi to Clarence Hay, and both of them announced to us that we had been elected members of the American Ethnologist (and Anthropologist) Association, as fellows . . thus being placed as professionals.[14]*

Journal entries from this period reveal a growing maturity in content and style. They include lengthy analyses of philosophical issues triggered by

Boas's lectures, other professors, or her reading. Comments about social gatherings, feelings, moods, and accomplishments were ongoing. The social whirl continued amid references to earning a living and new clothes. Work meant writing, as opposed to traditional academic endeavors such as teaching, which Hook and Trilling both did while in graduate school.[15]

Occasionally Anita registered comments about fellow students, recorded walking out of boring classes, bubbled with excitement over new classes, and suffered through all-nighters to finish papers.[16] She recorded major events in her academic career, such as attending a meeting of the American Ethnologist (and Anthropologist) Association in Andover, Massachusetts, in December 1927. She was impressed with being accepted as a member of the group, excited by the environment, yet highly irreverent in her description:

> A number of very important people staying. [. . .] Boas, summing up each session in a few words—astoundingly clear. He towers head and shoulders above them. Spinden is a wah-wah journalist. Nelson is very sound but does table-talk and this irritates some. Tozzer makes little Sunday school speeches. Kidder is the gentleman. Goddard with unusual dignity, and darn nice to us. Boas also extraordinarily considerate. He gives me mental or rather intellectual humility such as I seldom feel. Big kick out of the eno-archaci blah-blah between Spinden and versus George [Vaillant] and Lothrop. Spinden just ignored all their proofs, and brought in some pretty little bats to fly over the ruins of his theories. [. . .] Throughout, terribly proud of Boas and of being presented by him.[17]

Another highlight was overhearing professors' favorable comments about her review of Boas's book in *The Nation*.[18] Anita felt honored by an invitation from Boas in the fall of 1928 to help with preparations and translations for the Americanist Congress, a prestigious group which brought professionals from many countries together.[19] She had been at Columbia for one year, and gradually integrated Boas into her own private extended family. She included him in her "list of worries," and wrote, "Boas is sick, exhausted, and stays home, which for him is grave indeed."[20] The most illustrative statement about Anita's relationship with Boas was recorded in the journal on May 18, 1929. Classes were over and the topic for her dissertation was set.

This means that I may about do as I please with more or less the material I please and sometime next year whenever I am ready I present my papers and take my exams; no traveling back and forth and no uncertainty about the "finds." If it works out as apparently acceptedly planned, I shall have my degree at about this time next year. PhD at 24! I shall feel somewhat ridiculous. I am most proud of Boas' confidence. He never asks me what I am doing and never tries to make me change my course. Can I expand the subject, he asks? Expand, then. Do I want to select only portions of it? Select, then. And all he does is offer little additional suggestions. I just about weep with emotion. Ruth and Boas . . . we're all of us Ruths.[21]

Anita's play on words alludes to her colleagues Ruth Benedict and Ruth Bunzel—also followers of the Boas tradition at Columbia—and associates them with the biblical Ruth, who was known for her loyalty and who married a man named Boaz.

The most outstanding passages written during this period reflect Anita's intellectual stimulation. She recorded questions and ideas from classes, such as the contrast between the processes of social development and the role of individuals and science.[22] She used her journal to clarify thoughts about art, film as an art form, and literature. A detailed comparison of contemporary literature and art describes the ways writing fell behind. The "art for art's sake" controversy recurs, with a condemnation of "pure art" as nonsense. Boas is her authority: "Science looks sick beside art, to me . . . And Boas says he would rather have written a good poem than his 'Kwakiu' and rather a good symphony than all his work."[23] She threw in others' opinions and conversations and frequently used the image of words going around her head: "My head goes round when I try to put the world in order, the more I get the Boas air (my personal application of it, of course. Boas would distrust me deeply if he thought I'd go and get philosophical on him)."[24]

The journals also reflect Anita's effort to integrate ideas and concepts with previous experience:

The reasons in the U.S. sex is emphasized so much is because the only other way of emotional function is religion and art—are because of social reasons inhibited. Science cannot be a substitute, nor business, except only to a certain point; the technique is too limited . . like an academy . . against which necessarily there must be

constant reaction . . The limitation is exterior, and too great . . be-
cause it is exterior, it is real.

The connection between art and love is one of "conditioned re-
flex." They cannot be completely substituted one for the other—But
a stimulus which in a "goat" may produce a rape may in a painter
produce a picture . . The difference between the two passions exists
psychologically however, and although there can be such a thing
as an artistic or creative rape (as such) in this case it is a shifting
of emotional mechanism.[25]

Anita maintained that people not in contact with Boas would find her
musings incomprehensible. The journal entries, however, were very much
a part of her time. She integrated Freud's pleasure-pain concept and was
trying to clarify her philosophy of life.

Many ideas that Anita expressed came together two years into her Columbia experience, on November 1, 1929, in a long passage that she described as "receiving the call to heal." She reported a mystical experience
that fits the description of Abraham Maslow's "peak experience."[26] The
episode initiates the shift from an "anthropological participant-observer,"
who reported events, to a political crusader determined to make a difference in her environment. In Erik Erikson's structure, Anita's experience
corresponded to the culmination of an identity crisis.[27]

Anita never mentioned the stock market crash of 1929. Savoring the success of *Idols behind Altars*, she was in love and engaged to be married, but
also exhausted, elated, and deeply concerned about the morality of her
environment. The outside mood of despair and confusion influenced her
thinking, generating a yearning for principles and a dissatisfaction with the
world around her. Charlot soothed her, identifying her experience as that
of a true artist. Anita analyzed her projects and recognized that they were
"part of another period or that they are all elaborated by a 'scientific' mind,
[. . .] and they seemed to me incomplete; what I looked for now was for
the ethical implication. For the first time too, I understood what Jean
[Charlot] meant when he said most of my stories are immoral. Unmoral
is what he meant. And therefore to him, immoral." She described the
emotional upheaval with great lucidity: "A psychiatrist might call what I
had a 'paranoid panic,' and a theologian would call it an 'intellectual vision.' Whatever the name, it at once bridges a great many months of thought
and it seems, rather about-faces my whole trend of work."[28]

The process started while reading ancient history to prepare for a conference with Boas. Anita picked up

> the Bible to check up on Chaldean history—later Babylonia, period of captivity—and as I read more and more I suddenly and abruptly came to this thought: Well, what a simple-minded moron I am, looking for literary models, "influences" and such things, when obviously here is the model and the source for me, even in questions of form . . Then I had the queerest series of sensations, which mentally were translated into question and answer, much as this: Question: But what exactly must I do with my abilities . . Answer: Pick up the thread of uncompromising spiritual and ethical thought . . which means fight against nearly everything in modern thought around you . . which also means keep yourself as pure and lofty of mind as you can . . It grew and grew, and I had feelings of faintness and a tremendous sensation of being out of the world . . If I had seen anything "supernatural" I would not have been in the least surprised . . That was my mood . . And then I got a sensation of reluctance, because I realized the full implications of what the proposal was . . and I nearly said aloud, "No, no, I am just an ordinary normal craftsman," and I got burning sensations in my mouth, and my head felt much expanded . . and not until I "submitted" did it stop; after which I was thoroughly exhausted.[29]

Farther along the same passage she goes into detail about her explosive reaction to a comment by *The Nation*'s book editor, who thought her reviews too strong and her opinions too forceful. Anita identified her outburst as a reaction against the mellowness around her: "he represented in his attitude that outlook of compromise of which Dewey is the exponent and most American intellectuals the followers . . and which fairly makes me boil."

Two months without entries followed the experience. On February 20, 1930, she recorded, "I pick up 'this personal life of mine' where I left off several months ago. It has seemed that I have been marking time, insofar as work goes, possibly because I have done comparatively little writing . . an article here and there . . or a review . . I finished [. . .] the research for my dissertation. Also, a nervous breakdown cut off my *Nation* work definitively."

The dissertation was very short (93 printed pages), with ample illustrations of the designs found on a collection of potsherds that Boas had brought from Mexico and stored at the University of Pennsylvania library. Anita was relieved not to have to do field research, instead examining artistic patterns. The process seems to have been more of a necessary but insignificant chore, without the excitement of previous work.

In time, Anita widened her political involvement and commitment to include the causes of her time, especially the struggle against fascism and on behalf of the Republicans in Spain. The shift implied moving on from an identification with the Mexican Revolution and the underdog, fighting foreign absentee landowners who imposed cultural patterns. Up to this point Anita's position had been to listen and learn about politics without expressing her own views. The closest she came to taking a stand was the defense of Mexico as an appropriate place for Jewish immigration. She identified as a Jew and mixed socially with people who held many different political affiliations.[30] It was time to take a stand.

Anita's intellectual growth was probably influenced by her admiration for Boas. He was a pacifist, politically identified with those described by John Patrick Diggins as "the Lyrical Left."[31] Anita was familiar with his political ideology because of her relationship with Ernest Gruening. She had heard Gruening, Charles Erwin, and John Dos Passos reminisce about the good old "socialist" days over dinners in Mexico.[32] Their political affinity was confirmed a few years later when both Anita and Boas were members of the National Committee for the Defense of Political Prisoners. She does not mention discussing politics with Boas or anyone else in her journals. The visionary experience triggered the process of integrating her intellectual growth into political action.

Anita, the restless, rebellious daughter of a foreign landowner, finished her course work and wrote her dissertation in 1930. She applied for and received a Guggenheim fellowship to pursue her studies of Aztec art. Her Guggenheim travels served double duty as a prolonged honeymoon. She and her bridegroom toured European museums that had important Aztec art collections and then traveled through unexplored hills in Mexico in search of the roots of the creators of the same art.

ten

Flirtations, Relationships, and Love

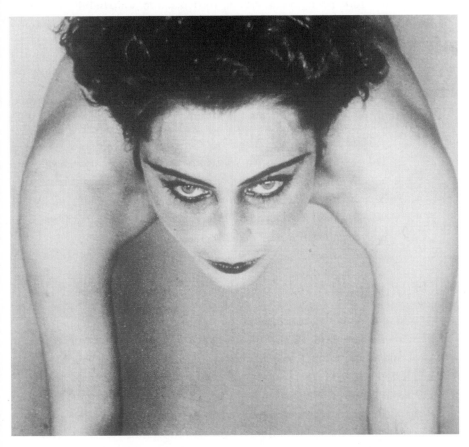

Nahui Olin. Photo by Edward Weston. Courtesy of Center for Creative
Photography, University of Arizona.

"IT IS very simple. Since anthropology is the science that studies man, it seems natural to me that a woman be interested."[1] That was how Anita answered a journalist who asked why she studied anthropology.

Anita's journals reveal a steady stream of male friends and suitors and a wide variety of relationships with men until she met David. The wallflower days of Texas were behind her.[2] In Mexico they came to lunch and in New York they took her out to dinner. Some just dropped by, both in Mexico and in New York. Beginning in 1923 in Mexico, parties were in full swing, and in New York Anita and her roommate, Lucy, entertained old friends from Mexico and new ones from Columbia.

Anita was concerned with her appearance, perhaps to offset her mother's affirmations that "it was too bad she wasn't pretty." She mentioned it repeatedly and recorded the feeling in her correspondence with David.[3] A letter applying for a job presented the information and provided the title for this book:

> Duly casting all modesty to the winds, [. . .] I can meet the specifications for your journalistic dream woman. [. . .] For over a year I have been conducting a cultural potpourri column, smart young woman's angle in Mademoiselle. It is called "A Mind of Your Own" and was named thus by the editors to describe the author. [I . . .] use my brains on face and clothes as well as on paper, but I have not quite forgiven God yet for the fact that I don't look like Dolores del Río.[4]

Anita had a number of friends who were older men and played the role of mentor. Carleton Beals encouraged her to write, helped her with contacts, and stayed in touch in a supportive fashion.[5] Ernest Gruening hired her, introduced her to the world of the "early socialists," and recommended her to publishers.[6] Franz Boas played a similar role; he and Gruening both demanded excellence, which stimulated her to stretch her intellectual skills and produce. Anita learned through her research for Gruening to provide him with raw and analytical information about Mexico. She had a straightforward professor-student relationship with Boas, embellished by his respect for her.

One of Anita's most complex relationships was with Jean Charlot. They shared creativity, mutual admiration, and a major stumbling block—religion. Charlot's roles as teacher, father, and mentor evolved naturally into one of a frustrated admirer.

Sexually, Anita was ultraconservative for her time, yet she recorded the efforts suitors made to woo her with a sense of humor. Her reactions varied depending on the gentleman in question. She did not enjoy being put on the spot but did not harp on the issue. She took it in her stride, dealt with it, and moved on. Anita did not mention any incidents of sexual harassment or pressure where she risked losing a job, but she did describe some clever maneuvers to maintain friendly relationships while turning down advances. One she refused on the grounds of not wanting to be number 179.[7] Another she sidestepped with drama: "He grew tender and passionate by turns and (since he has already paid me) I unfolded my remarkable ironic-naivete on him. It never fails to mystify. He tried to kiss me, so I put out my cigarette and arose dramatically; whereupon he followed me, and then I did a regular *Gaona capoteo* [bullfighter's maneuver], remarking as I hitched up my right shoulder and flung out my left hip—'Me siento torero!' [I feel like a bullfighter!] What does he take me for?"[8]

Sometimes Anita participated actively and was not an innocent bystander. As a young woman actively in search of Prince Charming, she described men with sensuality, focusing on attractive features. Rufino Tamayo "has very strong attraction for most women. Slim and terribly sensual, wide mouth and the savor of things apparent on it. He rouses desire."[9] She also noticed that "Diego [Rivera] in his suave moments [has] a sort of sweet-oil swimming in the eyes—as if they had been toasted in butter and floating—a vast and sensuous romanticism."[10] The search for the right man led to flirtations, conquests, and setbacks. The journals mention a formal *novio* (boyfriend) at one point, falling in love, and the ongoing relationship with Charlot. Her attitude was exploratory and contradictory. On the one hand: "Let my craving for excitement run, and my extreme pleasure in cat-mouse tactics (me being the feline). Almost got an over-dose. I don't give much of a damn, having been bored for some time now. Jean kisses beautifully."[11] On the other hand, she was genuinely in search of answers. "I wonder about sex; if you yield do you conquer it or does it conquer you? Am I freer now, abstaining completely, than I would be opening up these reserves that sometimes torment me?"[12] Sometimes she approached the issue from an intellectual angle; at other times she drew parallels between creative energy and sex. She mused about losing her virginity and consulted friends, such as Nahui Olin, known for her defiance of sexual and social mores. After a visit from Manuel Hernandez Galvan, she wrote, "I am embarrassed by the evident potence of my untouched properties, and would wish to be free of all this. Nahui says yielding does not give liberty."[13]

The quandary and inner conflict were strongest in late 1925 and early 1926. She thought she was "in-love" at the time and described the sequence of attraction, conquest, and heartache. She was so upset that she followed Nahui's method to get the man to appear:

> You take a candle and you do things to it with your finger nails, saying certain things, and you see what you want to know. White or red. Furthermore, you take a bath in male scents and wipe yourself with "pomo de limpias" [jar for cleansing] and you can give him certain things in his coffee. Finger nail filings, for instance. With a picture or handwriting or hair it is stronger. It works, absolutely. Nahui and I did it Sunday and Monday—6-8-12—and Tuesday at 4 P.M. he came—I did it this A.M. for a meeting at the P.O. and I met him.[14]

Anita expressed her yearnings and feelings in poetry, written in English and Spanish. Sometimes she repeated modified versions of the verses while working on the poem and sometimes she recorded a finished text. Many of the poems were about her love for Jean and the problem of religion.

PSALM

He was a Catholic.
And I a Jew.
How is that unique?
He loved me.

I did not know
One could love so
As he loved me.

And yet, never
Did we have a happy day.
I don't know whether it was because
He was Catholic, or I a Jew.

Oh my people!
Mother tormented by pain, and irony.

My great-grandparents, for thousands of years,
Stroked their beards and voiced their wisdom
In wandering magical poetry, sang God's praises
In all the tongues of apostasis.

At dusk my fathers stroll
In their slippers and caftan robes.
Their hands crossed on the sword
Calling troubles a nostalgia
For the land of Isaac and Abraham.

My father, King Solomon, said
That the world of gold and pearls is vanity.
And I with my cousins from all the lands
Pay to see them and make them with our lives.

Before, when there were prophets,
Women with breasts full of manna
Like mine
Nurtured with your strength and your devotion
Male children, hallowed by circumcision.

Their wide hips conceived
Like mine
My great-great grandfathers who together
Would create God's unity
So the Messiah might come.

Ardent race of Israel, your blood is the gift
Of love and of creation.

That Catholic who loved me
In the evenings would say
Why do you torture yourself, my dear?[15]

The relationship with Jean was intense, even though Anita saw other men and kept looking until she met and married David. There were times when she despaired and was ready to become a Roman Catholic. "A little crazy, I am tonight, probably because I haven't written anything for a little. It may be all right tomorrow. But it is because I am full on the crest of realizing how much I care about Jean. And I think that, notwithstanding the Pope,

Jean Charlot. Photo
by Edward Weston.
Courtesy of Center for
Creative Photography,
University of Arizona.

my family, his family, and no money, and the inconveniences of children,
I shall eventually or next winter, marry him."[16]

Sometimes she was more analytical than impulsive. Shortly before she
met David, she had been considering converting to Catholicism. The despair of feeling that she didn't belong recurred, and yet she pondered the
wisdom of following a religion and an ideology solely because of Charlot.
"Again, on the other hand, I don't know enough about Judaism to continue it into Catholicism. It seems the road, but I should begin farther back.
And I have a kind of racial feeling about desertion . . Which may also be
social embarrassment."[17]

Anita was fully aware of the contradiction between her feelings for
Charlot and the series of suitors. Nevertheless, she continued to flirt with,
provoke, and get involved with other men. After she left Mexico for New
York the search became less intense, and she recorded fewer emotional

ups and downs. She wrote about "going to dinner" and evaluated situations in a more cerebral fashion than in the earlier years in Mexico. Her attitude may have changed because she was older and took things more calmly, or perhaps she did not fall in and out of love as often. Charlot's absence and the lack of time for adventures are other possibilities. She did not, however, seem to modify her pace of activity.

Anita had dinner with Waldo Frank, a prominent writer among the radical New York Jewish intellectuals, several weeks before meeting David. The episode is significant because Frank was Jewish, available, and interested, and it was not the first dinner they shared. Religion was not the only factor under consideration; the chemistry was not there, and Anita returned to her impulse to marry Charlot.

> [Waldo's] *interest grew with the evening. He has a coquette's way of intimating himself, a venturesome way for women, [. . .]. This is not perhaps even a conscious thing with him. The idea is that the lady will suffer, and I suppose most of them do, on account of his abruptness, his way of suddenly chasing another thought or suddenly breathing another mood. All of which is too much like myself to surprise me, and anyway my usual attitude is to take quicksilver as quicksilver when quicksilver is there. A constant friendship, devotion, or whatever it is that is usually wanted, would not be there. But certainly vitality and sensitivity. I don't know about passion. He seems to have the same withdrawal, the same not wanting to give the self wholly, as I. My final reaction to the evening, which ended abruptly, was an impulse to write Jean* [Charlot]: *"Come and take me now, or you never shall!"*[18]

The same entry records spending a long evening in a philosophical conversation with David's brother, Alfred Glusker. She was intrigued but not interested in the young man whom she called "a youth" in a romantic fashion. Once Anita met David, the doubts previously recorded in her journals vanished. She was sure she had found her Prince Charming yet unsure about how long it would last. She felt safe with Charlot in the background. "The book finished, me thin, having clothes, and a warm sensation connected with the name of David and the sense of security given by Jean, standing by, I am really contented to numbness."[19]

Anita met David while spending the weekend with a group of friends in Williamstown, Massachusetts. They went wading in a brook, walked through a New England cemetery, and fell in love. Anita had the final re-write of *Idols behind Altars* on her desk and other work pending, includ-ing her dissertation. She had a full year to go at Columbia to complete her doctoral degree.

They had similar backgrounds, as children of East European Jewish immigrants.[20] Charles Glusker, David's father, was four years old when he arrived in New York. The story the Glusker family told was that Grand-father Solomon wasn't particularly fond of his wife. The marriage had been arranged by a matchmaker, who introduced Solomon to two attractive sis-ters. His bride, however, was to be the third, homely sister, who did not appear during the visit. Their eight children were all born in January, all conceived during the Passover holidays. (Perhaps Solomon was only home on Jewish holidays.) Charles taught English at Public School 6 in New York City. His sisters, Frances and Syd, were active in the women's suf-frage movement and with the Communist Party in New York. Anna Sims, David's mother, emigrated from Warsaw with her family. She was a self-educated woman who persevered, going to school at night, once family chores were done. Anna, remembered for her charm, her love of music, and her salonlike concert parties, was successful in insurance sales.

David was the elder of two sons. He grew up in Brooklyn and attended Boys High School (a school popular with Jewish immigrants), Brooklyn College, and the University of Pennsylvania. When they met, he too had one year left to complete medical school. Anita described him as a beau-tiful young person who had little experience with women: "I must seem mysterious and wise, but that is likely because he has had so little to do with women. It is all a little like the schoolboy and the actress. It comes so easy to me to dream about him, and I feel so secure and natural and at home with him, and yet in a way watchful because he is sensitive and ex-posed, and I seem to be able to reflect upon him so easily, reflect in the sense of form, stamp, or mold."[21]

Traditional courtship, wherein a young man called on a young woman living at home, gave way to more informal dating as more women attended universities. David called on Anita, took her to the beach, to dinner, and home to his mother. Before the summer was over, they decided to marry and informed David's mother in a formal fashion.

The vast correspondence between Anita and David during their first year of courtship provides an ideal vehicle for analyzing their relationship. They

David Glusker—
"Prince Charming."

wrote almost daily, and they both kept the letters, which record events, fears, concerns, and issues that would affect their future.[22]

Anita's letters to David provide an immense amount of information. First and foremost, they portray a woman in love. She designated a special chair for sitting and dreaming about David. She also described how difficult it was for her to work on articles or her dissertation while thinking about him. She was eager to spend all her time with him, to get away and be alone together, to have his children, promising to stop at five.[23] She was concerned about his chronic sinus condition, which he frequently wrote about "belly-aching," and with his relationship to his family. The letters gradually replaced Anita's journal. The journal records fewer events as the letters increase, even though some information is duplicated. The correspondence covers hard news, events, moods, feelings, and ideas. The hard news was about Anita's work, such as Jean Charlot's manuscript or her dissertation. The major events were the success of *Idols behind Altars*, the award of her Guggenheim fellowship, and completion of her doctoral exam.

Anita continued to lead an active social life, including meeting male friends (mostly artists she had known in Mexico) for dinner or seeing them when they dropped by her apartment. There were also dinners with new friends from the *Menorah Journal*, such as the Trillings, Elliot Cohen, and Waldo Frank. Anita was aware that her social life and friends made David jealous. Sometimes she tackled the problem by insisting on having a relationship where she could be open and honest. Other times she teased him: "And I will make a confession: which is, that I adore your being jealous. You see I boast about it. We'll both be primeval. If you ever stop being jealous I'll do my best to make you be jealous again. Wouldn't that be an involved situation? Seems quite impossible."[24]

David captures his wife studying maps. Photo by David Glusker.

Anita gave David a blow-by-blow description of each friend's reaction to the news that she was engaged. When she told Carlos Merida (who would illustrate Anita's guidebook *Your Mexican Holiday*), he

> *was so pleased to hear that you were dark, and jealous. And amused, of course, at what he calls the end of my romantic bohemian days. [. . .] He likes the idea of me being "disciplined" and taken care of. All of the things that you are going to do to me and for me are his idea of what a he-man (muy hombre) should do and does. I told him you didn't know anything about art, and he said, well, "you're marrying him for yourself, not for your friends." [. . .] Somehow, people in Mexico do sweep away the trimmings and see the fundamentals. If we had been in Mexico I would never have become so disturbed about our dissimilar personalities, orbits, tastes, what have you. It's the Nuyawk intelligentsia that did that to me, and to think I didn't realize it!*[25]

Their correspondence explores the importance of differences between them, differences in their lifestyles and interests. Anita vacillated, sometimes insisting that they were not critical, other times stressing them. She was interested in people and art; he was a scientist. He would be bored by her conversations and friends, and she would bore and be bored by his medical scientific types. One of her letters presents her fears in a remarkably lucid fashion:

> *As to me, there is a constant struggle going on in me. Part no. 1, which wants you and your body and quietness and security and babies, is fighting part no. 2 which wants to be wild and solitary and adventuresome and very hardworking and something of a bum and doesn't give a whoop how much it suffers and gets terribly excited about pictures and sights and people and sounds and such things; and since this is the part that has always had its way it is pretty well entrenched and hates to give anything of its privileges up, particularly, I suppose, being solitary, and kind of secret and independent. And part no. 1 says, as it kisses your letter, oh, I love him; I know how to love; I shall love him as no man was ever loved before and as few men are ever loved; I have the gift of love, and he has the gift of love too. And the drive, the emotion inside has al-*

ways been with no. 2, but it has absolutely shifted over to no. 1, so that no. 2 is mostly armed with habit, which is about the most powerful thing there is, except love; and since they are so evenly matched, it is a struggle. There it is.[26]

Anita and David were married six months later by Rabbi De Sola Pool, an orthodox rabbi, at the Spanish-Portuguese Synagogue in New York.[27] Members of the family corroborate Anita's not-very-hidden agenda to rankle David's mother with a "very Jewish wedding."[28] David had been brought up within the Ethical Culture school, an offshoot of Conservative Judaism which retains the ethics and the morality of the Jewish religion without stressing the role of God. David's mother had rejected her Jewish Orthodox upbringing by joining the ranks of Ethical Culture.

David's relationship with his mother was difficult. Anita was welcomed by her future mother-in-law, until it became apparent that the relationship was headed toward marriage. According to Anita, his mother was concerned that Anita, "tired of being a bohemian," wanted to marry a conventional and financially successful person.[29] The two women went to dinner, the theater, and concerts. Anita, concerned about the relationship between David and his mother, stepped into the middle of their conflicts. The issue was money. On January 30, 1930, Anita wrote,

> *Your mother is very bitter about you and I don't try to defend you. She told me something of your last letter and I must say it was straight from the shoulder. You are worse than I am. I think, too, a little unfair. After all, your mother is sick, nervous, upset, and will be getting older; she has borne most of the family burden, and she oughtn't to be just cut loose, you know; your father doesn't want any financial responsibility because he wants to marry again. Well, don't you think he wants too much by wanting everything? I had promised myself not to speak of all this stuff again, and I'll try not to. But your letter to your mother—what I heard of it—scared me. Some day perhaps you will talk to me with the same curt finality, the same lack of sympathy, the same—oh, I don't know what. But anyhow I feel rotten. And I wonder why my last letter made you feel guilty? This one will probably make me feel guilty. Which is the final ornamental loop on my black mood.*

Anita became involved with all the Gluskers: she helped find a job for Alfred, looked for insurance clients for Anna, and took Solomon Glusker's autobiographical manuscript to the *Menorah Journal*, reporting to David:

> the Menorah people find that your grandfather was a very intelli-
> gent and pleasant man, a little too intelligent, they say, so that he
> spoke of social theories and movements now without special inter-
> est. But the mss. is interesting as a human document . . curious Yid-
> dish, they say; half German. So? I mean Z—o-o-o-o-! How come
> your grandfather wrote that kind of Yiddish, living in Russia? You've
> been deceiving me. They may use some extracts from it, translating
> it themselves, I guess, because they say that its chief literary value
> is in its simplicity.[30]

Her role in the Glusker family was the same one she filled when she in-
terceded for her sisters with her father. She wanted them to communicate,
to hear each other and resolve issues. Her reaction to David's tone in 1930
was somewhat prophetic. After twenty years of marriage, David did address
Anita with a tone similar to the one he used with his mother.

The newlyweds spent the year following their marriage traveling together
in Europe and in the hills of Guerrero, a remote area on the west coast of
Mexico, largely unexplored in 1931 when they were there.[31] When David
returned to New York, Anita stayed in Mexico City to work on *Your Mexican Holiday*. Only after two years of marriage did the couple settle down
to live together. Even then Anita was in New York only about a year before taking off for Spain as a feature writer for the *New York Times Sunday
Magazine*. Their relationship was difficult. David wanted his Anita available in the evenings, at home, but Anita was working at full steam. She
published her first article in the *New York Times Sunday Magazine* in 1932.[32]

The letters written in 1931–1932 and in late 1933 deal with logistical
conflicts between their two lifestyles. David was adamant about having his
office within his home. Anita wanted privacy and her own space. She insisted on living in an apartment with more than two rooms, so she could
have a room of her own to work in, filling it with papers, files, and books.
David was upset because Anita worked at night, when he wanted to share
time after a full day's work.

Structuring their time was not the only problem. The Depression deeply
affected their lives. David, recently graduated as a physician, had a hard

Honeymooning in
Guerrero. Photo by
David Glusker.

time starting a private practice. He worked with several hospitals and colleagues, covering their vacation periods, without being able to find a niche
of his own that would pay the bills. The young couple survived on Anita's
earnings and on the funds that David borrowed from members of his family: his mother, father, aunt, grandmother, and others. Their correspondence in 1933, when Anita was in Spain, presents the situation clearly: Anita
was willing to stop working to have children, and David wanted them to
live within his income, but the painful reality was that he did not earn
enough to support them.

Their love for each other helped them overcome their difficulties. She
traveled to Spain again in 1936, shortly before her first child was born. In
1974, in an interview with Beth Miller a few months before Anita died,
she recalled the trials of being a working mother: "My own problem—when

my children were born—was having to be a housewife and a mother and at the same time make deadlines and so forth. Yes, that was a real problem. [. . .] Markel [editor of the *New York Times Sunday Magazine*] would once or twice make sneering remarks like, 'How's the great American Mother?'"[33]

Because Anita stopped keeping her journal when she married, the only documentation of their married life is their correspondence during periods when they were apart. They were together from 1936 until 1942, when David enlisted in the Army. Letters from his military days, stamped by the Army censor, explore concerns of a different nature: the war, the children, uncertainty about the future, and David's severe bitterness about anti-Semitism in the Army.

Interviews with their contemporaries did not provide much information about their life together. Memories of the couple's stormy break in 1952, when David was drawn into a relationship with another woman, seemed to blot out all else. Anita was heartbroken and focused on efforts to maintain communication, so that he would return, as she put it to me, "once he saw the light." Although she had many friends and male admirers, she never established an intimate relationship with a second partner. She was devastated when David died in July 1961; it meant that their relationship could not be mended.

eleven

Your Mexican Holiday

Photo by Marianne Goeritz.

ANITA AND DAVID arrived in Mexico on their extended honeymoon at the end of 1930. He had never been there, and she had been away for three and a half years. It was a different Mexico. The political scene had shifted to the right. Many artists had left in search of work; Rivera was working in New York and California; Orozco was in New York; Siqueiros was organizing unions in Mexico, going to jail for his political activity, and in and out of the country. *El Machete*, the wall journal published by the League of Revolutionary Writers and Artists, had gone underground.[1]

Labor had been maneuvered into docility by Luis N. Morones, a shrewd politician who headed the labor movement. Those who struggled for workers' rights went to jail or underground. Mexico was ruled by secondary figures controlled by the former president, Plutarco Elias Calles. They were not the revolutionary leaders who had been in power for the previous ten years. Business was slow and land reform stalled. The utopian euphoria of building a new society was gone.

Ambassador Dwight W. Morrow negotiated nonimplementation of the articles in the Constitution of 1917 that affected U.S. investors' interests. Morrow was also instrumental in deflecting radical left Mexican artists by putting them to work. He commissioned Diego Rivera to paint murals in Cuernavaca and promoted his work in the United States. Rockefeller funds were available to promote Mexican art through Frances Flynn Paine.

The Depression in the United States affected Mexico's economy until the industrial boom of World War II. Thousands of Mexican migrant workers were expelled from the United States and returned to Mexico. Demand for silver dropped. The same was true for oil and other minerals used by industry in the United States.

Anita's old friends had scattered. There were new ones on the scene, such as Sergei Eisenstein, who was working on the film that became known, in unfinished form, as *Que viva México!*[2] Katherine Anne Porter was back. Hart Crane was writing an epic poem on a Guggenheim grant. John Dos Passos visited Mexico frequently. Lesley Byrd Simpson was working on *Many Mexicos*. Stuart Chase was comparing *Main Street* to the village of Tepoztlan studied by Robert Redfield. Ione Robinson and Emily Edwards were there to paint. They gathered at Frances Toor's salon. Some had been in Mexico since the twenties. Those who came in the early thirties had a totally different agenda. The group in the twenties wanted to participate in building a new society. Those who came in the thirties were fleeing the Depression in the United States. They were in Mexico to write and paint.[3]

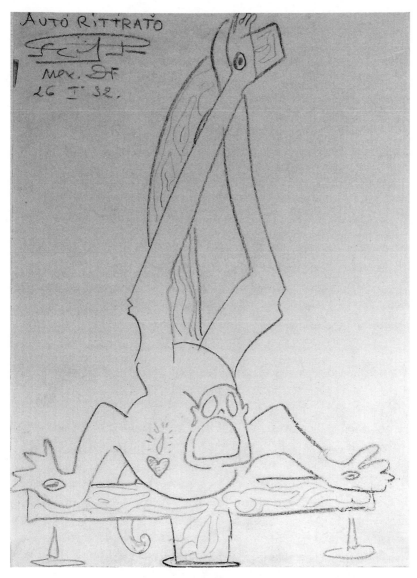

Self-portrait by Sergei Eisenstein. Photo by Michael Nye.

Anita contacted Bill Spratling to help her organize the trip through the largely unexplored state of Guerrero, to record the origins of Mexican art.[4] Spratling had traveled Guerrero and knew the routes. He developed an itinerary for the newlyweds and accompanied them for part of the trip. Anita recorded festivals and religious practices.[5] David inquired about medical

"A bit of savage, primitive, glorious honeymooning."

practices and took photographs. Together they worked on maps, adding lakes and rivers. The trip was as Anita had anticipated in her journals: "a bit of savage, primitive, glorious honeymooning."[6]

Anita applied for an extension of the Guggenheim grant, pleading that she needed more time because of the lack of information available for the Guerrero trip. She reported on the European phase of her project, mentioning the British Museum, the Trocadero in Paris, and several museums in Germany.[7] The Guggenheim Foundation granted the extension. After they returned to Mexico City from Guerrero, David went back to New York to start his practice and Anita stayed on to write her guidebook, *Your Mexican Holiday*. She saw Eisenstein often and also met with Alberto Mizrachi, who played a vital role in sponsoring the work for her guidebook. He had a combination bookstore and art gallery and helped her by lending her an apartment and advancing funds. Alberto Mizrachi was a Jewish immigrant from Greece, part of the YMHA group of Sephardic Jews that Anita was friendly with in the twenties. He was a patron of the arts who sponsored limited editions of lithographs and prints and purchased work to keep artists going.[8]

Your Mexican Holiday, first published in 1932, was so successful that five editions followed, the last in 1947. Still, there are fewer reviews of it in the archive than there are of *Idols behind Altars*, perhaps because Anita clipped less intensely; it was, after all, her second book. Ernestine Evans wrote a positive review in the *New York Herald Tribune*, complimenting Anita on a good job; the book, she went on, had "literally tons of information, about both past and present, [and] becomes at once the triple starred guidebook monopolizing the market, unless Frances Toor's forthcoming cheaper guidebook performs miracles of condensation. [. . .] Those who read [. . .] *Idols behind Altars* [. . .] will be surprised to find considerable humor in the book."[9] The two asides are in character for Evans. First, she plugs a competitor, and second, she remarks on Anita's sense of humor. Evans apparently hung on to her earlier mood.

Your *Mexican Holiday* reads like a letter to a friend describing sights and experiences. Anita combined information gathered for Gruening and for her "Mexican Decorative Arts" and "Mexican Renascence" manuscripts with her expertise as a journalist. She organized the book in independent chapters so readers could go directly to the information they wanted without having to read the entire book. There is clear information about what to see, where it is, how to get there, and who the main characters are. The book uses three different devices to present a skeleton history of Mexico: a brief narrative, a list of personalities and their roles, and a chronology of events. Each chapter follows a structure similar to those in *Idols behind Altars*: first, the geographic setting, what the visitor will see; second, a description of the people of the area; and, finally, the economic context. For example, when Anita presented *haciendas* (large feudal landholdings), she included the historical perspective, how Mexico was divided up among Spanish viceroys and notables. Once she had put them in a historical context, she followed with the geography, crops, and resources. Then she wrote about the legends, and provided anecdotes, as well as names of the current owners. Facts and figures about a particular *hacienda* are accompanied by maps and clear instructions about what to do and what not to do. Stories are woven into data with a transparent sense of irreverent humor.

Anita introduced the book with a definition of the visitor to Mexico, which was actually a description of her personal passion: "'Once the dust of Mexico has settled on your heart, you have no rest in any other land.' Mexico means something to you, in a queer personal way. You remember things about it at unexpected moments and with startling force. You are apt even to quarrel, resent most of the things said and written about it. You would like to write something yourself, full of your observations and experiences, things which you have not seen in print."[10]

She invited her readers to choose from a menu of vacation types, since there were no set recipes for tours and no beaten path. More than sixty years later her approach and the background information are still timely. There are, of course, many more roads, hotels, and restaurants, and many other guidebooks, but the basic philosophy for touring the country remains valid.

The book addresses fears and misgivings similar to those prevalent today. The second chapter takes on the question "Is it safe?" The reader is portrayed as facing a full array of pamphlets in search of somewhere remote, romantic, and glamorous, with a view of the ancient and a taste of Europe: "You hesitate. Some one has told you, or you have read somewhere, that it isn't safe. Bandits, hostile Indians, germs." That leads to what is today commonly referred to as Mexico bashing. Anita transformed the issue, turning danger into excitement: "Now a sense of danger is grand sauce to any undertaking. It changes a tour into an adventure and an ordinary trip into a story. The author hesitates, therefore [. . .] to do away too utterly with the tantalizing myth of Mexican dangers. An ordinary tour in Mexico *is* an adventure and a story, with plenty of shocks and surprises, but, unhappily for the very romantic, absolutely none of the conventional dangers." Anita proceeded to compare danger in Mexico with that in the United States: "you are as safe from bandits and hostile people as at home, probably a good deal safer; bandit gangs get rounded up and shot in Mexico. Unless, of course, you carry a very large chip on your shoulder. But even at that, foreigners being by definition mad to most Mexicans, you are likely to find yourself treated with astonishing consideration and gentleness—a little aloofly, indeed, as is necessary when dealing with the very insane."[11]

Anita added practical advice and information: what to eat, what not to eat, the effect of the altitude, the need for vaccination certificates, the climate, and a guide to Spanish pronunciation. The material is informative, light, funny, and it follows a pattern, just in case a reader might be reading the book through. The section on passport regulations warns women traveling alone that they would need a letter from a father, husband, or guardian to cross the border. The discussion of what to wear and what to bring or not bring tempts women with the news that French imports, perfumes, and cosmetics were less expensive in Mexico. Being comfortable with both the U.S. and the Mexican cultures, Anita was able to identify their quirks and address them with straightforward facts. The effect of the high altitude in Mexico City gave her an opening for comparing the two ways of life. "It becomes a virtue, almost a necessity, to do some loafing. The art of leisure is therefore one of Mexico's most stubbornly defended practices and one of her subtle appeals; a lesson in civilization which we of the hectic north need very badly to learn."[12]

Mexico City is described in detail: its history, weather, people, and entertainment options. The text is itself a tour, ending with routes to the suburban areas in the Valley of Mexico. Mexico City's geographical setting— it is surrounded by mountains and volcanoes—provides the perfect excuse to tell the legends of Popocatepetl and Ixtacihuatl, two snow-capped volcanoes still visible on clear days from the city. Surrounding areas include popular tourist spots such as Xochimilco (the floating gardens), the pyramids of Teotihuacan, and the Acolman monastery. Chapingo is described in sociological terms, as a hacienda that the government tried unsuccessfully to turn into a model village and that became the National School of Agriculture.

The guide shifts from places to peoples in the chapter "Ancient Civilizations." Besides noting the origins of the Maya, Mixtec, Zapotec, Totonac, and Toltec peoples, the book identifies major sites and outstanding samples of their art found in museums in the United States and Europe. The writing takes on a narrative quality as the reader is led from building to building. Ancient history is presented with humor in the description of the Mixtec-Zapotec peoples: "they are [. . .] related to the Mexican highland civilizations. (Which were probably just in rompers when Maya was growing up and getting married.)"[13]

Anita knew her audience and provided appropriate advice about which pyramids were worth climbing and which excursions the traveler could do without, such as the trek through the hills of Guerrero she and David had just completed.

The "Colonial Cities" chapter provides information on churches, missions, fortresses, and hospitals in the major cities of Mexico, including the people who built the structures and their legends. The text in this chapter is particularly rich with commentaries revealing Anita's interests. She twisted words and worlds while describing Pachuca as a city of the present and future and Taxco as a city of the past: "and ghosts are apt to be so glamorous."[14]

Anita was not an objective reporter. She was judgmental about the relationship between the Church and funds for building. She drew a parallel with mining towns, wealth, and colonial structures: "When you look at any one of these churches you are willing to believe true of it the story of La Valenciana in Guanajuato, built for God because God had facilitated a tremendously rich silver mine nearby." She delved further into Church wealth with a description of the mid-seventeenth to mid-eighteenth century that included the Inquisition, "administered most successfully by the Dominican Order and supported by all sorts of errant rich; Portuguese and Spanish Jews, converted moors, skeptical miners, witches, Irish soldiers of fortune, greedy priests and hysterical vision-seeing women. The magnificence of some of the Dominican churches built then, testifies to the sound business basis of the institution."[15]

Information gathered for "Mexican Decorative Arts" turns up here, colored by personal opinions. The Government Palace in Guadalajara "had a modern fresco (St. Christopher) by Amado de la Cueva, plastered over by a retrograde administration; to be discovered in future eras by some pleased archaeologist."[16] Other telling details are woven into the text about murals, such as the $10,000 that Ambassador Morrow paid Diego Rivera for a mural in Cuernavaca. Anita's irreverent attitude is at its best when introducing Sor Juana Inés de la Cruz. The excuse is the former convent and church of San Jeronimo, where Sor Juana took the veil and lived

> a not very secluded brilliant literary life. Sor Juana [. . .] was a very beautiful woman too intellectual to fit comfortably into the Mexican 17th century. She was one of the court ladies in her girlhood, which gave her the opportunity of begging the Viceroy to permit her to attend the University, even if in masculine clothing, women not being admitted. To discourage her the Viceroy had her thoroughly grilled by an entire learned faculty but she displayed so much skillful intelligence that the Viceroy declared "It was as if a royal galleon were defending herself from little shallops that attacked her, so readily did Juana Inés reply to all the questions, arguments and problems each professor propounded." She became a nun for reasons mysterious to her biographers; perhaps a love affair, perhaps merely the passionate wish for a room of her own and serenity for thought and writing.[17]

The passage about Sor Juana's room of her own is strikingly similar to Anita's letters to David about their apartment. Anita was finishing up the guidebook, ready to go back to New York to live with David, and adamant about

Amado de la Cueva's mural in Guadalajara. Photo by Tina Modotti.

wanting a "room of her own" in which to work.[18] Overall, however, she was happy and wrote David that marriage had made her feel freer than ever before. She expressed her interests, feelings, moods, and beliefs freely in *Your Mexican Holiday*. She wrote with joy.

The chapter on resorts is called "Honeymoon Places" for obvious reasons. Anita described the leisurely pace of beach towns with their respective legends. Acapulco offered the opportunity to tell the story of Nao China, a Chinese princess whose skirt became a national costume. Tepoztlan provided the entrée to discuss Robert Redfield's study of the town and Stuart Chase's comparison of it to the typical Main Street in the United States.[19] Lake Chapala, a favorite spot for D. H. Lawrence, was a good place to "dream, loaf, get brown, and write memoirs."[20] She was making her Mexico known.

The "Fiestas" chapter includes more legends and provides a calendar of official holidays and popular celebrations, along with a caveat that there was no "complete calendar of Mexican fiestas." More than twenty years

La China Poblana.
Courtesy of *Mexico/
This Month.*

later, as editor of *Mexico/This Month*, she published one. Each fiesta description includes instructions for finding the village and tidbits such as
"miraculous healings" available or "great gathering place of sorcerers and
medicine men." Anita provided information about routes as well as general introductory comments about what visitors could expect because she
felt that the fiesta experience was far removed from the culture of the average visitor from the United States. The chapter closes with an entice-
ment: "Presumably you will gain for yourself the favor of heaven, and you
may even witness a miracle or two; you'll hear of plenty."[21]

The "Arts and Crafts" chapter follows the outline for her "Mexican
Decorative Arts" manuscript closely, but without photographs. It describes
ceramics, textiles, costumes, leather, basketry, wood, glass, metal, stone,
feather mosaics, and toys. She provided historical background and sociological aspects of each craft, directions to the village, and recommended
artisans. Sometimes even the process of creation is traced. There is also a
tongue-in-cheek forecast of arts and crafts in Mexico: "Mr. Well-Mean-
ing Artist decides to revive Ancient Art, and takes pictures of idols and patterns of ancient temples to the potters, and tells them, 'This is it! Do this

and it will be marvelous!' [. . .] Mr. Tourist of course gets a great big thrill out of Indian idol-pots, and buys them by the dozen to send home to Aunt Emily and Uncle John."[22] Anita felt that the "sad process" had "rotted the edges of practically every Mexican craft," and she encouraged readers to select the "genuine." After an extensive presentation of arts and crafts, she closed the chapter with an aside, warning readers, "after all, this isn't an inventory!"[23]

Anita plunged into "Food and Drink" with an "Ah at last!" She led with a history of *tortillas* and how to make them. *Mole* was amply described, without the recipe. The information about "intoxicants" covered the socio-religious roots of *pulque* and *tequila* as well as their taste.

"Agriculture and Industry" is straightforward economic geography. The story of the revolution serves as background for a description of the *ejido* land tenure system, which meant returning to pre-Spanish tradition and rejecting the tyranny of absentee landlords from the *hacienda* system. A list of crops, with their origins and role in each part of Mexico, is followed by a list of *haciendas*, with brief presentations about the owners. Mines are treated in the same fashion. At the time, industry was limited but growing, and Jews were identified as among the initiators of small enterprise.[24]

"Education and Social Welfare" provided another opportunity to discuss Mexico's revolutionary philosophy. Anita explained Vasconcelos's rural schoolteachers program, as well as Manuel Gamio's approach of learning from the village, and suggested that visitors drop by the Casa del Estudiante Indigena (School for Indigenous Students) and the miracle school that John Dewey and Frank Tannenbaum wrote about. Universities, art schools, private schools, and charities are discussed, with a plug for the public health program for children from economically depressed areas.

The chapter on art relies on material from *Idols behind Altars* and "brazenly" recommends that book for more detailed information.[25] The chapter consists of a brief history of Mexican modern art and the development of the artists' organization known as the Syndicate of Painters and Sculptors that functioned as a union, negotiating contracts and running a school for apprentices, as well as publishing poster periodicals. She included a catalogue of artists (indicating where each artist's murals could be seen), and information about private galleries, sculpture, architecture, music, and literature.

Hunting, fishing, and exploring are covered in a separate chapter. Anita included detailed lists of equipment, including complex food supplies, needed to climb the Popocatepetl volcano. There are two white-water river trips, one down the Balsas River in Guerrero and the other a Papaloapan River adventure. Hunting is organized by geographical area and type of game. Anita recommended the fishing adventure: "Natives usually fish with nets, sometimes with harpoons, and sometimes they just dive in and grab their prey before the gull does. It's worth going fishing with an Indian just to see him do that. And you'll be telling bigger and better stories than that after you get home, but nobody will believe you except maybe this writer."[26]

Your Mexican Holiday closes with information about highways, warning readers about safety during the rainy season. Anita recommended sources of information and included a directory of general information about hotels, restaurants, repair shops, hospitals, transportation, currency exchange, and myriad other forms of data. Along with addresses and descriptions of restaurants and cabarets, she didn't hesitate to give readers orders: "Salon Mexico. Very low levels [. . .] Don't dress up."[27] She was adamant about not eating pork. The bibliography gives today's reader information about books available in 1932.

The book ends with a series of photographs by Sergei Eisenstein, Agustin Jimenez, Guillermo Kahlo, and others, each with a discreet sponsor credit. The high cost of producing books with photographs that made Anita merge two manuscripts into *Idols behind Altars* was a painful experience, so in her second book the photographs were sponsored by individual clients.

twelve

Identity, Commitment, and Activism

Anita at work in a room of her own . . . Photo by Lois Hobart.

ANITA RETURNED to New York in 1932, exhausted from having taken on too much. While working on *Your Mexican Holiday* she completed the translation of *Marcela*, a novel by Mariano Azuela, and wrote "Maria," a manuscript that was lost in the mail and never published.[1] She met frequently with Eisenstein, participating in his movie project, and launched her career as a politically active journalist.

David and Anita were happy to be reunited, in spite of economic difficulties and family problems. The Depression affected plans and expectations. David had not been able to establish a medical practice or find a job to support them. Money was tight. Anita spent the advance from *Your Mexican Holiday* on home furnishings in Mexico, where they were less expensive. They could not cover their expenses, even when combining his income with royalties from *Your Mexican Holiday* and *Idols behind Altars*.

Anita felt pressured to earn, adamant about not asking her father for help. The family in San Antonio was in the midst of a crisis created by the fracas between Isidore and Anita's brothers. It was even suggested that Anita's mother and younger sister Leah go to New York to get away. They stayed in Texas. Anita was limited to corresponding by letter back and forth with all the parties.

In New York Anita plunged into her professional writing with tremendous energy, turning the thirties into her most productive period. She published 86 articles and *Idols behind Altars* in the twenties; in the thirties, she published *Your Mexican Holiday* and 159 articles. After 1940 there were 31 articles, *The Wind That Swept Mexico*, five children's books, and seventeen years of editing *Mexico/This Month*.

During the thirties Anita wrote about art, Mexico, political issues, and the Spanish Civil War. The features she wrote about Mexico cover a wide array of subjects, including archaeological discoveries, art, artists, oil, and politics. She contributed a regular column reviewing art exhibits in the *Brooklyn Daily Eagle*. Her articles about political issues and the Spanish Civil War were published by *The Nation*, the *New York Times Sunday Magazine*, and *New Masses*, among others.

Her first venture as a political journalist began in 1931, two years after she recorded the "mystical experience" involving the morality of her writing. The issue was anti-Semitism in Mexico, where xenophobic groups were growing. The roots of the issue were economic and racial, parallel to the situation in Europe. Jewish immigration to Mexico increased steadily between 1921 and 1926, especially after the Johnson Act restricted immigration to the United States in 1924. Some immigrants came with the idea of getting across the border into the United States. The danger was getting caught and being deported back to Europe. Many immigrant Jews worked as peddlers in Mexico City and other major cities. They also traveled to small rural communities in search of installment-plan clients.[2] As revenues increased, they rented stalls in public markets. The next step was to rent a shop and then to establish their own small manufacturing plants.[3] Large department-store owners resented the competition, especially the loss of rural clients, who preferred dealing with friendly peddlers at home to facing taciturn city clerks. They felt more comfortable asking questions, making small payments, and looking forward to future visits.[4] Established European merchants chose the moment to fund a xenophobic campaign against Jews and Orientals. They supported Congressman Angel Ladron de Guevara, who organized demonstrations and launched a press campaign. He succeeded in getting Jews and Orientals expelled from the Lagunilla market in the center of Mexico City and was working on expelling them from Mexico.[5]

Anita went to work. She cabled *The Nation* to document the need for an interview with President Abelardo Rodriguez and Angel Ladron de Guevara. *The Nation* responded with telegrams pressuring for information. Anita got the facts about the anti-Semitic campaign and President Rodriguez's statement on the front pages of the local press. *The Nation* published her interviews as well as a statement from the president effectively stopping the campaign. Jews would not be expelled from Mexico. Their nationality would not be revoked; they were safe.

Anita had initiated her career as a journalist in the twenties writing about Jews in Mexico. Her role defending the Jewish community of Mexico was a bridge from her past to her future, writing in defense of people in trouble. Her identification with the Jewish people is closely related to her struggles as an independent radical—she was an independent Jew and an independent radical.

Anita's early relationship with her people is explored in the story "A Race of Princes," published in 1925 by the *Jewish Daily Forward,* which brought her a $50 prize. The autobiographical piece disclosed her experiences in the early days of the Mexican Revolution and the popular Mexican image of Jews as people with horns and long tails. It included her arrival in the United States, when she believed that she belonged to a very special people. After arriving in Texas, Anita discovered that her people "did not look like princes to me. The Jews seemed just like all the other stupid, impolite children who shrieked and pushed." The gulf between her fantasy of "robed prophets and gentle, blue-mantled Davids" and reality was confirmed in high school. She was bitterly disappointed: "I did not really believe they could be Jews, for they yelled coarsely, they were barred from the best clubs. Then I discovered that I, too, was barred. I had no friends. I was too proud to seek much intimacy where I felt undesired, and too queer for my own people. My own people. I got a good deal of rather dolorous ironic joy out of that phrase."

She felt alienated at the University of Texas in Austin and described going through an intellectual process of substituting religion with mysticism, then on to Emersonianism, and through various stages of pessimism, cynicism, fatalism, and agnosticism, to atheism. It was painful; she wanted to change her hooked nose and associated with Jews only "rather distantly." She "had a few Gentile semi-friends. I disdained scaling the barrier between Jews and Gentile, a wall compact as macadam. I was a lonely, absurd awkward person. I felt ugly and stupid. I was ignored. I resented and hated everything. A bewildered, unhappy nobody."[6]

The earlier romantic vision returned in 1923 when Anita returned to Mexico. "Fortunately Mexicans are splendidly indifferent to 'Jewishness' as a class distinction; I recovered some of the feeling of romance and glamour from them, and when genial little clumps of peddlers began filtering through Mexican streets, I became vastly and actively interested in them, and through them, in other things openly and interestingly Jewish."[7] It was in the twenties that Anita began to learn about her heritage. She delved into the files of Francisco Rivas Puigcerver, learning legends about Jews and the Mexican Inquisition.[8] As a child she had heard Madero accused of being a Jew. She recognized him as "the first wedge in the heartbreaking revolution that tore Mexico from feudalism into socialism. [. . .] After a time I strutted with my hooked nose again."[9]

In the thirties in New York, Anita socialized with the group of Jewish intellectuals who worked at the *Menorah Journal*, long before they initiated political activities.[10] She reported one occasion to David in a letter dated March 1930, before they were married. Her description of the guests and conversation hardly conveys their future radical position. The scene seems more like the Goldschmidt home she described in the twenties.

Last night had dinner at Lionel Trilling's. The other guests were the Hurwitzes [editor] and Maurice Samuels [well-known Yiddish writer]. He is a chattering little man with a compound British-Parisian-Yiddish accent. Affected but sincere. Reads too much Joyce and Proust to be a good writer; those guys are bad for Jews. I'm too tired to elucidate why. It was a charming dinner with many, many cocktails. The piece de resistance of the evening was a discussion of fidelity in marriage, which divided us into generations: both of which were surprised to find us, the third and youngest, so "puritanical." When Lionel stated his life's ambition he furthermore emphasized that by being a good writer he meant a moral one! Samuels said that he didn't know what he wanted from life—We three babies died [did], most emphatically. And none of us wanted anything world stirring—to have a comfortable living, to live with a person one loved, and to do well by one's profession. Mrs. Hurwitz thought us hardboiled and they decided that the trouble with the younger gen. is that it lacks vitality. Maybe so.[11]

The younger generation exhibited great vitality in fighting for their values a few years later. Their focus was on morality, not on power of or within a given organization. Their first battle was against the executive board of the *Menorah Journal*. It began when Elliot Cohen, the managing editor, asked for the support of his writers, among them Anita. Tight economic conditions in 1929 led the board to cut the journal's budget to increase funding for Menorah Clubs on university campuses throughout the United States. Anita responded with an autobiographical letter that did more than address the issue of the role of the *Menorah Journal* within the Jewish community. She defined her position as a Jew, contrasting two approaches to Judaism, the social and the intellectual. First she described the Menorah Club that she attended at the University of Texas: "the social atmosphere was strained, as evidently the Gentile distinction of fraternity and non-fraternity was weightier than the monthly bond. [The entertainment committee provided] a marvelously mechanical program of speeches, music, and club routine. We were all bored, but dutiful." She contrasted that image with her first impression of the *Menorah Journal*:

For the first time I was satisfied with the attitude of literate American Jews toward themselves as Jews. The Journal evidently accepted with a clear head and some relish, everything essentially Jewish, and

> *was not abashed at the accessory ideas of peddlers and pawnbro-*
> *kers and people with beards. [. . .] I found no maudlin sentiment*
> *of the "aren't we persecuted" type; but a good deal of genuine emo-*
> *tion, and above all, a subtle intelligence that thrust beyond the sugar-*
> *coating implied in reminders of how many great men have been Jews.*
> *It was written in muscular, poetic English; in spirit and form I felt*
> *it superior to most publications; I was flattered to write for it.*

Anita supported the institution that represented the values with which she identified. She felt that clubs and meetings could not provide the "spiritual leadership so badly wanted by hundreds of sensitive and intelligent American Jews."[12]

The *Menorah Journal*'s executive board pressured Elliot Cohen to shift to a more conservative position. Cohen resigned; Herbert Solow followed suit shortly thereafter.[13] Solow approached the issue from a social and political position.[14] He defended Cohen's policy of publishing radical views and critical writing that offended some of the journal's backers. Before money was tight the journal could find financial backers who did not object to radical collaborators. Now the *Menorah Journal* would shift to the right, forsaking critical writing for safe, inoffensive authors.

Anita collaborated with the *Menorah Journal* intellectuals, writing in defense of political prisoners and against fascism. They did not establish a formal organization; their ad hoc groups focused on specific issues.[15] Although there is a vast literature about the New York intellectuals, including many of the *Menorah Journal* crowd, a clear chronology of events, groups, and issues is yet to be published.

The struggle over the political position of the *Menorah Journal* was the first time the group fought conservatives with critical thinking. They were good friends and participated together in radical organizations such as the National Committee for the Defense of Political Prisoners, the Non-Partisan Labor Defense, and the American Committee for the Defense of Leon Trotsky. Many of the *Menorah Journal* collaborators, including Anita, were nonpartisan liberals who did not affiliate with any specific political party. Anita was familiar with radical thought, Marxism, and communism. Some intellectuals and artists in Mexico had been members of the Communist Party during the mid-twenties. Anita did not join the party or question her friends who were comrades. She was well aware of the Russian Revolution of 1917 but identified politically with the Mexican Revolution:

Due to having been born in Mexico, I have tended to side with the underdog and be sympathetic to rebellion and revolution whose deepest psychological, economic and social roots have always intrigued me and into the research of which I have put much time. This is also due to the fact that I am Jewish and although I was not an underdog on this account in Mexico[,] the minute we hit Texas as refugees from the Mexican Revolution (my father having been a landowner) the problem hit me full in the face when I was too small to know what it was that was hitting me.[16]

During the early thirties Anita was among the many intellectuals who were interested in Marxism, socialism, and communism. She discussed the issues in her correspondence with friends and colleagues in New York when she was in Mexico. She wrote David an enthusiastic letter after reading Leon Trotsky's autobiography: "What a book and what a man! Inevitably getting more and more interested in things Marxian; I'll have to delve and figure them out for myself; I know the sentimental crap offered in New Masses and such, isn't what I mean."[17]

Max Gorelik, an artist who had lived in Mexico in the twenties, was among those actively searching for answers. He wrote Anita early in 1932 from New York, where he worked as an illustrator for *New Masses*. His letter included news about Diego Rivera. The Communist Party had disrupted his lecture at the John Reed Club, arguing that he had sold out by accepting contracts for murals from American capitalists. The letter presented Gorelik's position: "I'm going completely Marxian and therefore getting thoroughly tangled up in radical activities. I can see plenty of trouble ahead. It will soon be the latest thing around N.Y. to be a Communist, and all the debutantes will be shocking each other with quotes from Lenin, and they will call each other comrade."[18] Anita's answer is not in the files; however, a second letter from Gorelik two weeks later revealed her position. Gorelik wrote,

I'm very much interested that you've hit the sawdust trail and are studying Marx; I see signs of a coming lineup among the intelligentsia as everywhere else, some going left and others right. The American intellectuals who are going radical are still hazy but are reading Marx and making progress; you can see it clearly reflected in the writing of Edmund Wilson. [. . .]

As to your hesitation about hailing Russia—I think you will ac-knowledge, if you are consistent, that Russia leads the world in political intelligence just at present. This doesn't mean that we must grovel before it; nor does the Third International lay down any me-ticulous program for the U.S. or any other locality; it merely sur-veys the world situation and makes suggestions from that standpoint. As to the Stalin-Trotsky break, it is far too early to decide which one's program would have been more effective. Even the Communists within the party are suspending judgement, apparently, and have no animus towards Trotsky except in so far as he carried the struggle into the camp of the bourgeois. In any case that schism has no bear-ing on the inevitability of Communism.[19]

Anita's doubts revolved around friends who had been to Russia. Carleton Beals returned from Russia shortly after *Idols behind Altars* was published. They met, and she recorded in her journal, "He got a jolt in Russia. It wasn't as pretty as he romantically had imagined the carrying out of his ideas might be. In fact, he found it distinctly ugly and irksome to his individualistic chip-on-the-shoulder short man's character. It happens with Russia that exactly the same kind of people who decry the superficial evils of capital-ism decry the superficial evils of the opposite system. They always think the system is to blame. They aren't entirely wrong, ultimately, but it is a very distorted view."[20]

thirteen

Full-fledged Menorah Journal *Radical*

Full-fledged professional. Photo by Erick Kastan.

ANITA AND HER community of writers and intellectuals struggled against injustice and the right wing. Some peers turned to Marxism or joined communist, socialist, and workers' parties. Others, including Anita, remained nonpartisan. She fought for workers' rights and Spanish Republicans and against German fascism and Stalinist terror. Hitler's rise to power was a major factor—fascism was increasing. Mussolini formed terrorist groups known as Black Shirts. The same political forces were active in the United States and Mexico (where they were known as Gold Shirts).

When Elliot Cohen left the *Menorah Journal*, he became executive secretary of the National Committee for the Defense of Political Prisoners (NCDPP). He wrote Anita on NCDPP stationery listing participants on the left margin.[1] Anita's name appeared on the letterhead from December 1932 to May 1933, when she resigned to join a group that later created the Non-Partisan Labor Defense in March 1934.[2] The participants in August 1932 included three familiar names: Franz Boas from Columbia University, the writer Waldo Frank, for whom Anita translated, and the artist William Zorach, about whom Anita had written earlier.[3] A statement attached to one of Cohen's letters identified the committee as an "independent organization of writers, artists, teachers, and men and women in the professions, associated on one ground and with one purpose." It specified that their political views were not alike; they were, however, united in the belief that "neither the laws nor the spirit of this country sanction imprisonment or other punishment as restrictions upon the freedom of thought, speech, and written word guaranteed in the Constitution of the United States: nor as penalties imposed, often in the name of justice, upon members of political minorities, socially outlawed races, and mass victims of the struggle for wealth."[4]

The NCDPP raised funds to hire attorneys and sent people to investigate situations. It focused on press campaigns about victims of racial or political discrimination, among them, unionized workers, especially African Americans, who were jailed, harassed, or murdered. Anita participated actively with the Scottsboro and Tampa cases, writing and leading a spin-off committee.[5]

The Tampa case involved the arrest of members of the Tobacco Workers Industrial Union. The superficial issue was allowing Cuban cigar makers to maintain their tradition of hiring a person to read aloud while they rolled tobacco, usually local political and labor news. Thirteen men were brought to trial after provocation turned a demonstration into a riot; two were serving sentences, and one had gone insane. Anita's article on the case in *The Nation* (December 7, 1932) focused on political persecution of foreigners and brought a flood of responses that led to the creation of a defense committee whose members included Waldo Frank, John Dos Passos, and Malu Cabrera.[6] The group expanded after Anita made a presentation at an International Labor Defense meeting in January 1933. Another group was organized to raise funds for a pamphlet and a mass protest meeting planned for March 31, 1933. Anita headed the defense committee and used her personal address for its correspondence.[7]

Anita's political activity was not limited to the NCDPP. She joined several groups. One, the United Committee for Struggle against Pogroms in Poland, published an open letter of protest after Jewish students in Polish universities were attacked by fascist gangs. It was signed and published by many people from the *Menorah Journal*, among them Anita, Louis Berg, Franz Boas, Elliot Cohen, Waldo Frank, Herbert Solow, Lionel Trilling, and William Zorach.[8] Anita may have signed other such letters with the *Menorah Journal* radicals, who worked as a close-knit group. They stuck to the issues and stuck together.

The group's falling out with the *Menorah Journal* was repeated with the NCDPP, when the committee refused to sponsor the defense of a person who was not a member of the Communist Party. The first to resign was Elliot Cohen. Herbert Solow, Elinor Rice, George Novack, Diana Rubin, Lionel Trilling, and Louis Berg resigned from the executive board of the NCDPP when the board defeated a motion demanding clarification at a general meeting. Anita was either not on the executive board or not at the meeting, because she wrote a long letter of resignation from the committee two days later.[9] Subsequently the entire group withdrew from the organization.[10] Elinor Rice sent Anita the resignation documentation for her to sign, with a friendly note expressing her interest in keeping in touch. Their friendship lasted for many years. In 1992 she vividly described shopping for clothes with Anita for years after they left the committee.

The new NCDPP secretary wrote repeatedly, inviting Anita, Solow, and the others to come back.[11] They, however, were putting their energy into creating a new organization, the Non-Partisan Labor Defense (NPLD), that included people from several political factions. Gathering a wide representation of the Workers Party and Socialist Party was particularly important to them. They were convinced that there was work to be done, but not as instruments of the Communist Party.

The mood surrounding their withdrawal from the NCDPP and the rallying of support for the new organization is documented in a letter Solow wrote Anita:

> explain to him [Waldo Frank] our position, tell him who backs us (including Dos Passos) and who opposes us (ILD [International Labor Defense] plus the iron Bolsheviks of Hollywood and the Left Bank) and ask him to throw his influence on our side. [. . .] Waldo should take the position that unless the Committee is reorganized on a broader and more independent basis, its value to the ILD will not grow. In fact it must decline, as it is no longer a good smoke screen. [. . .] All this will in the end lead to nothing. Moscow has ordered close control. The ILD wants the Committee as its private milch cow. They would prefer to kill it rather than let it stand on its own feet. Reform is possible but beastly slow and ignores the root evils, as reform always does, with the result that the root evils are perpetuated. I can't be active on this basis any more after I turn in my proposed Constitution, I'm through for some months even if I don't go to Germany. My name can stay but I won't be active. I'm not even sure that I will submit my frazzled nerves to Wednesday night's repetition of the recent performances. I wish you luck, kid, and admire your nerve. Regards to David.[12]

Anita chaired the NPLD committee on Cuba.[13] She also participated with Carleton Beals and Waldo Frank on the Peruvian committee of the International Committee for Political Prisoners, chaired by Roger Baldwin.[14] They were joined by a few Menorah Journal friends as well as Salomon de la Selva, a Nicaraguan poet who had lived in Mexico in the twenties.[15]

Her political activity as a New York radical was interrupted in July 1933 when she sailed for Spain. She had a double assignment: she would act as a foreign correspondent for the New York Times Sunday Magazine and write for The Nation. (Her writing about Spain is covered in the next chapter.) On her way back to New York she interviewed Leon Trotsky in Paris.[16] Her role in getting him to Mexico was an important part of her life as a radical.

Anita wrote an article about Trotsky for the New York Times Sunday Magazine that focused on his ideas. (The interview appears in Writings of Leon Trotsky, 1933–1934.[17]) Lester Markel, editor of the magazine, did not like the angle and wrote her that it "seems to me to miss. I am much more interested in Trotsky's present status and manner of life than in his ideas."[18]

Anita's interests centered on Trotsky's opinion about the effect of the European political crisis on American life. She asked about the role of democracy, the contribution of the USSR, and Hitler's position in Europe. Trotsky spoke of "a great war (I do not speak of a small, preventive war)" once Germany completed its rearmament. To the closing question about the time frame for the transition from capitalism to socialism, Trotsky replied that it would be measured in generations, not years.

There are no traces of continued contact between Anita and Trotsky, although she was part of the Committee for Asylum for Trotsky. She wrote letters seeking support for allowing Trotsky to come to the United States. Waldo Frank informed Anita that he would participate only if the group was specifically nonpartisan.[19] A few years later Anita was instrumental in obtaining Trotsky's asylum in Mexico. George Novack, a socialist member of the *Menorah* group, alerted Anita that Trotsky's life was in danger in Norway, where Trotsky had been granted asylum. The new Norwegian administration included Jonas Lie, head of the Norwegian-German SS, as minister of justice. The Norwegians, under pressure from Stalin, were considering placing Trotsky under house arrest. He needed a new haven.[20] Anita cabled Diego Rivera that it was a question of "life and death" to get Trotsky out of Europe.[21] Rivera went to see President Lazaro Cardenas and asked him to give Trotsky asylum, and Cardenas accepted. The Mexican Stalinists rallied to oppose his decision. Cardenas overrode all the objections, and on December 7, 1936, Trotsky was granted an entry visa to Mexico.[22]

The American Committee for the Defense of Leon Trotsky raised funds for his passage.[23] In letters calling for contributions and telegrams congratulating Mexico's president, Anita was listed on the official stationery.[24] The committee raised $1,284 at an event attended by more than three thousand people.[25]

Anita was also among the intellectuals who formed the Dewey Commission to investigate Stalin's charges against Trotsky. Their mock trial was held at Diego Rivera's house in Mexico in 1938. Some commission members traveled to Mexico to present or to hear evidence relative to Stalin's accusations against Trotsky, then they returned to New York, studied the testimony, and ruled in Trotsky's favor in the fall.[26]

The decision called for a celebration. Anita and David hosted a Halloween party for the group, which became a popular footnote in U.S. political history because it was there that Whittaker Chambers came out from the underground. By 1938 many radicals had become disenchanted with

the Communist Party and its tactics. Solow, then an independent journalist, struggled to expose cases of people who had worked as agents and
disappeared after breaking with the Communist Party. Chambers, Solow's
classmate at Columbia University, contacted him for help in coming out
from the underground as a Communist agent.[27] He felt it was a dangerous situation. He too could disappear, just as others had after talking about
quitting. Solow brought Chambers to the party. The event has been mentioned by Sidney Hook as well as Diana Trilling (among others) and is
the subject of several letters to Anita from scholars hungry for further details.[28] Diana described the party at Anita and David's: "Her celebration
of Halloween had indeed all the paraphernalia of a pagan festival: masks,
pumpkins, skeletons were everywhere. When Solow shepherded Chambers around the room, it was as if he were introducing yet another appa-
rition. More than one guest mockingly greeted him 'Whose ghost are
you?'"[29] Anita and David decorated their house with Mexican Day of the
Dead motifs; Carlo Tresca, the anarchist, made his usual tub of spaghetti.
John Dewey was present, as were Elliot Cohen, Dwight and Nancy Mac-
Donald, James Farrell, Sidney Hook, the Trillings, Frida Kahlo, Noguchi,
and Lucienne Bloch and her husband Stephen Dimitroff.

Ten years later Whittaker Chambers accused Alger Hiss of being a Communist agent. The long battle that ensued is well documented.[30] The Halloween party was mentioned because Chambers was said to have been inspired by its decor to choose a pumpkin on his farm as the hiding place
for some secret film known as the "Pumpkin Papers." Anita replied to one
query:

> The only time I ever saw Whittaker Chambers was that night at my
> house. [. . .] At this time we were what has since been called "pre-
> mature anti-stalinists." [. . .] It became evident to us we were being
> bamboozled. Some of us were taken aside confidentially and asked
> to help along, on the theory the rest were simple-minded liberals
> and had to be deceived. Being of an explosive nature, I told them
> to go to hell, what had I been doing in those outfits in the first place
> [. . .] We had vague friendships with some Trotskyites, but nothing
> very much came of this either, as we really weren't very sectarian
> types.[31]

Anita defended Trotsky actively, although she did not join a Trotskyite party.
She was often labeled a Trotskyite, yet curiously, it was Trotsky who iden-

tified her position as that of a nonpartisan radical.[32] Trotsky praised her writing about Spain, almost as an aside, while trying to remove Carleton Beals from the masthead of *Modern Monthly*.[33] Beals had incurred Trotsky's wrath during the trial in Mexico City, and Trotsky refused to be published while Beals was a contributing editor.[34] During the conflict Trotsky mentioned Anita: "We have naturally not the slightest interest in repulsing such valuable people as Anita Brenner, for example."[35]

Two years later, in 1939, the Mexican artist Siqueiros led a failed attempt to murder Trotsky. A confidential memorandum from Robert McGregor, American consul in Mexico, reported that "[Siqueiros' brother-in-law] had visited Miss Anita Brenner (whom Trotsky describes as on the fence between being a Third or a Fourth Internationalist) in New York early in June before any suspicion had attached itself to him."[36] In the thirties it was popular to identify radicals with party labels. Sometimes, people were labeled to invalidate their arguments. It is therefore critical to identify the labelers and their hidden agendas before taking those labels seriously. Even as a nonpartisan, Anita was not immune to being labeled; she was a woman of her times.

An exchange of letters in *New Masses* early in 1934 illustrates the intensity of infighting among groups. The issue that triggered the letters was a confrontation of forces at a meeting at Madison Square Garden on February 16. The Socialists called the meeting in support of the Austrian revolutionists and did not invite Communist groups, but the Communists came anyway, as part of the "united front from below" strategy.[37]

The Communist Party demanded discipline; membership was not open to everyone, and known radicals were not always welcome. Scott Nearing, a well-known pacifist, applied several times and prepared a long written statement swearing loyalty to the party, yet he was not accepted.[38] There is no record of Anita's making an effort to join. She was known as an "independent, and they would not have had her."[39] Anita struggled to keep radical groups nonpartisan, fearing their use as Communist Party fronts.

Anita's letters to *New Masses* reflected her political convictions rooted in the Mexican Revolution. She and her colleagues felt that they could change the world. They sought to empower the working classes and eradicate racism, poverty, and injustice. The Madison Square Garden meeting ended in a near riot, with chairs flying and blows being exchanged.[40] Twenty-five people signed a letter to the editor of *New Masses* protesting the Communist Party action. Anita sent the letter to Dos Passos to sign,

with a note mentioning that she had seen similar tactics used in Spain.[41]
New Masses published the letter, but the editorial response was addressed
to Dos Passos. Anita and others protested, yet her letter was the only one
published.

> *Your Open Letter to John Dos Passos, in answer to an Open Letter*
> *to the Communist Party, which I signed along with many other*
> *friends of militant labor, seems to mean that if Dos Passos had not*
> *also signed it, the letter would not be worth answering because the*
> *people who wrote it are not worth serious attention from a revolu-*
> *tionary writers' and artists' magazine. Your letter slanders us as a*
> *group and attacks several of us specifically, myself among them, for*
> *presuming to criticize the Communist Party without being revolu-*
> *tionary leaders. You also imply that all the signers except Dos Passos*
> *belong to one of two categories: either we are shady people maneu-*
> *vering against the Communist Party, or else we are stupid people*
> *allowing ourselves to be used for that purpose.*
>
> *[. . .] First, I want to state that to my knowledge, the letter was*
> *signed by each of us as independent individuals, not as members*
> *of a group. We knew who had written it and we believed it to ex-*
> *press sincerely and clearly, our own position. [. . .] I do not see why,*
> *if we are asked to support certain Party activities and if our assis-*
> *tance as sympathetic intellectuals is accepted, we should not also*
> *be entitled to ask questions and make criticism of those policies or*
> *acts of the Party which we feel to be harmful to the militant labor*
> *movement as a whole. The Party does not claim to be infallible, you*
> *say; is it infallible then only so far as the questions and criticisms*
> *of sympathetic intellectuals are concerned?*[42]

Anita's response confronting the Communist Party and the editors of *New
Masses* was charged with energy because of her experience in Spain. Her
convictions are clearly presented in her biographical statement:

> *I think writers wherever we can get the chance and in whatever ways*
> *have got to fight the Age of the Lie in which we are living and which*
> *is beginning to overwhelm and destroy even our reason for existence.*
> *For this reason I was involved in the 1930s in the famous John Dewey*
> *Committee which was among the first attempts to uncover and make*
> *public the Lie which makes things run so brutally in the Soviet*

Union and which then was picked up by Hitler as a modus ope-
randi and did the entire world an immense amount of harm. We
have by now become accustomed to it as a commercial gadget and
as a political way of life and it has made a climate that is as poi-
sonous to the mind and spirit as the junk that gets dumped into
the sea is to the lives of the fishes. This activity with the John Dewey
Committee earned me the honor of being attacked in Pravda along
with many of the other members of this group which included the
most vigorous writers of the time.[43]

fourteen

Spain

Walking with Miguel de Unamuno.

ANITA WAS ALREADY familiar with many aspects of the situation she encountered in Spain. She transmitted her sense of excitement with a hint of ideological disappointment in a long letter to David, shortly after she arrived in August 1933:

> The most thrilling thing in Spain are the workers. Revolution and all that really means something here. Makes all our intellectuals' committees and the I.L.D. look awfully silly, because from this distance it is plain that we were doing everything in a vacuum, and all the people who were doing it were miles away from being workers. Bourgeoisie and petty bourgeoisie, a lot of failures; anyhow a big fake, as everything that the P. does officially. Here it is different. You talk to a worker—take a waiter in the hotel, for example, or even a head-waiter—and they know what it's all about. Labor meetings, strikes, are news and big news. If they see you on the street with a priest they surround you with unfriendly silence. They're all ready to go . . . they were within an inch of getting there, but one thing and another—the Socialists and the Party—messed it up. They sing the International in the streets—hundreds and thousands of them; everybody knows the song. The best of the lot are the anarchists. They have childish ideas but they're not afraid of the devil himself and they're not easily fooled, either. Now they're putting them in jail, but there are a couple of million outside. In Andalucia they're burning the crops—setting fire to mile after mile of harvest—because the landlords are "hoarding"—sabotaging by refusing to harvest or plant for the new season, to force the gov. to take it all back about the land laws. And it will. And then the picnic. That's why I must get to Andalucia. The papers—they're not usually so poetic—say the air is hazy with smoke; and what do you think? The Minister of Agriculture says it isn't so, that—literally that it just isn't happening! With the landlords and the deputies and the peasants and the papers raising hell and one state after another going up in blooey. [. . .] Jail, concentration camps, what have you. What I wanted to see, and what I expected to see [. . .] was the movement going forwards. None of the stuff that comes out of Spain, in the news, is so. It's a lot of boloney, and none of the stuff that is so comes out. I've sent a good load to the Nation—sweat rates, but I want it published somewhere and nobody else would—and I think it will make

a little splash, because it is pretty sensational and out of such a rosy sky! [. . .] I'm more and more pleased about the book. It will be a good one, and it will give me a push forwards on the way I want to go. One has to change and develop, but I am beginning to feel now, for the first time, completely mature and completely sure of my control of ideas and techniques. Ready for business. And I'm pretty cheerful about personal things. So we don't have a house? So we don't have a house. We can try to live humbly, and anyhow it's a bum idea to get accustomed to having too much. So we have a house? Swell. Fact is the only reason for a "house" is children, and I still want them—more than ever—do you?[1]

The Spanish Civil War was a complex confrontation which has been the subject of many books.[2] There are more than 45 manuscripts and clippings of articles written by Anita between 1933 and 1937 in her files. They do not include her work as a radical or the material she wrote about art or about Mexico, the bread-and-butter work that brought income as opposed to the time spent as a radical in the same period. An in-depth study of her articles would become a full-length book, not a chapter in her life.

The early articles focus on getting information out about the reality in Spain, breaking stereotypes about the country and its people. Their tone is reminiscent of the articles in defense of Mexico. She presented history, cultural factors, and economic realities. The first articles were published by the *New York Times Sunday Magazine* and by *The Nation*, where her friend Gruening was back as an editor.[3] Her writing conveys the following story.

Spain tried to carry out a bloodless "revolution from the top" almost a century after the French Revolution.[4] The battle between those who had been in power (the monarchy and the Church) and the socialists led to giving people what the leaders believed the country needed, independently of what the people wanted. While the Republican constitution was being written, emergency measures were taken canceling freedom of the press, freedom of speech, and freedom of assembly guaranteed by the document they were drafting. Some articles capture the flavor of political discussions in cafés and skillfully shift to debates within a parliamentary process, weaving the dialogue back and forth.[5] Anita addressed two themes: a narrative description of people and events and a report on the ideological conflict on the left with Soviet communism. The narrative dealt with land, workers, political orientation, and the role of the Church. Her term for the situation was "class war."[6]

The war involved peasants, who worked the land for absentee landlords, and workers who formed strong unions. It was a natural sequence for Anita because land tenure was a primary concern in the Mexican Revolution of 1910. The concerns that paralleled the interests of New York radicals were political: the welfare of the working class, the struggle against fascism, and the defense of political prisoners.[7] Land tenure in Spain was an unresolved issue underlying political upheaval. Most of Spain's land was held by the ruling class, foreign and local absentee owners, or the Church. There was a strong resemblance between land tenure in Spain and in Mexico; a feudal system was in place in both countries.

The Church in Spain enjoyed economic privileges and social authority. It owned and operated schools and hospitals. It kept citizens' birth and death records. It owned large tracts of land and enjoyed tax privileges and subsidies. In both Mexico and Spain the Church was allied with the conservative political positions of wealthy landowners, but Spain had not had a Benito Juarez to check the power of the Church.[8]

Western Europe, including Spain, faced the same type of economic problems that brought on the Depression in the United States. Further, the flow of about $100 million a year, which Spanish émigrés had been sending home, dropped drastically because of the Depression.[9] Spaniards were well aware of the consequences of the rise to power of Mussolini and Hitler and the fall of German and Italian socialism.[10] They knew that the stakes were high; in this they were joined by people from all over the world.[11] Anita participated by describing the situation with great lucidity.

Individuals were not the only ones who participated and took sides. Germany and Italy supported the right-wing military: Mussolini supplied troops; Germany provided ammunition and military aircraft. The Church provided funds to buy arms and even allowed churches and monasteries to be used as military bases for the right. Mexico was the only country that supported the Republicans and supplied arms with no strings attached. England, France, and the United States formally assumed positions of neutrality. Labor unions, workers' parties, and anarchists from England, France, Germany, Mexico, Italy, Soviet Russia, and the United States fought for the Republicans within the international brigades.

British business and government did not remain totally neutral. They worked behind the scenes with Moscow to make sure that their economic interests would be protected. The Soviets participated with the British because they were interested in keeping Spain aligned to Russia and not to Hitler's Germany.

Soviet Russia supported the Republicans after the struggle had been going on for a few years and the Republicans desperately needed arms and funds. Stalin demanded and received Spanish gold, shipped to Moscow. Then he sent strategists and troops to bolster the badly depleted Republican ranks.[12]

The left in Spain was in the midst of a fierce battle with the military right when it tangled with Stalin's policy of a "united front." The Soviets wanted to control Spanish labor unions, especially the POUM (Partido de Obreros Unidos Marxistas); the anarchists, among others, did not agree.

The Soviet Communist Party in Spain formed small guerrilla police groups, known as Chekas, to round up leaders of the left who did not accept the united-front strategy, especially writers and labor leaders.[13] They worked with the support of the minister of justice to set up an elaborate system of clandestine prisons. The confirmation of their strategy was published in December 1936 in *Pravda*: "As for Catalonia, the purging of Trotskyites and the Anarcho-Syndicalists has begun; it will be conducted with the same energy with which it was conducted in the U.S.S.R."[14] Important Spanish and foreign leaders and journalists who would not be controlled began to disappear. Some were found dead, others died in prison, and a few were rescued by groups sympathetic to the Republican cause. Outstanding leaders from many countries were murdered by the Chekas.[15] Anita was deeply involved with those who worked to raise money and public awareness to save political prisoners from clandestine jails. Although she had anticipated being able to write more openly for *The Nation* than for the *New York Times Sunday Magazine*, it was Lester Markel, editor of the latter, who was more open to publishing her material about the Soviet Chekas.[16]

When Erwin Wolf disappeared, Anita signed a letter of protest addressed to the Catalonian Generalidad. Wolf, a Czechoslovakian citizen, was in Spain as a representative of the London *News Chronicle*. He was a member of the Journalists' Club of Barcelona, with an official journalist's card from the Catalonian Generalidad. Wolf had acted as secretary to Leon Trotsky during Trotsky's stay in Norway and was framed during the Moscow trials.[17]

There is ample documentation in Anita's files about the struggle to free

Jose Escuder and Russell Blackwell (also known as Rosalio Negrete), friends from New York.[18] They were American journalists of Spanish descent who joined the Republican struggle. Both were released after long, intense efforts.

Escuder and his American wife were picked up with a group of POUM leaders. She and the other wives were held hostage until all the men had been rounded up.[19] Escuder's wife kept Anita posted with letters that he was able to smuggle out of prison.[20] He also wired Anita after the June 16, 1937, arrests, informing her that the POUM had been banned and several friends' lives were in danger, and asking her to "intervene immediately" and inform others.[21] She called the Spanish consul in New York, asking for an investigation.[22] She addressed a mass meeting at Union Square sponsored by the United Libertarian Organizations, and participated in a wide publicity and letter-writing campaign.[23] Herbert Solow identified 30 non-Spaniards among the 250 POUM prisoners in a letter appealing to Norman Thomas, head of the Socialist Party, to participate in united action.[24]

When Anita, Solow, and Carlo Tresca tried to form an umbrella organization of left-wing groups to free political prisoners—the Provisional Committee for the Defense of Workers' Rights in Loyalist Spain—all three organizers were told that they could participate only if they agreed not to belong. The demands were made by Norman Thomas of the Socialists and Bertram Wolfe, head of the Lovestoneites. Solow seethed. After all, he was the one who had called everyone to the first meeting to create a defense front along the lines of the Sacramento, Herndon, Tampa, and Cuba committees, and now he was to be excluded. He warned Anita to beware of the committee and encouraged her to circulate a letter to friends, "Berg, Rorty, Farrell and Walker."[25] Alliances among New York intellectuals were complicated. Anita's position appears consistent, but a full rendering of the period and its personalities remains to be done.

Anita shared friends and interests with Russell Blackwell before the Spanish Civil War. Blackwell knew Diego Rivera and asked him to support *Claridad*, a Spanish-language Bolshevik journal. His return address was *The Militant* in New York. He was also friendly with Paul O'Higgins and Abel Plenn, part of Anita's group in Mexico in the mid-twenties.[26] Blackwell was arrested in Spain and held in Valencia by the secret police. The U.S. State Department gained his release and put him on a British vessel, with documents in order. Then he was detained a second time. The Blackwell Defense Committee focused first on learning what the specific charges were against him.[27] The Communist Party press alleged that he was a "Franco agent," but a telegram signed by Anita and others noted that others "against whom similar allegations have been made by the Communist Party because they differed with its policy have been kidnapped and killed."[28] Blackwell was accused of being a Trotskyite, of having written several Trotskyite books, and of having worked as Trotsky's secretary, as well as of being a homosexual.[29] Anita clarified the facts:

> Blackwell's political antecedents are typical of those of many who are now being persecuted by the C.P. He was at one time a member of the Communist Party and was an organizer for them in Mexico and later in Central America. He took a prominent part in the early struggles of the Mexican C.P. and is well known by all those who were associated with it then, such as Bertram D. Wolfe, Diego Rivera, etc. Later he was a member of the Communist League of America, which fused with the American Workers Party to create the Workers Party. He went out of it together with Oehler when their group broke with Trotsky. [. . .]
>
> He has always been more of an organizer than a theorist and writer, and to my knowledge has never written much except articles in his party press. He has not written any books—whatever kind of crime that may be—of Trotskyite or any other tendency. Even though it is no crime to have been secretary to Leon Trotsky, the fact remains that Blackwell was never his secretary. In fact, they have never met. Blackwell's trip to Spain in October, 1936, was his first to Europe, and Leon Trotsky left Norway in December, 1936, and went by boat directly to Mexico. As for his sexual habits, he was married to a girl I know quite well and, as a matter of fact, I was one of his witnesses at his wedding three or four years ago.[30]

The letter reflects the times but did not change Blackwell's immediate situation. Anita served as executive secretary of the Russell Negrete Blackwell Defense Committee, which included more than fifty "independent comrades, whose pressure eventually achieved his release."[31] They welcomed Blackwell home and then wrote a report comparing the actions of different organizations.[32] The committee had achieved its goal in a nonpartisan fashion, even to the extent of getting Trotsky to write the American consul in Mexico denying that Blackwell had been his secretary.[33]

A manuscript in Anita's files presents a detailed account of the end of the Spanish Civil War. Refugees who sought passage to Mexico were screened by people known to be members of the Soviet Communist Party, who issued passes for the limited number of ships. Anita described a complex web of activity, including smuggling Spanish jewels to Mexico, the effort to murder Trotsky, and the role of Tina Modotti and Margarita Nelkin as liaisons between Germany and Russia.[34]

Letters and notes in the Brenner files indicate that Anita planned to write a book about Spain. The book was never finished, but she did write a pamphlet published by the Socialist Labor Party of Australia in 1937.[35] Several drafts of the introduction to "Today the Barricades" are in her files:

> This book begins in June, 1933. It begins like this: I, a member of what is calling itself the lost generation, sit in the bottom of a pit in New York watching the life I was taught to assume would be mine strangle. I mean what everybody under thirty knows—doors slammed. We are not the people who lost their possessions in 1929. We are the people who were brought up planning fine lives of accomplishment, with no idea that the economic foundation for such lives was cracked up under us. Now in 1933 I, equipped with an elaborate university training which gives me the highest academic standing, cannot find a way to live that will produce the two satisfactions I seem to need. One, the security that my work will feed, clothe, shelter me and allow a surplus for recreation and study. Two, the sensation that I am participating in and contributing to some common good.[36]

Political activity as part of the New York radical community in relation to the Spanish Civil War was only one aspect of Anita's output as a writer during the thirties. Parallel to the Tampa protests, meetings, committees, demonstrations, and articles about Spain, she wrote about Mexico and produced a weekly article about art for the *Brooklyn Daily Eagle*. The thirties saw a peak in her productivity, as a writer and as the mother of two children.

fifteen

Art Critic in the Thirties

Woodcut by David Alfaro
Siqueiros. Photo by
Michael Nye. Courtesy
of Adriana Siqueiros.

ANITA WAS an independent spirit, personally and politically, not just a nonconformist opposing the mainstream. She simply did things her way. The same woman heavily involved in political struggles persisted in her interest in clothes. In 1933 a contemporary woman journalist reported that

> Petite vivacious, dark-haired Anita Brenner is more like a college girl than a full-fledged author, registered anthropologist with a PhD from Columbia. She greets her guests in green lounging pajamas, topped with a brightly flowered coat. She bubbles with girlish enthusiasm, talking eagerly and shaking her short curls. Her apartment fits her. With its bare floors, Mexican scatter rugs and low comfortable chairs, it forms an excellent background for her colorful personality and costume. And she is living just where she has always wanted to live—on Columbia Heights overlooking the river. "It's the most beautiful spot in New York," she says.[1]

The interview took place after Anita returned from Mexico and before she left for Spain. It featured a review of *Your Mexican Holiday*, the book that temporarily assuaged Anita's need to make Mexico known and released her energy to fight political realities. Mexico was by no means out of Anita's system. She wrote about its politics, art, and artists throughout her life.

Just as her role in the Spanish Civil War could easily become a full-length book, so could her work as an art critic. She began writing about art in the twenties. The bulk of the material she wrote in the thirties was published by *The Nation* (17 articles), the *New York Times Sunday Magazine* (20 articles), and the *Brooklyn Daily Eagle* (50 articles). There are more differences than similarities between Anita's earlier work about art and her later articles in *The Nation*. In the thirties, she had widened her horizon beyond Mexican art and artists and considered herself a full-fledged art critic and connoisseur. Her writing seemed more in tune with where she stood as a radical.

The articles that were published in *The Nation* were written from a politically combative stance. Just as art had offered her a way of describing Mexico, art became a way of dealing with political issues. Even the titles of the articles reveal confrontation: "Art and Big Business," "Revolution in Art," and "Aesthetics and Agitation." Anita took on art patrons, museums, and galleries as irrational authorities. She dealt with political perspectives, historical contexts, and styles. She wrote as a critic and as an art historian. The issues she explored in *The Nation* paralleled her political activity and revealed her Mexican background. Art and artists were an integral part of a social revolutionary process. The origin of her approach was her familiarity with Mexican artists, who felt they were responsible for contributing to the process of the revolution.

Anita discussed Mexican artists' influence on artists in the United States but focused on the generic function of art within an American setting. Her position is clearly established in "Revolution in Art," an article in *The Nation* in 1933. It assailed art critics who believed that good art was detached from a meaningful subject, or that technique was all that was required to provide pleasure. The peg in one article was the review of a Forain show, because he expressed "rage at the white-slave traffic, the lecheries of courts, the horror of life for the bottom dog." She compared Forain's work with the exhibit at the John Reed Club, where "the pictures and sculptures [. . .] emphasize social distress rather than sensory pleasure."

Modern art, for Anita, reflected a revolutionary process. Artists in the United States and Europe rejected conventional and imposed forms, just as Mexican artists turned against that which was foreign. Anita wrote about European artists who felt "a determination to smash the cage of prescription, convention, and dogma in which artists performed like trained monkeys for the edification and benefit of Victorian morals."[2] Artists broke away from serving religion, "civic virtue and domestic duty," and turned their attention to science. They experimented technically, searching for method and "aesthetic discovery." Traditional society reacted with antagonism to those who broke with established conventions, labeling their work as propaganda, which in turn was meant to invalidate the message and the artist.

Anita opposed the "art for art's sake" school and agreed with those who felt that art was part of social expression. She was concerned with artists, whom she considered socially responsible human beings, struggling to earn a living. This too was a carryover from Mexico. In the twenties she had lobbied government officials to reinstate Orozco's contract. In the thirties and throughout her life she defended artists in print, in order to help them survive. When she exposed the Whitney Museum's treatment of Thomas Benton ("alas, the painter was paid just about what the job cost him, and less than the rate per foot paid to commercial decorators for restaurant and hotel jobs"),[3] *The Nation*'s board of editors received a letter of complaint dated a week before publication.[4] Juliana Force, director of the museum, threatened legal action. Anita defended herself and saved a draft of the letter she wrote to the board of editors. Her article contrasted the Whitney with the New School for Social Research, which had commissioned Benton murals at "cost," noting that the school had the artist's consent. The New School was open about the agreement, and if the director of the Whitney felt that the museum's reputation would be affected by releasing the information, then she should explain why. Anita's position was, "As a rule all leeway is given criticism of an artist. Why not of a patron? It was the business of this critic, having seen the murals, and valued them, and having then been shown the distressing correspondence between patron and artist, to choose between silence embroidered by notes on the aesthetic of Benton, for the glory of the patron; or protest for the sake of the artist. No credit is claimed for the choice because my head is due for one platter or another anyhow."[5]

The Nation editors responded to complaints about Anita's work by postponing articles and then advising her that they hoped to run them in the following issue.[6] Sometimes they suggested changes or questioned the wisdom of publishing "an unfavorable review of an exhibit that is over." Yet they wanted more articles from her.[7] One such postponed article reviewed Malvina Hoffman's sculpture, touted as anthropological documentation. The material was right up Anita's alley, and she blasted Hoffman: "As a hardy traveler, persistent researcher, competent recorder of the ultra-picturesque and humanitarian propagandist, Malvina Hoffman deserves all praise. She is not a first-rate artist or a very good anthropologist, however. Her sculptures belong to the sentimental school which prettifies to glorify, and in prettifying loses beauty and truth but makes a successful appeal to facile emotion." Anita critiqued her portrayal of racial attributes: "a frizzy-haired Mediterranean, a crinkly-haired Chinese, a wavy-haired Maya, [. . .] very handsome but hardly 'pure racial types.'"[8]

Anita saved a letter attacking her for her scathing critique of an exhibit and a Lewis Mumford review. The lively exchange started with Anita's article "The Clinical Eye," in May 1933: "What Lewis Mumford calls 'the pulse of the nation' is on view in this year's Independents' show at the Grand Central Palace. If he is right, then the nation is a bad cardiac case, and the ambulance should be called. The show is small, which means most likely that fewer amateurs this year had the seven dollars necessary for entry. [. . .] The show as a whole exhibits the American earmark of technical skill, and points to emotional breakdown." The second exhibit featured in the same article didn't fare much better than the first: "Throughout there is nothing that is not well made, as is a good chair or a good shoe. There are many picturesque and pleasant pictures and nothing emotionally indecorous except a few socio-mystical things as introverted as an intestine." Her closing repeated the offensive metaphor: "The suspicion grows that an art gallery is no place to take the pulse of the nation, and this reviewer is willing to stop and cast a clinical eye instead at automobile shows, for example, where surely the nation's aesthetic joys are in active evidence. As for excitement caused by painting, it has been seen in the small mobs of watchers who somehow crashed the formidable gates of the unfinished R.C.A. tower in Radio City, to watch Diego Rivera and his gang doing big things in a big way."

Critic Lionel Reiss countered with, "Is it therefore any wonder that Miss Brenner [. . .] manifests her trivial impatience at the work she reviews? Hers is just as much a lost voice crying in the wilderness of the American art nightmare as the many pictures doomed to perdition. [. . .] Puffed sleeves being now in fashion she believes that she would not appear to the best advantage in them. A Mexican adaptation of the Mother Hubbard seems better fitted to her figure."[9]

The archives also contain a complimentary letter from Walter Pach, an artist and writer who was supportive of her efforts to publish *Idols behind Altars*. Taking aim at Lee Simonson in "Impurity in the Modern Museum," Anita may have been settling an old account, dating from 1928 when Simonson was at *Creative Art* and asked her for several articles about Mexican art. She registered her reaction in her journal on July 2, 1928: "Letter from Lee Simonson (*oh, que animal!*) [oh, what an animal], with demands for the first article, about *niños al aire libre* [open air art schools for children], and instructions about what to put in it. I'll do it, and with a vengeance. Boomerang at least."[10]

It was a slow, powerful boomerang that took almost six years to get back. Simonson curated a theater art exhibit at the Museum of Modern Art in New York that included sketches of set designs. Anita took him to task for his view that stage designers were "content to be necessary craftsmen who rarely needed as an incentive the conviction that they were producing a work of art or contributing to the development of art history." Her article refuted his classification of art as "pure" and "impure" and critiqued his derogatory remarks about "artisans." She used Picasso as an example, because he "couldn't be bothered to look for the designs of 'Le Tricorne.'" She also mentioned Derain, who "refused categorically to send any of his ballet designs. They were too unimportant." She closed with, "Well supposing Joyce were asked to publish his outlines and notes for 'Ulysses'?"[11] Pach congratulated Anita, assuring her that her "article is not personal— it is simply just, as I told an audience at Columbia last night, recommending them to read your lines."[12]

Anita's writing for *The Nation* reflects her self-image as a cocky, straight-shooting, confident professional. On another occasion *The Nation*'s editors suggested she modify an article that was "based largely upon generalizations and suspicions, which are no doubt justified but which are not very strongly supported."[13] The editor at *The Nation* returned "Private Art and Public Interest" for a second time. He closed his letter with, "Don't be sore."[14]

Anita responded by accusing him of censoring her writing because he did not agree with her, asserting that her book reviews and political writing were not questioned. She demanded the right to her opinion and the privileges of an "old contributor," stating clearly that "if my work is worth having it is worth having as work done according to my judgment and ability." She gradually toned down her protest with,

> I believe I have made it quite clear that I want very much to write about art in the Nation, and I think I can write about it from a fresh, informative, vigorous viewpoint. I know my pieces are read and discussed, and it is only for that reason that I write them, hoping to contribute occasional shocks of life to the vast inertia of picture painting and image carving among us. [. . .] So, this is a kind of sweetly reasonable ultimatum. I won't be insulted if I'm fired, either, knowing there are excellent reasons for it. I shall be relieved and very sorry.[15]

She wasn't fired, but "Private Art and Public Interest" was not published. The exchange coincided with the letter of protest she sent *New Masses* about the Madison Square Garden meeting crashed by Communists early in 1934 (see chapter 13).

The article was combative, focusing on art patrons who determined which art would be available to the public. She took on the Rockefellers for exerting pressure on art and artists, and she compared the destruction of Rivera's Rockefeller Center mural to Hitler's burning of books. "In other words, if the Rockefellers want to exercise a dictatorship over American art—in the New York market anyhow—they may do so whenever it suits them."[16]

The quality of art and the citizenship of artists was another point in her caustic attack. The artists exhibiting at the Rockefeller Center gallery were American in that they were "all entitled to American passports"; however, the extensive exhibit, which Anita identified as a "mile" of their work, included nothing American. "The names sound like an international roll-call, and the objects are individual variants of the school common to all the western world." The works exhibited were slated for private ownership and enjoyment; hence, "In form, idea, function and aesthetic quality they follow the tradition of nineteenth century Europe. [. . .] As a whole they contribute nothing new, independent, vigorously moving to American or world art, and yet they are put before us as a whole, constituting a public interest."[17]

In the end the article draws a parallel between art and oil (Rockefeller owned Standard Oil). A few years later oil became a thorny issue when Mexico expropriated European and U.S. interests; Anita contributed her views in articles and in *The Wind That Swept Mexico.*

One of Anita's prime considerations in evaluating art was its ability to evoke emotion. A review of machine art emphasized a recurring theme in Anita's art criticism in *The Nation.* "It is a given, that machines are used to make more machines, not to evoke or express emotion and therefore be considered art."[18] Evoking emotion was linked closely to another pet peeve: landscapes and still-life studies.

Anita was unrelenting when it came to landscapes. In "Art and American Life" she identified the lack of emotional content in the exhibit she was reviewing by praising only one piece done by Zorach, which illustrated that "such a thing as love between man and woman was known in our part of the western world."[19]

Two articles in *The Nation* in 1934 focused on the relationship between artists in Mexico and the United States: "American Folkways" and "Some Artists Lose Some Chains." They carried the earlier message, which promoted Mexican art, while integrating American artists into the process. She did not explain the involvement of Mexican artists in the revolution but simply identified common goals and circumstances to bridge the gap between Mexican and American artists, thereby facilitating their relationship.

Anita reviewed American murals favorably in "American Folkways," classifying them as a movement and stressing the social content: "a vague general sympathy for the 'plain man,' usually exemplified by the rugged farmer; a love of the idea of labor, again usually represented by agricultural labor; and a sympathetic emphasis on American Folkways, with 'American' underscored." Equating the sense of freedom experienced by artists sponsored by the U.S. government with that felt by Mexican muralists, she took the opportunity to state categorically that the Mexican Revolution and Renaissance were over, with a veiled warning about the role of government in art.

> *The Mexican muralists were paid by a government anxious to prove itself revolutionary, therefore willing, for a while at least, to give their spokesmen great leeway; furthermore it was a government put in power by an agrarian, anti-feudal revolution (the classic "bourgeois revolution") and therefore the distribution of land, the glorification of the native peasant, and the expression of nationalism as against foreign domination, which were the stuff of Mexican muralist content, were political, economic, emotional current issues corresponding to a national reality. And finally, American artists ignore, or forget that the Mexican Renaissance died because the Mexican revolution, when only half over, was throttled.*

The second article, "Some Artists Lose Some Chains," explored the relationship and influence between government and art from a more technical perspective. She complimented the Works Progress Administration (WPA) program in a backhanded fashion, saying that there was no indication in the artists' work exhibited that they had received relief funds from the government. Two artists were singled out, James Michael Newell and Lewis Rubinstein, both said to have been influenced by Rivera. Newell's picture *Science Destroying the Past and Building the Future* was described as "quite without Rivera's significant punch." Rubinstein's works *Chlorine* and *Nitrogen* were praised for the way they "combined the impersonal and personal, the abstract and the concrete, more successfully than Rivera is usually able to do," because the artist was the child of an industrial scientific culture. He featured the abstract, "whereas Rivera invariably puts human beings in that place of honor."

Anita praised the exhibit of American art for its expression of emotion. "Too, there was something else as hard to describe. It was a kind of freedom, as if the artists had sighed with relief to be rid of the shadow of patrons and markets, and had simply let go and painted. And the quality of the work was higher, freer, stronger, as a whole, than in any of the exhibits that galleries have so far managed to put on sale." The bottom line was the "temporary, but quite real, freedom from sale-anxiety, with its accompanying conscious or subconscious leaning toward marketable goods."

Anita published twenty features about art in the *New York Times Sunday Magazine*, a little under half of the total number of articles she wrote for that publication. The earliest articles were about Mexican art; however, she went on to write about contemporary art in New York. Whereas Anita's art criticism in *The Nation* was limited to 1933 and 1934, her work in the *New York Times Sunday Magazine* spanned more than ten years. Most of those articles were written more than once. There are revisions, rewrites, and, in one case, nine different drafts of an article about Mexico's oil expropriation. Her tone was not combative, rather straightforward, and somewhat mellow.

Anita's relationship with Lester Markel, editor of the *Sunday Magazine*, was good. He had responded favorably to her articles about the Spanish Civil War. Although Anita was fond of reminiscing about Markel as a "difficult person" and a tyrant, she recognized that she learned more about writing from him than from anyone else. She was proud to have survived his supervision and bragged about her ability to get along with him. She respected his point of view. His notes and comments throughout were encouraging, complimentary, and apologetic when he cut an article.[20]

Both Markel and Anita suggested subjects for articles. Her ideas for stories were not always accepted, but the door was open for further exploration. Sometimes an idea was rejected initially and then retaken. In "Arts Storied Debate Renewed" (sent from Spain in 1934), she presented the "art for art's sake" issue in historical context, beginning with the eighteenth century and discussing the artist's involvement with social and political struggles at each point. Her presentation was subtle, stressing that Mexican art was not social propaganda.

Once they agreed on an article, Markel would keep after her with notes, prodding her into delivery, especially after she had children. The subjects paralleled those she wrote about in *The Nation*, but with a significantly different tone. "Art is a living stream which flows through the finest works of every century and period" reflects her position.[21]

She wrote about WPA programs, murals, exhibits, and artists such as Picasso and Eilshemius, the Mexican influence on art, the differences between art in Europe and the United States, and the general panorama, including the jazz movement in New York. She reported the donation of the Widener Collection to the National Gallery in Washington, still under construction in 1941, without digressions into politics, and reviewed the "Independents" group of artists favorably.[22]

Anita also wrote about Trotsky, labor unions, and socialized medicine for the *Sunday Magazine*. The information had to meet Markel's standards. Her readers commented, critiqued, and praised. Samuel Allen sought her out to discuss Soviet communism and splinter groups because he did not agree with her article "Stalin and Trotsky." He invited her to talk about their differences of opinion.[23] John Beffel, from the Brotherhood of Utility Employees of America, on the other hand, wrote an enthusiastic response to "The Labor Duel," on April 1, 1935. He posted her article on the union's bulletin boards, praising her recognition of the union's rights.[24]

Her work in the *Brooklyn Daily Eagle* combined the styles in *The Nation* and the *New York Times Sunday Magazine*. The bulk of the articles were dated between November 1935 and April 1937. There were periods when she contributed an article every week and adopted a conversational tone with her readers, similar to the one she used in *Your Mexican Holiday*. The subjects included movies, photography shows, art exhibits, and artists, from Picasso to the lesser known Houmere. There was a balance between exhibits praised and those panned. Her political concerns were constant: sometimes she plugged public housing, other times she commented on the cost of an exhibit. The Gauguin show impressed her with its entrance fee and security, which she claimed scared little old ladies on Fifth Avenue.[25]

Anita integrated political history into discussions of art schools and their origins. One example was this comparison of surrealism and proletarianism:

> *Every time the question of what to paint involves a moral problem a new school of art is born. Today the two newest are surrealism and proletarianism, whose doctrines repudiate the art for art's sake maxim that an artist's business is exclusively to have and give aesthetic enjoyment; [. . .] which in its day of revolt turned against the still older belief that the function of art is to preach. [. . .] And since both surrealism and proletarianism reject the present social order, the artist's duty, they say, should be to aim his work toward a new one. [. . .] their job was to protest. They divided at the same point,*

precisely where Marx and Bakunin parted. And the question that divided them was this: Is an artist primarily a social unit, exactly comparable to any skilled or unskilled worker, or is he important primarily as a special kind of individual.[26]

She criticized intense political party types, singling out a "cheerful" communist, "not full of despair like the John Reed Clubs," but neglected to mention that she lectured on art at the John Reed Club School of Art.[27] By 1936, Anita was pregnant and impatient with group infighting and violence. She had been back to Spain, where the situation had gotten worse. In a review of an exhibit on war and fascism at the Artists Congress, she commented that "one needs more clarity and some specific truths. Above all some pictorial indication of what can stop war and how fascism can be routed. Fear and horror don't; they just make ostriches of us."[28]

Sometimes Anita let her hair down and allowed her personal feelings to show. She was friendly, yet apologetically brutal. When she panned exhibits, she communicated the reluctance of a good friend who must transmit bad news. For instance, an exhibit of WPA easel work and a Whitney Museum show were too refined:

The tune at the Whitney assemblages of contemporaries goes like this: landscape, landscape, landscape, nude, still-life, landscape, still-life, nude, landscape, landscape, landscape, genre; nude, landscape, landscape, still-life, nude, landscape, landscape, genre, nude . . . And so on, or you could put it this way: indoors, outdoors, indoors, outdoors, outdoors, outdoors, outdoors, subjective.

Well at the WPA it is even more monotonous. It goes like this: landscape, landscape, landscape, landscape-city, landscape-country, country, country, water, genre, genre.[29]

Anita also wrote about the role of an art critic, as if she needed to focus on her function within a larger framework. The taciturn tone of many of her reviews may have motivated her to put her goals out in the open, clearing the air. Once she put it this way: "the critic's job is no longer a question of taste at all. It is much simpler and, at the same time, much harder. What he has to judge is how far the work is performing its allotted function. And he may also want to go beyond, and examine the social and ethical character of that function."[30] She acknowledged criticism and dealt with the issues raised. The tone might be called apologetic, but not in the least

Frida Kahlo.
Photo by
Anita Brenner.

humble. When she covered an exhibit at the Brooklyn Gallery, she mentioned being "called names" because she reviewed too many shows in Manhattan, across the river: "Besides, we're crabs. We're always criticizing. We sometimes go so far as to say not-so-hot even about things that are shown in Brooklyn[. . . .] So our nice castle is all in ruins. Here we thought we were doing a pretty job."[31]

Gender issues made their appearance in her critiques of artists, favorably and negatively. Georgia O'Keeffe was reviewed positively, Anita believed, solely because she was a woman. Anita considered an artist a person. A woman, as defined in her article about the artist Angna Enters, "is really creative, really new and original, it is hard to define[. . . .] Feminine in the sense of what women are really like, not what they are supposed to be. They combine something like this: basic vision, sympathetic; method of understanding, highly rational, unsentimental; style, precise, intellectual, subtle, and with much malice; materials, imaginative, ingenious, luxurious."[32] It is safe to assume that her vision included herself. A quality she omitted was her irreverent sense of humor, and the art of good parties and clothes. Her review of the Dada show at the Museum of Modern Art led with: "There is a rumor that a prize, the fur-lined cup and saucer No. 452 in the show of dada, surrealism and fantasy at the Museum of Modern Art, is being offered for whoever writes the most reasonable and rational account of that show; because anybody who tries to be rational about these

things is thereby madder than the maddest of the competitors in lunacy now at the Museum for your serious consideration."[33]

Mexican art and artists were a recurring theme in her work for the *Brooklyn Daily Eagle*. Sometimes she quoted Diego Rivera or mentioned Siqueiros's favorite piece in a show. She was sensitive about exhibits billed as "international," especially when they did not include Mexicans. She heaped scorn on one exhibit advertised as international that omitted Mexicans "for the whimsical reason that the sponsors or collectors of the Cosmopolitan Club show 'just felt tired of seeing Mexican stuff; we've seen so much of it . . !' It only included artists from the United States!" The show was de-

Lucienne Bloch's mural at the
Women's Detention Home in New York.
Photo by Lucienne Bloch.

scribed as the first comprehensive exhibit of government-sponsored art. The
result of government financing—walls, materials, wages, and liberty—was
a technically significant but "emotionally timid" sample. The one redeem-
ing note Anita found was, "Our architectural artists have emulated the
Mexican school and have proved their capacity to create one of their own."
She went on to qualify the experience, bringing in her opinion about the
situation in Mexico: "For political reasons, the government cannot allow
them complete freedom of expression. The Mexican government did, but
that was a government committed to revolution, and completely indifferent to the cyclone its artists raised in polite society. [. . .] The Mexicans

found that mediocre-to-good artists rapidly outgrew themselves when given very hard work to do. The big talents too, were revealed for the first time in their public work."[34]

Anita brought Mexico in again in her article about Lucienne Bloch's murals at the Women's House of Detention in New York. Lucienne had worked with Rivera, grinding his colors for the mural at Rockefeller Center. The passage summarizes Anita's philosophy of art and politics:

> It is the first crystallization, in our idiom, of a new approach to painting that stems from the Mexican revolutionary muralists. Article one of this philosophy is that the artist is a creature of social responsibilities. Article two says that, since the artist is as a rule economically one of the masses, his work should be directed toward their enjoyment, instruction, and benefit. This implies a repudiation of the intellectual and social snobbery that determines much of the appearance and character of "modernist" work. In fact it requires so complete a revision of the function of the artist that it brings about a new school and new style: as also new forms, and even new instruments and new techniques and materials.[35]

Anita's articles in the *Brooklyn Daily Eagle* that mention Mexican art are similar to her earlier writing that promoted Mexico. She identified with the early years of the Mexican Revolution, before it was "throttled."

sixteen

A Radical Looks at Mexico: The Throttled Revolution

Man at the Crossroads by Diego Rivera, in progress, at the Rockefeller Center in New York. Photo by Lucienne Bloch.

MEXICO is woven into most of Anita's writing. Good examples of the chronological and thematic overlap are her articles on Diego Rivera during the Rockefeller Center episode. The issues again were art, politics, and Mexico.

Rivera played an important role in Anita's story. She learned about art and the position of revolutionary artists from him in the twenties. The pattern of listening and learning while remaining independent was set then. Their relationship lasted until he died in 1957. They had their differences, often provoked by his intense competitiveness with other artists. By the early thirties they had known each other for ten years, and her views about revolutionary artists had grown closer to the ones he had expressed in the early twenties. She shared Rivera's definition of art as an expression of the people and that of the artist as a worker.

Rivera had been in and out of the Communist Party since the twenties. When it came to rescuing Trotsky, however, he set aside party affiliation. The party expelled Rivera in 1929 when he chose to continue painting on government walls rather than go underground with the artists and intellectuals who produced *El Machete*.[1] In 1933 Rivera was not committed to a specific party. His position was somewhere between the American Communist Party (known as the Lovestoneites), which Bertram Wolfe joined when he broke with Stalin, and Trotsky's Fourth International.[2]

The Rockefeller Art Commission hired Rivera to paint a mural of 1,071 square feet on the central panel wall above the bank of elevators at Rockefeller Center. He was paid $21,000.[3] The commission defined the theme as "Man at the Crossroads, facing the future with uncertainty but with hope, looks toward a better solution."[4] Thematically it involved the "liquidation of superstition by science." Rivera asserted that he was inspired by Jefferson's speech praising Benjamin Franklin as the man "who snatched the bolt from heaven and the sceptre from the tyrant."[5]

The problem centered on a portrait of the Soviet hero Lenin that Rivera placed in his mural. It took John D. Rockefeller II three weeks after Lenin appeared on the wall to object in a letter to Rivera.[6] The complaint was ostensibly that Rivera's work "did not harmonize with the building and was not suitable for public view." Rockefeller did not admit openly that "most business men object to renting space in a place where they and their customers must look at Lenin."[7] Anita wrote:

> By a strange coincidence on the same day that Hitler was having
> Germany purged of everything Marxist, modern and Jewish in its

literature, the Rivera murals at Radio City were nailed within a curious structure that may very well turn out to be a coffin. The funeral on the night before was attended by a body of resolute gentlemen whom the doorman said were tenants, two representatives of the owners, a multitude of guards and some mounted police, and we guess fifty carpenters. The mourners were Rivera and his assistants, three students who stayed outside when all visitors were ordered out of the building, and this writer, who did likewise. Also by a photographer who was surprised to learn at the door that there was a ban on pictures and reporters.

The operation was dramatic. It was plain that the operators meant to be quick, efficient, and still. It was plain too why, for the Rockefellers were caught between two nasty choices. Either they allowed the mural, Lenin notwithstanding, to remain on public view as a monument to their financial and intellectual generosity as patrons of the arts, and faced the probable loss involved in not renting much space in the building, which meant seventy stories of real-estate debit; or they removed, destroyed, or wall-papered the painting and suffered a considerable loss of prestige as public uplifters and benefactors, which no doubt was the ideal they meant to serve when they engaged Rivera, one of the recognized greats among living artists, to decorate the most prominent wall in the biggest building of the Radio City ensemble.[8]

The New York press exploded with protest. Some took a nationalistic approach, wanting to eliminate all works by foreign artists. Their attitude was not new; Anita had discussed it in an article before the Rockefeller Center episode.[9] She picked up the theme in an editorial defending Rivera in *The Nation.*

The ban on the Rivera murals has made much good copy, and has added one more comic foot-note to the pages of the history of art. It has also encouraged a body of academicians to form a kind of society for the suppression of foreign art. They are going to break a lance in defense of [the] highly startling idea that an artist born outside of the American tariff wall is not necessarily superior to the artist sheltered within it. In the name of American Art, we shall hear, down with purchases and contracts rewarding the talent or labor of creatures not citizens of the United States. We note with patriotic alarm

*that one of the founders, Ulric Ellerhusen, was born in Germany,
and we wonder about Jes Schlaijter; and would it be exactly proper
for a New Yorker to purchase the work of Dean Cornwell, who hails
from California? [. . .] and let us start at once to build a glass en-
closure over and around Woodstock—and whom shall we put in it?*[10]

In a story in the *New York Times Sunday Magazine* before the conflict
emerged, Anita discussed the scandals surrounding Rivera's earlier murals
in Mexico City, San Francisco, and the Detroit Institute of the Arts, where
the panels featured the automobile industry and workers, which were not
considered beautiful by the people of Detroit.[11] Critics focused on the panel
depicting a vaccination in a manner strongly reminiscent of the Holy Family:
the doctor with a syringe ready to inject the child, who sits angelically in
the nurse's lap. Religious and community leaders felt that the Trinity, with
animals that provided the serum in the foreground, was insulting.[12]

Anita stressed the fact that Rivera enjoyed scandals and controversy. He
took great pride in regaling friends with his long history of sensational public
upsets, which, according to a document that he dictated to Anita, began
when he was four years old.[13] Rivera knew full well that Lenin's portrait
would create a problem. Nevertheless, his rage drew Anita and many others to protest in support of a friend and freedom of artistic expression. Anita
spread the word to colleagues at the *New York Times,* translated for Rivera
at a dinner meeting of the Menorah Group of Writers and Artists organization, wrote in the *New York Herald Tribune,* the *New York Times Sunday Magazine,* and *The Nation,* and joined an ad hoc committee organized
by Suzanne La Follette to defend him.[14]

A second article in the *New York Times* mentioned the student vandalism at the National Preparatory School murals in the twenties. However,
Anita neglected to mention the incidents in which Rivera was the exter-
minator and not the victim. Rivera was not competing for walls in 1933 in
New York as he had been in the twenties in Mexico, but it was now his
turn to experience the outrage he had provoked in Jean Charlot and Amado
de la Cueva, after succeeding in eliminating their murals at the Ministry
of Education.[15]

The theme of "revolutionary artists" appears in Anita's review of Bertram
Wolfe's book about Rivera's work in the United States, *Portrait of America.*[16]
Her review included a complex critique of Rivera, Siqueiros, Wolfe, the
Communist Party, and Mexico's shift to the right. She wrote the article four

months after the Madison Square Garden confrontation and after seeing the Chekas at work in Spain. She seems to have been clarifying her own position as a revolutionary writer vis-à-vis the Communist Party and the bourgeoisie. She examined the relationship of revolutionary artists and intellectuals with the bourgeoisie, the bourgeois aesthetic code, the role of the Communist Party in the Mexican Revolution, and the status of the Mexican Revolution in 1934. The peg was Rivera's murals at the New Worker's School, reproduced in Wolfe's book, depicting "class-struggle in America." She declined to review the book solely as an art monograph because that was the job of "bourgeois reviewers." Instead she took the opportunity to answer Siqueiros's article in New Masses:[17] "Siqueiros in this article takes 75% truth, 20% significant omissions, and 5% untruth, pours the mixture into the social-fascist mold, and serves up a dish jelled transparently around the word 'counter-revolution.' The final garnish is this pretty little thing; 'With one arm he (Rivera) embraced the Lovestoneites and with the other, he embraced the Trotskyites. Thus he demonstrated that in this trinity there was counter-revolutionary unity.'"

Anita pursued her interest in the relationship between artists and intellectuals who were party "sympathizers" with revolutionary parties. Siqueiros's solution did not satisfy her because his proposal for professional revolutionary artists worked only for a "minority willing to cut themselves loose from the bourgeoisie," which meant leaving "sympathizers and semi-recruits" out, in a vulnerable position as "liberals," who could be used by the Stalinists. The relationship of revolutionary intellectuals to the bourgeoisie was an intricate part of Anita's life, as a landowner's daughter who was not averse to shopping sprees at highly bourgeois establishments.[18] The bourgeoisie were clients for artists and writers; they selected work and paid for it. Anita defined the situation:

> An artist tied economically to the bourgeoisie tends inevitably to orient his language to a bourgeois audience, therefore is likely to talk and think in a bourgeois way himself, even though he may be sincerely in sympathy with proletarian revolution. This is one of the big problems artists and writers face today. If, moreover, he calls himself an active revolutionary, and is accepted as such by a revolutionary party, he tends to compensate for his bourgeois ties by taking wild leftist attitudes and making wild leftist moves.[19]

Your Mexican Holiday was selling successfully at the time; there is no ques-

tion that it was oriented to a bourgeois audience. Her writing for *The Nation* could be considered more revolutionary. Anita's description of the bourgeois aesthetic included an analysis of style and its relation to the reality of revolution. "The core of the bourgeois aesthetic is this formula: never touch concrete current issues. Hence cubism, art for art's sake, still-lifeism, surrealism, etc. The corollary to this formula is, if you do touch current issues treat them reassuringly, as solved problems, which turns out to be another form of evasion." Rivera's major murals fell within the evasion specifications. The exception, when he broke the rule at Rockefeller Center, was "destroyed because of the *concreteness* of the Lenin portrait." His Detroit murals demonstrated the nature of Rivera's adherence to the bourgeois aesthetic, Anita pointed out, by depicting "the grandeur of industrial

Man at the Crossroads by Diego Rivera at Rockefeller Center in New York. Photo by Lucienne Bloch.

development, with Edsel Ford among the engineers, and nowhere the Ford rubber plantation slaves."[20]

Anita compared the Detroit mural with the one at the New School. Rivera had worked on the New School mural with Bertram Wolfe, who had broken with Stalin and joined the Lovestoneites. The mural, however, followed the party line and therefore allowed Rivera to regain his

> *official status as a revolutionary painter. And the inevitably neces-*
> *sary relation between artist and party comes out sharply; they are*
> *each responsible for the other. And there are a number of happy co-*
> *incidences. For example, Rivera's nationalist bourgeois-revolutionism*
> *matches nicely Wolfe's efforts to give proletarian revolution Ameri-*

*can ancestry, and one result is a very sympathetic portrayal of the
left-wingers of '76—Jefferson, Franklin, Paine, Adams. And in the
last panel, Rivera's two-master habit meets the Lovestoneite dual-
personality theory of the C.P., so that the final "high-note" of the
series is a masterpiece of equivocation. Wolfe gets Stalin in prominently, and Rivera, Trotsky.[21]*

The Communist Party's role in Mexico was complex; the party as such did
not exist when the Mexican Revolution of 1910 erupted. Once the party
was established, many artists and intellectuals joined. Wolfe came to Mexico
to help establish the party and met Rivera, who was back from Paris.[22] Rivera
was invited to join the Central Committee of the Communist Party in the
mid-twenties; however, when he had to choose between the party and continuing to receive contracts for murals sponsored by the Mexican government, he chose to paint murals. Anita stated that Siqueiros was aware of
the contradictions in Rivera's position: "and the fact that one foot in the
C.P. and another in the nationalist government was the quintessence of
opportunism, makes Rivera the prime exponent of all the elements in the
Mexican movement that separate it from a straight Communist position."[23]
Siqueiros attacked Rivera for not reinforcing the Communist Party's emphasis on the glorification of the native peasant, calling his work "Rivera's
mental tourism."[24] He also called him every name the Communist Party
used for those who were not disciplined followers. Anita took Siqueiros to
task for sidestepping issues:

> *For reasons of his own, Siqueiros leaves the C.P. pretty much out
> of the discussion, or rather, he builds up a picture of an infallible
> Something continuously tricked and betrayed by a born villain. He
> states, correctly, that Rivera is the most complete and mature ex-
> pression of the Mexican muralist movement, and that this move-
> ment is an expression of the Mexican revolution, but he omits analy-
> sis of the C.P. relation to both—indispensable in view of the fact
> that Rivera was a member of the C.P. central committee at the time
> he did most of his work.[25]*

The last point in Anita's article was the status of the Mexican Revolution,
which she described as that of a typical Latin American revolution. "What
happened in Mexico is also typical: the petty bourgeois, small-farmer government raised to power by the revolution became almost immediately a

Two Women with Child by Diego Rivera. With permission of Dolores Olmedo.

government of landlord generals allied to American imperialism, and not that counter-revolution involved no actual great shifts of power, but merely psychological changes in the leaders. They kept their revolutionary vocabulary of course."

Anita's realization that the Mexican Revolution had been throttled did not affect her passion for the country. She wrote for the *New York Times Sunday Magazine* about Mexican archaeology, silver and mining, the new Pan-American Highway, and of course politics. Her tone was informative, with ample historical background; however, her writing about political issues was not as mellow as her descriptions of Mayan astronomy.

Anita wrote about both the Spanish Civil War and the political situation in Mexico. Spain, however, was in the limelight among radicals in New York, and Mexico was not. When the Spanish Republic fell and the outcome of the Spanish Civil War was clear, Anita expressed concern for Mexico's future. In an editorial paragraph in *The Nation* Anita reported on the murder of government officials by "bandits" and the efforts of peasants and workers to overthrow Calles and get rid of American industrial and financial imperialism.[26] Another manuscript, written in 1935 for the *New International* under the pseudonym "Jean Mendez," described the betrayal of the revolution by the Obregon-Calles group, who had become landowners, "producing for export, and hence interested in maintaining the semi-colonial land situation."[27]

Mexico in the thirties was far from the Utopia it had been in the twenties. The most important revolutionary leaders, such as Emiliano Zapata, Venustiano Carranza, Pancho Villa, and Alvaro Obregon, were dead. Plutarco Elias Calles, president from 1924 to 1928, played the role of a dictator who made and unmade presidents. Anita described Calles as a Chinese warlord who "has loomed indestructibly in the Mexican picture, like a Toltec pyramid — huge, harsh, mysterious. His name adds naturally to the list of dictatorial gladiators that the world watches with mixed feelings, with its ancient admiration for the strong. He has been called a Mexican Mussolini, an Indian von Hindenburg, a Latin-American Lenin, and many other names equally picturesque and superficial, and often more derogatory."[28]

Workers were among the most affected. Unions, which had achieved a minimum-wage law, insurance, pensions, and labor boards to settle disputes, saw their benefits curtailed. Calles also stopped distributing land. Cristeros (guerrilla bands sponsored by the Catholic Church) renewed their activity, in spite of the agreement in 1929 that U.S. ambassador Morrow had negotiated.

When Lazaro Cardenas took office as president at the end of 1934, he faced a struggle with the Calles machine to put the Mexican Revolution back on track. Anita, writing as Jean Mendez, drew parallels with the situation in the United States: "The men now in power can be compared to the Rooseveltians, with the difference that imperialist pressure pushes them farther toward the left—much farther, in speech; a little farther, in action. Nevertheless they provide the opportunity for organization and struggle, and for victory in immediate gains, true of a social-democratic regime. In this sense the exit of Calles constitutes a step forward for the Mexican working class; not, as C.P. theorists assert, the prelude to fascism."[29] She issued a passionate call for the creation of a workers' party to support the shift toward socialism and avoid fascism. In an editorial written for *The New Republic*, she brought up popular anti-American feelings prevalent in Mexico, analyzing the fear of an American imperial conquest as well as the outcome of securing benefits for the few to the detriment of the many.[30]

Anita supported Cardenas. One of the prime issues was land, because "the bulk of Mexico's good arable ground is still held in huge haciendas run semi-feudally, and more than half of it belongs to foreigners[. . . .] This means that for the majority of Mexico's population, and especially for that part of it which formed the backbone of the revolutionary armies, conditions have not changed very much. With minor exceptions, Mexico's peasants are still living on a coolie level."[31] She and many others considered Cardenas the "agrarian messiah." He was known for supporting peasants; it was said that he would drop everything to travel to a remote village to help solve a particular problem. One of the earliest actions he implemented was transforming the largely foreign-owned Laguna cotton area in the north into a vast cooperative community. His policy of putting the revolution back on track meant defending peasants' and workers' rights, even if it antagonized foreign and local capital.

Many of Anita's articles combined views of art, politics, and Mexico during the thirties. Her *Creative Art* review of Alma Reed's book about Jose Clemente Orozco is a case in point. She praised the book: "The rockbottom of it is that Orozco is profoundly a moral man, an indignant man, and he stands by that. [. . .] that his murals, which have always a plain, immediate social meaning, at the same time stand out powerfully as fine, sound painting."[32] Her article in *New Masses* about Orozco's work goes even farther.[33] She considered it the role of a critic to go beyond appraisal and appreciation of the "technical, emotional and intellectual excellences of his work." Orozco met her definition of a "revolutionary artist."

> *His work identifies him at once as a critic of the social order under which he lives. His antagonism is translated in two modes: satire, when he turns his attention to the individuals and classes which represent social oppression; and profound emotion of a semi-mystical character—backed with anger—when he looks upon the oppressed. In that all the forces of his nature set him squarely against the social status quo, and in that he does not espouse any liberal or reformist cause, he is a whole revolutionary.*

seventeen

The Wind That Swept Mexico

Working on the first edition with George Leighton.

THE WIND THAT SWEPT MEXICO, written from 1934 to 1943, is a synthesis of many of Anita's ideas on Mexico. First published by Harper and Row, it was reprinted twenty years ago by the University of Texas Press, which now advertises the book as one of its best-sellers.[1] For Mexicanists, it is Anita's most important book. Anthropologists and art historians consider *Idols behind Altars* her best contribution.

The Wind That Swept Mexico presents the Mexican Revolution of 1910 in 100 pages of text and close to 200 photographs. It was first published as a series of articles in *Harper's Magazine*.[2] The groundwork was done in the thirties, especially in 1934, with a series of articles published in the *New York Post* and several radio broadcasts on WEVD.[3] Anita used the story of the Mexican Revolution of 1910 to warn the United States to focus on

Mexico before it was too late. *The Wind* was published in the midst of World War II. Mexico, Anita felt, could become embroiled in a situation like the Spanish Civil War.

In her *New York Post* series, Anita discussed the failed revolution, land tenure, labor, and the role of the Church, drawing parallels between Mexican and U.S. historical figures to get her point across. For example, she asked rhetorically whether George Washington would have been excommunicated "by the Inquisition for declaring independence," as was Morelos.[4] Anita looked at the conflict through the eyes of the poor, the peasants, women, workers: "People want schools, land and the things they fought for in the revolution."[5]

The Church, identified with economic power (landowners and industrialists), supplied arms to bands of Cristeros and opposed unions and the Constitution of 1917.[6] Anita widened her perspective to the international scene with a description of the Jesuits' role in Spain, Europe, and Latin America. She stressed the importance of the political role of the Church, the denial of freedom of religion, and the people's quest for civil marriage, divorce, and the right to choose their own teachers.[7]

A subsequent article discussed political forces such as fascist sympathizers, known as the *Camisas Doradas* (Gold Shirts), and left-wing intellectuals. Anita described a growing dissatisfaction among workers and the anticlerical mood among practicing Roman Catholics. She traced the history of U.S.-Mexico relations, interventions, and policies, discussing Roosevelt's Good Neighbor policy, and presenting the role of Nazi Germany's influence in Mexico.

The *New York Post* articles unleashed the wrath of the Knights of Columbus and the U.S. Catholic Church hierarchy. A lively exchange of letters and opinions ensued between Peter Arno (the managing editor of the Catholic weekly *Brooklyn Tablet*), Anita, and supporters such as Katherine McNally Beehman and Horace Casselberry, who wrote, "Your articles in the Post on the Mexican Catholic show down are as lucid as they are honest. [. . .] Your knife is clean & true, the operation urgent & vital—do not delay the book."[8]

Anita registered her perception of her situation in a letter to the *New York Post*:

This morning I was accused by a Communist friend of being pro-Catholic. I am beginning to feel like the calves on our ranch when

Villa's boys arrived. They tied a rope to each foot of the beast and then got together and pulled—in four directions—to see which was the strongest. For the Strange Coincidence Department: Numerous pieces on Spain and Mexico appeared without arousing a Catholic ripple. Yet in the last few weeks, we've had two complaints, both based on evidence I should call extremely subjective. Can it be that the Post series (in which Brenner insisted on exercising Times training-discipline and telling the facts on both sides) has aroused some sort of organized effort at punishment. I am now taking bets that almost any article I may write in the future, will bring back a Catholic demurrer. I said any article. So should I retire and write a mellow essay on the gentle art of taking it on the chin?

[signed] *She who got slapped*[9]

In the four years between the controversial *New York Post* articles and the nationalization of Mexican oil properties in 1938, Anita reported events in Mexico, traveling there early in 1935 to update *Your Mexican Holiday* and research future articles. Her reports recorded struggles between fascists, communists, and liberals in Mexico. Lazaro Cardenas had taken over as president and battled the Calles group from within and fascists from abroad. He sent former president Calles into exile (arrested while reading Hitler's *Mein Kampf*), along with labor leader Morones and the leader of the fascist Gold Shirts.[10]

The struggle between U.S. private enterprise and Cardenas came to a head in 1938 when President Cardenas nationalized Mexico's oil. British, Dutch, and U.S. corporations had been battling the oil workers' unions for some time. Cardenas was familiar with the abominable living conditions and wages paid to oil workers, because he had been stationed in the oil-producing areas of Mexico as a young general. By nationalizing oil, Cardenas enforced the laws of the Constitution.

In 1938 Anita was caught between President Cardenas and *Fortune* magazine in a different kind of controversy. She wrote an unsigned article for *Fortune* that was edited in New York, without her consent, changing her message from a positive to a negative image of Mexico.[11] Her efforts to rectify the situation included letters of explanation to Cardenas and subsequent articles about Mexico, including those in *Harper's* that became *The Wind That Swept Mexico*.

The original story proposal presented Mexico as the "David against

Soldaderas on the lookout. Courtesy of *Mexico/This Month.*

Goliath of foreign interests." She stated that "The warp of Mexican economy, history, politics, art is—land. About 95 percent of the people live from the soil or subsoil: sugar, coffee, wheat, hennequen, rubber, tobacco, corn, fruit. [And the] Sub-soil: gold, silver, copper, oil, antimony."[12] The upheaval against large landowners and industrialists was part of the revolution. Her sympathies were with the workers, against exploitation by foreign oil companies. She asserted, "The role of exploited, expropriated, resisting Indians is so deeply a part of the Mexican mind that it in turn shapes politics and history."[13] She drew a parallel with conditions in the United States and brought up the revolutionary artists, who were "Deeply influenced by Marxist theory, not unlike the current generation of American intellectuals. Due, however, to the government's need of revolutionary color, they figure more prominently in political life than their contemporaries here, and have more real influence. The young men around Cardenas belong to the same revolutionary-Bohemian group which produced modern Mexican art (Rivera, Orozco, Siqueiros). No longer in existence as a group, it nevertheless crystallized a cultural and political outlook."[14]

The memorandum outlining the story for *Fortune* included the first of many warnings to the United States, repeated in *The Wind That Swept Mexico:* Mexico could become another Spain.

The Cardenas government zig-zags between the revolutionary ideas of the intellectuals, and the economic-diplomatic realities of Mexico's position. Its trump, on the side of the intellectuals, is the fact that [the] U.S. government must, for military reasons, have a stable and friendly government in Mexico. Its trump on the side of the capitalists is the fact that perhaps 85 per cent or more, of Mexico's productive capacity, is in the hands of big foreign concerns. Its fate can be decided one way or the other by Washington's policy. [. . .]

A Mexican "Franco" would play, from a military and industrial viewpoint, the same role in Mexico against the U.S.—as in Spain against France and England. Considering the strategic importance of the Panama Canal, this would be a major danger to the U.S., in the event of anti-German, anti-Japanese alignment including U.S. in the next year.[15]

Fortune omitted the above text. Anita delivered a long, well-documented piece with extensive charts and economic data. (Her extensive research is documented in her files, as listed in appendix E of this volume.) The article published, however, was a derogatory, paternalistic presentation of Mexico, its history, and economic development in the light of the recent oil expropriation.

Securing her interview with President Cardenas had been difficult; she finally won him over by writing a ballad for him (transcribed in appendix C). Once the article was out, she wrote letters of apology to Cardenas, his private secretary Ramon Beteta, and Frank Tannenbaum, their mutual friend who had recommended her. *Fortune* refused to return the original text so that Anita could document the difference between her draft and the published article. In the midst of the apology, she took the opportunity to reproach Cardenas for refusing entry to Mexico of 500 Jews from Europe. Anita took him to task for his words and actions, stating that they made it difficult to answer the accusations of fascism made by the president's enemies.[16]

Anita's emotional and intellectual identification with Mexico added to her difficulties. At approximately the same time, she struggled with a story about Mexico for the *New York Times Sunday Magazine*. There are eight drafts of the oil story in her files written between July 1938 and February 1939. Clues about problems include a note suggesting she rewrite the first paragraph and another asking her to "eliminate the slant [. . .] against the oil companies."[17]

In the drafts, Anita juxtaposed the Mexican who produced lacquer trays with the one who tinkered with automobiles, portraying a change in modern Mexico from the romantic image of the indigenous artisan to one who built dams and roads. Beauty and poverty are contrasted with socialism and capitalism. She traced the history of Mexican oil from the concessions awarded by Porfirio Diaz to British, Dutch, and U.S. companies; through the Constitution of 1917, which confirmed the nation's ownership of Mexico's subsoil; to Ambassador Morrow's deals with Calles to overlook the laws. She described the conflict and the political issues underlying the friction. Germany was buying Mexican oil. The United States wanted European interests out in order to maintain control of oil in Mexico in light of the situation in Europe.[18]

At the end of November Anita wrote a long letter to Markel, editor of the *New York Times Sunday Magazine*. She was frustrated, weary, and depressed at not being able to get Mexico's reality across. She presented her position, defining the Mexican Revolution as a "progressive phenomenon, recapitulating in great part U.S. developments," and included her roots as the daughter of a landowner who had suffered "considerable" losses. Further, she did not want to jeopardize the reputation of the *New York Times*:

> *anything I wrote which deviated markedly from this attitude would at once be seized upon as more proof that the Times is a "Fascist" paper and is in on an American-capitalist-international-Jewish conspiracy to prevent Mexicans from doing what they please with their country. What appears in the Times has an enormous effect there, even on policy making. I think that the attitude of the American press since the oil expropriation has all been pinned on the Times, and that in turn has been pinned to anti-Semitic propaganda, which has now convinced enough government people to make Cardenas reverse his policy—as he did in the deportation of the refugees a few weeks ago. I hesitate to write anything that can in any way intensify the nationalist bitterness and sense of persecution and betrayal which is now in Mexico virtually hysteria.[19]*

The negative experience with *Fortune* was still fresh. She made her position clear, leaving the ball in Markel's court:

> *If you really think there is any possibility of re-working the piece to meet your idea of what is wanted, without putting me down among*

the belligerents giving aid and comfort to the Nazis and Esso (alas,
in this situation their ideas coincide!) I'll be glad to try again.

There are three more drafts written after that letter. The new angle was
foreign relations between Mexico and Europe, with an emphasis on
"Mexico for the Mexicans" (a phrase used as a chapter title in *The Wind
That Swept Mexico*). Anita stressed that Mexico did not have "progressives,"
rather "revolutionaries," who built schools, highways, created industry, and
distributed land; she added a favorable description of Cardenas visiting villages.[20] Anita changed the focus of the article to Mexico's foreign relations
in order to get her message across. It was published in 1939.

The series of articles about the Mexican Revolution in *Harper's* presented
Anita's traditional position with renewed eloquence and skill. The material
was amply reviewed after it was published as *The Wind That Swept Mexico.*
As anticipated, it drew threatening letters from members of the Roman
Catholic community in the United States.[21] Anita responded to the editors of *Harper's*, defining the position of the Church in Mexico, specify-
ing the Church's mistaken policy of protecting "the few against the many."[22]

Church authorities were not the only ones who took issue with the book.
Orville Prescott, the reviewer for the *New York Times*, praised her "smooth,
graceful, spirited prose" but objected to her views. The Mexican Constitution, he wrote, "*sanctions all revolutionary acts and effectively prevents
conservative ones.* This, Miss Brenner seems to think is a good thing, failing to distinguish between much-needed democratic reforms and *the men-
ace of a socialist totalitarian State, which Mexico is well on the way to
becoming.* Her confusion of values is part of a world wide delusion of our
time—namely, that freedom is less important than bread and circuses"[23]
[Prescott's emphasis]. Anita responded, "I am not a socialist revolutionary
believing in an all-powerful state. An all-powerful state is the thing I am
most afraid of. I was not writing a book about my views, I was telling a story.
[. . .] I do not think the significant achievement of the Mexican Revolution is that more people have been able to get more corn, [. . .] now the
people are not afraid to speak out, and that they feel they have a right to
participate in how the country is run, whether or not they are always able
to make their weight felt."[24]

Several reviewers identified Anita with the "partisans," underscoring that
her sympathies were uncompromisingly with the revolutionaries.[25] She got
her message across to others who chose to highlight the role of the United

States, such as Lewis Gannett: "Whether the revolution was ebbing or flowing, most of the Mexicans, Miss Brenner says, have become accustomed to expecting the United States to be against it. [. . .] The revolution, she is sure, will go on: whether gently or as a tornado will depend largely upon the attitude of the United States. The Mexican people instinctively identify counter-revolution with North American influence, she says; they are intuitively anti-fascist, but bewildered to find us their allies in that fight."[26]

The Wind was published after the United States had declared war on the Axis and created a stir among Mexicanists. Some questioned Anita's position, and others, such as Katherine Anne Porter, felt she could have gone farther to the left:

> *I think Miss Brenner yields again to her old temptation to give too pretty and simple a picture—for, mind you, this terrible little story she tells is a mere bedtime lullaby beside the reality—and in general, to treat individual villains, whom she really knows to be such, too gently. [. . .] I think the deeds of the oil companies could have been exposed with somewhat more vigor. [. . .] within the more multiple and complicated limitations of the present international political situation, she has perhaps ventured as far as she might and still have her book published at all.*[27]

Anita presented the Mexican Revolution as an ongoing vigorous drive. *The Wind* is not limited to the period of armed struggle between 1910 and 1920; it carries the reader through 1942, unraveling forces and outcomes.

Anita kept in touch with friends from Spain who were in Mexico.[28] They were aware of the activities of many Stalinists who had arrived in Mexico as refugees from the Spanish Civil War, and they urged her to make the information known.[29] Anita repeated warnings about Mexico's future and the relationship with the United States. Although a Mexican by birth, she clearly identified herself as an American in the early lines of *The Wind*: "We are not safe in the United States, now [1943] and henceforth, without taking Mexico into account; nor is Mexico safe disregarding us. This is something that Mexicans have long known, with dread, but that few Americans have had to look at."[30]

eighteen

Epilogue: New York, 1942

Anita with her children, Peter and Susannah.

WE CROUCHED under the dining-room table beneath thick blankets so the light of the radio bulbs could not be seen. We listened for the siren signaling the end of the blackout. We were glued to that radio. I remember it happening over and over. It was terrifying. Was it a bomb? Was it practice? It is still real, more than fifty years later. My mother wrote:

> *Last night I crouched*
> *Breathless within myself*
> *And called on God*
> *An image focused dust,*
> *Dust on a vacant shelf.*

O dreadful symbol
Let it not be a signal of catastrophe.
Let it not cancel time's account,
Red-inked and overdrawn.

The nightmare years stretch back,
stretch on,
The work to do, the courage needed.
For my son's sake, o for my smiling daughter,
Have mercy Lord. Lord let there be a Lord.
Strengthen me.[1]

World War II changed the course of everyone's life, people and countries. The Allies were on the defensive when Anita wrote that poem. David left a growing private practice and a teaching post at Cornell University Medical School to enlist with the U.S. Army in 1942. He was sent to Washington, D.C., for training in tropical medicine and then was shipped out to Tingo Maria, a small village in Peru. He established a clinic as part of a public health program sponsored by the U.S. Army to offset pro-Axis sentiments in South America. His contribution was documented in *Time Magazine*.[2] His letters to Anita were bitter, angry, and disappointed: he saved the life of a Japanese pilot, the enemy; he wasn't in Europe; and the U.S. Army was plagued with anti-Semitism. After his mission was accomplished in

David Glusker goes to war.

The family reunited.

Peru, David was transferred to San Jose, Costa Rica, to head the U.S. Army Public Health Office. His letters transmit a sense of community with other Americans in San Jose. He found a house so that Anita and the family could join him.

Anita remained in New York until late 1943. She finished *The Wind That Swept Mexico* and was there to refute the critics when it was published. Economic survival with two young children was difficult on David's military salary and what Anita could earn. Further, New York City presented the stresses of war: rationing and blackouts. Anita negotiated her fees, mentioning that her income had to cover child care. She hustled for work, sending out story ideas on the advice of her agent.[3] She worked with James Rorty as a ghost writer, did translations, and landed a contract with Simon and Schuster for a history of Mexico, which meant an advance.[4]

The situation was so bad that Anita agreed to work for her father, running errands and getting information in New York to send to San Antonio, Texas. She also drew up an inventory of her art collection in order to sell it.[5] Anticipating a short wait, Anita packed up the house, bundled the children into a 1939 Ford, and headed south to wait for military orders to join David in Costa Rica. The first stop was San Antonio with her family, then Mexico City. David didn't stay in Costa Rica, though; he was sent to California to recover from pleurisy and remained there until the war was over.

Anita was fairly productive in the early forties, considering she was virtually a single parent for two young children. Her writing, its subject matter and tone, shifted with the changes in her personal life. There is a sharp drop in the volume of published work after *The Wind That Swept Mexico*. Moving to Mexico meant a transition from intense activity as a radical, journalist, and art critic in New York to life in Mexico. She was removed from the scene where contacts and contracts were made, and her subject matter revolved around Mexico. She had nineteen articles published in the *New York Times Sunday Magazine* between 1940 and 1943 and only one after that, in 1948. Approximately half of the articles are about art; they include reviews of exhibits and significant events in the art world in New York. Other features cover a wide spectrum of subjects, including a racehorse and the Brooklyn Dodgers. The correspondence about her work is lively and complimentary.

The quest for work that Anita initiated in New York in the early forties continued into the fifties, with sparse results.[6] She contributed several articles to *Holiday*, one about the Paricutin volcano, which became the vehicle for telling the story of the people of Michoacan.[7] The *New York Times Sunday Magazine* published a feature on Miguel Aleman in 1948, when he took office as president of Mexico. Anita was optimistic about his program and wrote a positive presentation of his professional cabinet.[8]

Articles about Mexico, or the relationship between the United States and Mexico, were not of prime interest in the forties and did not sell. Anita kept trying anyway: in an article about mosquitoes and public health she presented the need for improving communication between the two countries and peoples. The *Saturday Evening Post* objected:

> We read Anita Brenner's article with a good deal of interest. It started to be a good medical article dealing with various diseases coming into this country by a greatly expanded air traffic and the means taken to combat them; but after that slid off into a piece about the Good Neighbor policy with South America. We have had an awful lot about the Good Neighbor policy and are not interested in any more of it. The article would have to have some of this, I agree, but nobody here can sympathize with that business of turning a promising medical article into that sort of thing. We would be glad to read this again, if she would care to take another crack at it in the light of the comments above.[9]

During this period Anita wrote several incomplete autobiographical novels and mentioned wanting to write a novel. She coauthored a manuscript, "Doctor in Petticoats," with Louis Berg. It was a love story, which may have been intended as a script, about a woman who traveled to Paris to become a doctor, fell in love with a French doctor, but returned to New York, alone and unmarried. She practiced as a doctor in New York, establishing a woman's teaching clinic. The French doctor followed tradition and married the young woman his mother chose for him. The couple met many years later when he visited her in New York.

A second story, "Love," presented an almost opposite situation. The story is reminiscent of the life of Dolores del Rio, a Mexican movie star. A young pianist fell in love with a beautiful woman from a traditional, proper Mexican family, who married in order to go to Hollywood and work as an actress. The pianist pursued her with flowers and letters until they met again in Mexico City. Again, the story was written as a script; however, here Anita included the names of real people such as Carlos Chavez, Claudio Arrau, and Diego Rivera. The woman in this story was a true femme fatale, a professional actress, adventuresome and daring, who married several times.

Anita addressed women's issues in story ideas she sent out, such as the life of an ideal foster mother in New York. *Woman's Home Companion* was not interested.[10] Anita was now a mother focused on children. She referred to her writing as "paper babies" in a presentation to the Women's National Book Association in New York in 1943.[11]

Anita's only fiction was published in the *Menorah Journal* (in the twenties) and as children's books. *The Boy Who Could Do Anything* is a collection of indigenous Mexican stories that Anita heard from Luz, Diego Rivera's model, and retold.[12] *I Want to Fly* is a story about children who take an airplane trip while sitting in cardboard boxes. Anita shared this project with Lucienne Bloch, who had married Stephen Dimitroff and also had young children. They tested stories on their children; Lucienne laughed as she remembered how bored we were, after hearing the same story over and over. *A Hero by Mistake: The Story of a Frightened Indian* (1958) portrays the capture of dangerous bandits by mistake.

Anita's last children's book, *The Timid Ghost, or What Would You Do with a Sackful of Gold*, is a story about a friendly Mexican ghost who wants to reveal a treasure to someone, if only he can find the right person. The book brought Anita and Jean Charlot, who illustrated it, the Boys' Clubs of America Junior Book Award. Charlot illustrated three of the children's books and Lucienne Bloch illustrated one (plus a second that was never published).

Anita's confrontational writing faded in the forties. She translated and introduced an article by Indalecio Prieto for *American Mercury* about the role of the Soviet Union in Spain.[13] She warned her public about the European Communist Party's activities in Mexico. The last effort to get her message in print was a book review in the *New York Times* focused on Argentina's fear of idealism and preference for fascism.[14] The low volume of published writing at this time does not reflect Anita's concurrent active involvement with political issues.

Her files are full of documentation about activities defending the underdog. She participated with Herbert Solow and others in demanding a full investigation of the murder of Carlo Tresca in 1943. Tresca, an Italian anarchist, shared struggles with Anita and Solow during the Spanish Civil War.[15] Solow sent her a report of the dinner of the Joint Anti-Fascist Refugee Committee at the Hotel Biltmore in May 1944, mentioning the "Audience: Suckers toward the front. I was at a rear table, largely occupied by under-disguised Communist hacks."[16] Anita's response was a long letter with details of her trip to Mexico as well as an explanation of the conditions for her contributions to the *New Leader*:

> *Would not want to do it on any spec basis, as the person I would have to hire to stick around at home with kids, would be paid, spec or no spec. Don't see how the NL can afford to pay that dough for marginal stuff only, since apparently they do not want any Mexican news at all—some of the hottest items might not get thru. Besides, I will have to be extremely circumspect because the censorship goes on at the American Embassy, where there are some 500 employees, of all political complexions, and I can't afford to get balled up in the kind of intrigues such folk might cook up. So I'd have to use my judgment as to how much I could relay, in view of the above. The NL has to be told this, and might not be willing to accept it; might do better with someone freer to take more risks. [. . .] Things do happen as you know.[17]*

Anita shared causes with friends in New York and made new friends in Mexico with new struggles. Jose Bartoli, a Catalan artist who was a refugee from the Spanish Civil War, put it this way: "Anita was a liberal. [. . .] She was never a militant loyal to a given political ideology. [. . . She] knew

Mathias stayed in
Mexico. Photo by
Marianne Goeritz.

more or less directly the comrades who made up the international group
in Mexico, however, never collaborated with this group in the political
ideological sense, that I know of, it was always on a level of personal friendship, intellectual because she was a democratic, liberal anti-fascist."[18]

Artists remained favorites. Although Anita was friendly with Diego Rivera,
she rescued artists when he went after them. Goeritz described meeting
Anita after Rivera attacked him in the Mexico City press. He was packing
when Anita knocked on his door. She told him that he was not in Europe,
that he need not flee from Diego's tirade. Goeritz stayed and became one
of Anita's closest friends, there for her during crisis periods, designing her
home and adopting her daughter as his own.[19]

Anita visited friends in prison and helped many who were persecuted politically. The adrenaline flowed, priorities were shifted, and she was off to the rescue. A crisis was a crisis; nothing else mattered, not even picking children up from school.[20]

New York friends stayed in touch.[21] They exchanged news about activities, children and grandchildren, with an occasional mention of their shared history. I found one of Felix Morrow's letters the most poetic. "I am well and so is my wife and three children and two grandchildren. In these past years I have finally learned to relate to people instead of ideas. So I am happy. I feel fortunate to have lived long enough to have come to this understanding. Most of our old friends are dead and they never did get to it."[22]

Elliot Cohen encouraged Anita to write about the Jewish community in Mexico for *Commentary*, where he worked. They corresponded about fascist and Nazi activity in Mexico.[23] Anita identified as a Jew and was consistent in her efforts to help when trouble brewed.[24] Her archive includes reports, clippings, and correspondence about anti-Semitism in Mexico. She also participated in the drive to raise funds for Israel. "She helped the American League for a Free Palestine present their case to the B'nai B'rith organization of Mexico in spite of tremendous opposition."[25]

Anita's bond with Judaism went beyond troubleshooting; she pursued and enjoyed the study of the Bible and Cabala.[26] From a professional perspective, she carried out extensive research on the Carvajal family, who came to Mexico persecuted by the Inquisition. Unfortunately she did not complete the project. When she died, she had completed a first draft of the story of Moses for young people. Her identity as a Jew led her to include the following statement in a biographical narrative: "if I had to be a refugee again I would unquestionably go to Jerusalem."[27]

Judaism for Anita was not a series of rules and regulations. One friend recalled her flexibility: "The servant was posted on the street as a lookout for the Rabbi. She was a good lookout. She came running down the steps, 'Here comes the Rabbi.' All the shrimp and ham canapes disappeared like magic. As soon as he left they reappeared—all great fun. Respect for one and all."[28]

Correspondence between Anita and David provided valuable information about their thoughts, lives, and plans after the war. New York meant a high cost of living but good research possibilities. Mexico had a lower cost of living but less sophisticated and fewer libraries and laboratories. They opted for Mexico, and Anita lived there until her death in 1974. David became the first foreign-trained physician licensed to practice in Mexico. Anita coped with two children and worked on several projects, constantly drumming up trade.

During the fifties, Anita wrote several articles for *Art News*. She presented a panorama of galleries, without any political agenda, reporting about old friends and new favorites, including Francisco Goitia, Frida Kahlo, Miguel Covarrubias, Roberto Montenegro, Carlos Orozco Romero, Ricardo Martinez, Rufino Tamayo, and new names on the scene: Mathias Goeritz, Leonora Carrington, Pedro Friedeberg, Alice Rahon, Jose Bartoli, Pedro Coronel, Myra Landau, and Vlady. Almost ten years later, Anita wrote a long article, "Art and Artists in Mexico Today," for *Atlantic Monthly*. Here, she traced Mexican art historically and outlined the political context.[29]

A series of personal blows in the early fifties contributed to lowering the volume of her writing. First, her prophetic fear that one day David would give her the cold shoulder came true when the couple separated in 1951. Second, her father died early in 1952 after a long bout with cancer, unleashing a long, brutal battle among the Brenner heirs. Third, she was diagnosed with cancer and underwent a hysterectomy within the same year. The situation was dramatic and difficult. I vividly remember her gazing out the window, crying. When I asked what was the matter, she responded with, "I'm trying to decide whether to live or to die." I was fifteen.

Loving friends, her drive to make Mexico known, and financial difficulties brought her back into professional ventures. She contributed profiles of artists and intellectuals in the Sunday edition of the local *Mexico City News*. Rather than photographers, Anita took young artists, among them Jose Luis Cuevas, to sketch the person being interviewed.

Bartoli and other artist friends encouraged her to start a Christmas-card venture.[30] One thing led to another and pretty soon Anita had launched a monthly magazine, *Mexico/This Month*, which continued to publish for seventeen years.[31] Anita threw herself into developing the publication with many admirers but no capital. The Comité Norteamericano Pro-México, a binational group of entrepreneurs focused on improving the relationship between Mexico and the United States, was one of the earliest supporters.[32] *Mexico/This Month* became a vehicle to get back into action. In a monthly editorial called "Person to Person," Anita dealt with the things uppermost in her mind. She created a revolving team of collaborators, some young and unknown who were first published in *Mexico/This Month* and others who were established writers and artists.

Queries from "Loving readers," who wanted information about everything from where to retire to how to start a dairy farm, were answered by the fictitious Juanita Jones. Friends from New York provided feedback, visited, and sent people to meet Anita.[33] It was not uncommon to run into celebrities or visiting journalists at the magazine office. Henry Moore was in town to do a mural in a bar that Goeritz and his friend Daniel Mont designed. Jack Beck, a CBS news correspondent, taped Anita, the economist Edmundo Flores, and Carlos Fuentes in Anita's living room. Richard Condon wrote Anita into his novels. Laura Bergquist, a reporter for *Look*, came in and out on her way to Cuba. Fletcher Knebel, married to Laura, used Anita's name in his novels. Bud Schulberg, a frequent visitor, lived in an apartment behind the office. His apartment had a large terrace, as one staff member wrote:

> We could see him in the mornings, having breakfast on his terrace which must have been a couple of floors below the editorial offices of MTM. She [Anita] talked with him fairly often and always by screaming across the back alley to him. One time he complained to her because one of her employees, the great looking blond whose name I've forgotten, had sent him a message he didn't like. The blonde was the one MTM "raffled off" as a magazine promotion one summer. She really wanted to get to know Schulberg and was trying desperately to arrange a way to do that. She decided with my assistance, to send him a note. In the note, she introduced herself and told him she really wanted to talk about the Jazz Age and Paris, etc. The message was delivered, by wrapping it around one of the old advertising offset blocks we had in the office and tossing the package down to Schulberg's balcony. He was not happy about this, since I think that on landing the package broke a window or something. He complained to Anita during one of their screaming conversations across the back. Anita laughed about this but warned us about future communications with the good Mr. Schulberg.[34]

Mexico/This Month put Anita back into a productive mood; she was busy, with dozens of projects going on all at once. Bartoli, who worked in the art department, recalled a typical scene:

Like a captain at the helm of a ship in a storm, Anita, in the midst of incredible chaos in her office, talks on the telephone, reads papers, hands out articles to translate, answers questions, gets mad in English or in Spanish, laughs. Anita, surrounded, almost buried under papers, insults some licenciado *on the telephone.*[35] *The tic, tic, tic, tic, tic of the typewriters, telephones, and the yelling are not sufficient to drown out the voice of woody woodpecker, a manager, accountant, cashier, who calls out for someone to give him a piece of paper. You can hear Anita: "Tell that bastard to come back next month! If he wants to collect!" [. . .] "Jennifer, please do this caption over again, and please remember that Yucatan is a state of the Mexican Republic, not an Indian costume! For God's sake, Jennifer!" [. . .] "Alice, take this article about Oaxaca that you translated into English and take out the forty-seven 'sombreros' and thirty-two 'señoritas.' Please." Anita's desk and the two side tables are covered with photographs. Anita, with a telephone on one ear and Vlady standing next to her, with unquestionable skill and speed chooses the photographs for the coming issue, always a time for great fun, good laughs, amid "Yes. . . . Yes. . . . Very kind of you, Licenciado. Thank you. . . . Yes. . . . How could that be? . . . Ha! And please tell that dunce that I will not release a cent until January. . . . Yes. . . . Yes. . . . At Sanborns. . . . Yes. . . . Thank you, Licenciado. . . ." And while she talked on the telephone she passed the photographs that she chose from amid the multicolored ocean of paper to Vlady: photographs of ruins of pre-Columbian civilizations, Colonial churches and palaces still in use, Acapulco! [. . .] Anita slipped Vlady the picture of a tortured individual with dark glasses, carefully coiffed to make his shiny black hair appear uncombed, sporting the mustache of a lady-killer, his dark skin bathed with shiny oil, his shirt open for a view of an elaborate necklace. . . . Vlady looked at the picture and asked Anita: "This jerk? What for?" "Vlady, don't be dense, pictures like these move mountains . . . of flesh . . . provoke passion and even orgies. Come on, many potential tourists see this, roll their eyes and take off for the travel agency."*[36]

Anita carried on the battle of the Brenners, took charge of the family property in Aguascalientes, and published *Mexico/This Month* at the same time. Sometimes editorial meetings were shifted to Aguascalientes, eight hours away by car, overnight by train, and there was no airplane service at the time. Letters provide progress reports and crises, such as financial crunches to pay for paper or the printer.[37] Pedro Friedeberg, a staff artist, was among those who went to Aguascalientes. Pressed into service on Anita's project to identify Brenner land, he described suffering a cabalistic number of seven nervous breakdowns while placing colored thumbtacks on a city map.[38]

Mexico/This Month was not always on time, but it was lively. The paper wasn't glossy, but the content was first rate. Anita included articles about every imaginable aspect of Mexico. Centerpiece maps designed by artists presented Chapultepec Park, the pyramids of Teotihuacan, native dress, and other illustrations. A calendar of events and a shopping service were started, and soon the staff was boxing rebozos to be shipped to a myriad of readers.

The magazine survived by selling a block of subscriptions to the Mexican government for distribution at embassies and consulates throughout the world. The subsidy was withdrawn in 1972, and the magazine folded, in spite of Anita's effort to keep it alive. Her own writing had been on the back burner for seventeen years. Her perennial rationalization was the need to solve financial problems, claiming that later she would find time to write. Promotion, advertising, and funding were major concerns. Money was always short. Once, Bartoli stormed into the office determined to be paid, and without knowing that Anita was there, he yelled to Vlady, his colleague, "If Anita doesn't pay me today, I'm jumping out the window." Then he heard Anita's voice: "Vlady, open the window."[39]

The office was an interesting, busy place, and Anita's temper was infamous. She took on the role of the tyrannical editor that she said she had learned from Lester Markel. There was always grumbling; people stormed out, came back to work, and left again. Some tangled with her so often that one never knew if they were working or "mad."[40]

Anita's return to Aguascalientes, where she was born, revived her spirit of adventure and creation. She put the family farm back into production, introducing asparagus and new varieties of apricots and nectarines into Aguascalientes. She brought Israeli scientists to provide technical assistance for local wineries and fought bitterly with the oligarchy, who kept slicing off pieces of the Brenner land for themselves. Her worlds overlapped.

Anita loved to lure friends to Aguascalientes and show them the farm and the town. Now, instead of books to sign, there were crates for exporting asparagus and garlic. The son of one of Anita's closest friends, Leonora

From signing articles to garlic boxes.

Pablo Weisz says: "I woke up every morning ready for pasta!"

The artistic influence
on the farm. Courtesy
of *Mexico/This Month.*

Carrington, was among the visitors. Pablo remembers the permeating smell
of garlic. "I woke up every morning ready for pasta."[41]

Anita was killed in a car accident on her way home to Aguascalientes,
on December 1, 1974. She had an appointment to sell the farm, which would
give her economic freedom to return to her writing. She left many irons
in the fire and three major unfinished projects: the story of Moses for young
people; the story of Gonzalo de Guerrero, a shipwrecked Spaniard who
integrated into the Maya world; and a history of Mexico in the twenties in
collaboration with Bambi (Ana Cecilia Treviño, a journalist working at
Excelsior).

I believe that there is a strong analogy between Anita's spirit and the
last children's book she wrote, *The Timid Ghost.* The ghost Teodoro haunts
roads looking for a person who can handle receiving a large amount of gold.
The criteria match the values of the indigenous peoples of Mexico. The
candidate must not be interested in amassing a fortune for personal gain.
Greed is not acceptable. Simplicity is of the utmost importance. Anita's

spirit is said to roam the land where she was born, where she planted asparagus and orchards. She may just be looking for the appropriate person
to carry on in her spirit—growing fruit, making Mexico understood to a
foreign audience, and fighting injustice—someone to receive the gold, to
continue the struggle.

appendixes

Unpublished Documents by Anita Brenner

appendix a
Letter to Joe Krutch of *The Nation*, March 18, 1934

Dear Joe Krutch,

I think I have been unfairly treated. After all, I was asked to write a piece about the Municipal Art business. I spent a lot of time seeing the show, getting information, writing, discussing, and rewriting the piece. Your refusal to print any of it on the basis that it does not exactly follow the line discussed brings up a number of fundamental questions. Your objections—one, length, and two, limiting the piece to one instead of two subjects, are not I think valid enough to justify the wastebasket, especially as we agreed that the subject I wrote about needed to be discussed in the Nation and was to be written about at length. I wrote Peggy I thought it should be cut but could not do it because I was afraid I was too close to the material and might sacrifice clarity. I separated the Machine Art show because I found that both could not be written about clearly in the allotted space, and that the Machine Art piece constituted a review in itself, which could be used two or three weeks later, since the show runs to the end of April.

Heretofore I have been treated as a writer responsible enough to produce articles more or less according to my own judgment. In writing about art, however, my judgment is often questioned, and in this case completely scrapped. It is my opinion that the reason for that is that you do not agree with my fundamental point of departure, dislike my viewpoint, and are not willing to give me the same latitude that I get in writing editorials or articles. In other words, I am in a special position and subjected to special restrictions as an art critic which I do not meet as a political writer or book reviewer.

This is what I cannot understand. I do not see why you apply to reviewing pictures, standards any different from those you apply to reviewing books. It has been my experience that, having satisfied yourself with the general intellectual solvency of the reviewer, you hand the book over and print the review without asking for either previous consultation or revision. Yet in reviewing pictures, I am asked to consult each piece beforehand, and sometimes to rewrite, and finally in the present case the piece is discarded entirely.

I find it on the whole too uncomfortable and irritating to work under tutelage to be willing to continue. You know by now whether or no I can write competently and interestingly about art, whether or no my judgment is worth trusting, or worth having. If it is, I think I should have exactly the same freedom you would give me in reviewing books; if it isn't, I think the Nation should have someone who can be given that freedom. You know that as a rule, I am not temperamental about my work. I don't insist that everything should be printed as written. I am willing to adjust myself to space limitations, I don't wail when wording and punctuation is changed, and I am reasonable about rewriting when I can see for myself that rewriting is needed, and I think I see it about as quickly as anyone else does. But just the same I do expect the kind of latitude and guarantee that is given to an old contributor, and if my work is worth having it is worth having as work done according to my judgment and ability.

To settle the question I propose: a given amount of space per month, or if you like, a maximum and an average, and consultation in every case when I think I need more than the allotment, but freedom to write as I like within the allotted space. If you don't think I can use that freedom well, then clearly that means that you prefer me to write under supervision, which is comprehensible enough in dealing with a new writer on a new project, but not with an old contributor on a project that has already been tried.

I believe I have made it quite clear that I want very much to write about art in the Nation, and I think I can write about it from a fresh, informative, vigorous viewpoint. I know my pieces are read

and discussed, and it is only for that reason that I write them, hop-
ing to contribute occasional shocks of life to the vast inertia of pic-
ture painting and image carving among us. The time and trouble
involved far outweigh the cent a word I am paid for them; add su-
pervision to that, and my only reason for writing the things disap-
pears. I can't possibly write comfortably always with your possible
reactions in mind, knowing that your aesthetics differ radically from
mine, and knowing that in each case, I am risking a complete waste
of my time and energy.

I am sorry to accuse you of censorship knowing how you dislike
the word, but that's what it amounts to. It is an unhappy business
for both of us, but you would feel and behave the same way, I think,
if our positions were reversed. So, this is a kind of sweetly reason-
able ultimatum. I won't be insulted if I'm fired, either, knowing there
are excellent reasons for it. I shall be relieved and very sorry.

Sincerely,
Anita Brenner

appendix b
Excerpts from "Private Art and Public Interest," March 1934

[. . .] escorted by our Mayor, American art [. . .] serves a private interest, the Rockefeller real-estate project of Radio City, by helping to establish it as a cultural center, thus making rented space in it worth the while
of all business which profits by the arty and luxury trades. This has been a
paramount problem in Radio City. The Rivera murals interfered with the
renting of space in the RCA building, and were covered over for that reason, as the management itself said. The adverse effect of this choice in favor of business and against art made some sort of reconciliation between
Radio City and the artists and art-public advisable, for business reasons. A
semi-official, all-American show serves the purpose admirably.

[. . .] In the Rivera matter, they were plainly guilty of vandalism; yet
they had just spent large sums to make the all-American show possible.
Were they or weren't they public benefactors? A considerable section of
the artists included in the show thought not, and withdrew on the ground

that ownership of a work of art could not mean the right to destroy it. Moreover, this work was by its nature and place intended as art for the public, and was paid for by the Rockefellers as philanthropists, public benefactors, and yet it was destroyed by them as unquestioningly as you and I might discard an old hat. The artists who withdrew from the show questioned their right to do so on the traditional ground that a work of art is the property of civilization over and beyond the accident of its private ownership; they viewed art as a public interest, they protested on much the same ground as we when we censure Hitler's burning of books and suppression of free scientific and artistic activity. [. . .] "Oh, well, Rivera is a Mexican anyhow." [. . .] since the Rockefellers are the biggest modern art buyers in the New York market, wield an enormous influence in the galleries and museums, they could if they wished easily ruin who they chose. In other words, if the Rockefellers want to exercise a dictatorship over American art—in the New York market anyhow—they may do so whenever it suits them.

[. . .] It consists of a thousand sculptures, painting, prints, produced by artists all living, and all entitled to American passports. Other than the artists' citizenship, and the fact that there is a mile of their work, there is nothing specifically American about it. The names sound like an international roll-call, and the objects are individual variants of the school common to all the western world. They are things made by independent artisans for private ownership and enjoyment. In form, idea, function and aesthetic quality they follow the tradition of nineteenth century Europe. [. . .] As a whole they contribute nothing new, independent, vigorously moving to American or world art, and yet they are put before us as a whole, constituting a public interest. [. . .]

In censuring and throttling its manifestation for business reasons, are the Rockefellers acting for the benefit of the American public and American art? We come [to] the same question in art as in the other oil business—is their public power a private or a public interest?

appendix c
Corrido del Periodismo Americano Castigado

"Written June 1938. Dedicated to Lic. Ramon Beteta."

Corre petróleo, corre
Corre a la refinería
Que aquí ya se acabó
El mando de la gringuería.

Pero luego las empresas,
Viendo que perdían el hueso,
Dijeron ay Lázaro Cárdenas,
Te quitaremos el pescuezo.

Entonces dijo Beteta,
Conque con esas andamos,
Pués al diablo los periodistas,
Ya ni noticias les damos.
Ay mire licenciadito,
Licenciado castigador,
En esto y en toda la vida,
Paga el justo por el pecador.

Corre petróleo corre,
Enchapopotado vas,
A mí también ya me corrieron,
Por ser una gringa más.

appendix d
Letter to Lester Markel, editor, *New York Times Sunday Magazine,*
November 22, 1938

Dear Mr. Markel,

*I've been looking that Mexican piece over and for the life of me I
can't find the "defense of the present regime" in it. It seemed to me
that its abstract and heavy effect was due precisely to a strenuous
objectivity, which simply described and reported the Mexican revo-*

lution as it has worked out historically and as Mexicans feel it. I don't see how I can lean over backwards any further with it, so I wonder whether it is worth while to try a rewrite. It begins to feel as if almost anything I wrote about Mexico at present would be unacceptable. My own view, that the revolution is on the whole a progressive phenomenon, recapitulating in great part U.S. developments, is based on pretty thorough knowledge of the country and the facts; and is held in spite of the fact that it has cost my own family a considerable investment. It is bound to color anything I write and since I believe I report truthfully, and base my views on judgment of an objective character, I don't see why such color should be removed, even if that were possible for me to do.

And another thing: my ideas, that the revolution is a progressive phenomenon but that the present regime, like the others, is full of crooks and all kinds of unscrupulous careerists, are so well known in Mexico that anything I wrote which deviated markedly from this attitude would at once be seized upon as more proof that the Times is a "Fascist" paper and is in on an American-capitalist-international-Jewish conspiracy to prevent Mexicans from doing what they please with their country. What appears in the Times has an enormous effect there, even on policy making. I think that the attitude of the American press since the oil expropriation has all been pinned on the Times, and that in turn has been pinned to anti-Semitic propaganda, which has now convinced enough government people to make Cardenas reverse his policy—as he did in the deportation of the refugees a few weeks ago. I hesitate to write anything that can in any way intensify the nationalist bitterness and sense of persecution and betrayal which is now in Mexico virtually hysteria. One can criticize or comment, in a friendly tone; but anything else looks like abuse to them and unfortunately produces effects quite out of proportion to the incidental cause.

There is a pretty serious crisis developing now in Mexico, that begins to look like another Spain. The Nazis have recently changed their anti-Cardenas policy to a boring-from-within tactic, meanwhile continuing to back opposition in the press and elsewhere. They figure they will be in on the ground floor no matter who gets the upper hand in the struggle that will probably become violent on the electoral issue; and preparations are already being made. The Mexican *progressives are going to have their hands full, Cardenas included, and due to the anti-American wave of feeling there is a real possibility that a Nazi-dominated dictatorship will emerge next door. Unfriendliness here to the sincerely progressive and honest men in Mexico, and their programs and ideas, helps to build up that possibility in a manner which is not quite conceivable here, where there is so much press, and so many conflicting ideas about everything as to cancel out any definitive influence, from one source.*

I hope I've made myself clear. All these things may be irrelevant to the handling of a story, but the facts aren't, and I feel responsible on both counts. If you really think there is any possibility of re-working the piece to meet your idea of what is wanted, without putting me down among the belligerents giving aid and comfort to the Nazis and Esso (alas, in this situation their ideas coincide!) I'll be glad to try again.

Cordially,
[copy in files not signed]

P.S. A peg for the sculpture piece: Whitney Museum showing of contemporary sculpture in January. Would you mind outlining briefly to me how you think the piece should be handled? Angle and points. It will be encouraging to turn to such subject-matter again. This Times-on Mexico-on-Brenner series of complications has upset and depressed me very much.

appendix e

Contents of a file of Mexican economic and industrial information from July 1938, relating to an article published in *Fortune* magazine

Bach, Federico, "The Agrarian Question," 11-page document describing the history of landholdings in Mexico from the Spanish Conquest to the current figures of largest holdings, giving the number of hectares. Brenner Archives box 207-61.

Department of Commerce Foreign Trade Statistics, "Trade of the United States with Mexico," 11-page document with statistical information about imports and exports between Mexico and the United States. Brenner Archives box 207-71.

Mexico's Banking and Credit Structure, table showing structure of banking and credit institutions. Brenner Archives box 207-71.

"Fuerza," ballad about the union movement. Brenner Archives box 207-62.

Notes and statistics, 22-page document, tables of figures on specific industries. Brenner Archives box 207-71.

Secretaria de Hacienda, "Informe de las instituciones nacionales," 24-page document describing financial institutions in 1937 and 1938. Brenner Archives box 207-71.

Brenner, 10-page document with agriculture and industry production figures. Brenner Archives box 207-71.

Gonzalez Aparicio, Enrique, "Las nuevas formas de organización industrial en México," 24-page document about economics in Mexico, the effects of revolution, establishing banks to finance oil, railroads, and sugar. Brenner Archives box 207-71.

Brenner, notes and statistics about cotton production from 1935 to 1937. Brenner Archives box 207-61.

Censo industrial de 1930, 7-page industrial census report listing type of industry, number of employees, production, and taxes, with Brenner's notes on oil and mining production included. Brenner Archives box 207-71.

Ingresos del gobierno federal, table of income to federal government from 1900 to 1937. Brenner Archives box 207-71.

notes

introduction

1. Steffens, *The Autobiography of Lincoln Steffens*.
2. Turner, *México Bárbaro*.
3. Britton, *Carleton Beals*, 60.
4. Sergio Aguayo's dissertation on *New York Times* reporting on Mexico mentions Brenner and Paul Kennedy.
5. Brenner, two-page document with biographical statement written in 1972, Brenner Archives box 219.
6. Interview with Stephen Dimitroff. Response to the question: If everyone broke, why is there no record of Anita breaking with the Communist Party? "They would not have had her; she was too independent" (16 May 1989, San Francisco, Calif.). [Information confirmed with Ella Goldberg Wolfe.]
7. Brenner, "Centuries Clash in Many-Sided Mexico," 1934. Brenner used two ellipsis points frequently in her writing, especially in her journals. To distinguish between her punctuation and SJG's elisions from direct quotations, the elisions are enclosed in brackets.
8. Brenner to Gruening, May 11, 1961, Brenner Archives box 202-G.
9. *New York Times*, Dec. 8, 1929.
10. Brenner to Cass Canfield, Jan. 4, 1956, Brenner Archives unclassified.
11. Departamento de Turismo, Homenaje a los Pioneros del Turismo en México, 1967, Brenner Archives box Q.
12. IBM, *Golden Circle Memoir* (booklet about the Golden Circle Convention Meeting in Mexico City in 1969), Brenner Archives box B; Brenner, "Mexico as a Developing Country," typescript, Brenner Archives box Q.
13. Smith, *Pig in the Barber Shop*, 199–200.

one. *Nana Serapia*

1. Brenner, interview by Beth Miller, Aug. 30, 1974.
2. Ibid. (See also Brenner, *The Wind That Swept Mexico*, 1971, 17.)

3. Ibid.

4. Gruening, *Mexico and Its Heritage*, 124.

5. Brenner, *The Wind That Swept Mexico*, 25.

6. Ibid., 31.

7. Britton, *Carleton Beals*, 52–54.

8. Brenner, *The Wind That Swept Mexico*, 41.

9. Ibid., 41–43.

10. Ibid., 46.

11. This was the climax of a series of events that involved the U.S. Navy on Mexican soil. The policy of the United States had shifted from neutrality to one of isolating General Huerta from foreign aid and sympathy in order to force him out. One of the incidents took place in Tampico, where members of the crew of the whaleboat the USS *Dolphin* were loading gasoline. They were arrested and jailed for an hour and a half and released with an apology. U.S. Admiral Mayo demanded that the Huerta government hoist the American flag and present a 21-gun salute. Huerta refused. A few days later an orderly from the USS *Minnesota* was arrested briefly when he went ashore in uniform to pick up the ship's mail. Later that same night President Wilson was informed that the ship *Ypiranga* was due in Veracruz with weapons, and ordered Admiral Mayo to take Veracruz. See Gruening, *Mexico and Its Heritage*, 577–582.

12. Brenner, *The Wind That Swept Mexico*, 47.

13. Ibid., 49–50.

14. White, "Quietude of Heights Home."

15. Salas, *Soldaderas*.

16. Brenner, "Race of Princes," 1925.

17. Brenner, unfinished autobiographical novel, 1923.

18. Ibid.

19. Brenner journals, Aug. 29, 1929.

20. Brenner, unfinished novel, 1923.

two. *Mexico Welcomes Anita*

1. Frances Toor was an American writer and editor who taught at the National University's summer school and received a stipend from the Ministry of Education to publish *Mexican Folkways*.

2. Brenner to Jerry Aron, Sept. 24, 1923, Brenner Archives box 6-B. The writer Bertram Wolfe (1896–1977), mentioned in this letter, was persecuted in the United States for organizing unions (Bolshevism). He and his wife, Ella Goldberg, were brought by their friend and comrade Bob Haberman in 1922. They worked as English teachers and Wolfe organized the Communist Party. During the Stalin years he broke with the Stalinists and joined the Lovestoneites. In later years he worked for the State Department and at Stanford University, from where he retired. Ella worked as the Tass correspondent while in Mexico City. See Wolfe, *Life*.

3. Dick Oulahan, story proposal for *Time Magazine*, 2 pages, 1958, Brenner Archives box B. Brenner, "Vacation without Pay," Brenner Archives unclassified.

4. Bokser, *Imágenes*, 79.

5. Hexter, "Jews in Mexico," 2–13. See Brenner bibliography for articles in *The Nation, Jewish Morning Journal, Menorah Journal*, and dispatches sent to *Jewish Telegraphic Agency*.

6. Charles Hale, "Frank Tannenbaum."

7. Ross, *Gruening of Alaska*.

8. Beals arrived in Mexico in 1918 and taught English. Venustiano Carranza, a future president of Mexico, was among his students. See Britton, *Carleton Beals*.

9. Herbert Croly edited the liberal journal *The New Leader*.

10. Brenner, interview by Beth Miller, Jan. 20, 1974.

11. Manuel Gamio is known as the father of Mexican anthropology. He worked on integrating indigenous peoples into the mainstream. See Gamio, *Forjando Patria*, and Gonzalez Gamio, *Manuel Gamio*.

12. Brenner, "Mexican Renaissance," *New York World*, 1928.

13. Brenner, "Muralist Lucienne Bloch," 1936. This article describes Bloch's mural at the Women's House of Detention in New York.

14. Isidore Brenner divided his land into 100-hectare parcels and sold adjacent lots so that he did not own more than the 100 hectares allowed by the new laws.

15. Rosalie Evans was married to a British investor who became ill and died while in Mexico tending to his interests. She came to Mexico to pick up where he left off, trying to prevent agraristas from distributing her land. She visited the American and British embassies and enlisted their help. Her efforts are known because her sister published her letters after Rosalie was killed. See Caden Pettus, *Rosalie Evans Letters*.

16. Weston, *Daybooks*.

17. Brenner journals, Dec. 30, 1925. Reference to the wife of Alphonse Goldschmidt, a German socialist who wrote a book about Mexico and taught economics at the university.

18. Brenner journals, June 22, 1926.

19. Brenner journals, Dec. 2, 1925.

20. Salvador Novo was a major literary figure in Mexico. He was a poet, dramatist, and novelist identified in the late twenties and the thirties with the Vasconcelos group known as the *Contemporaneos*. He and Gabriel Fernández Ledesma edited and produced the magazine *Forma*. Alicia Azuela describes their relationship in "La Vanguardia Mexicana."

21. Brenner journals, April 11, 1926.

22. She hosted great parties and enjoyed the process up until her death in 1974. It was great fun to discover descriptions of Anita's parties, especially those I had attended. Aide-mémoire from Mary Elmendorf, Wendy Holden Tolksdorff, and Dr. Bernie Zuger; Hook, *Out of Step*, 286; Smith, *Pig in the Barber Shop*, 199–200.

23. Brenner journals, April 17, 1926. Tatanacho, whose real name was Ignacio

Fernandez Esperon, was a musician and songwriter who spent time in New York. He was part of the circle of intellectuals, especially close to Adolfo Best Maugard, and one of the people who encouraged Katherine Anne Porter to come to Mexico. See Walsh, *Katherine Anne Porter and Mexico.*

three. *A Family of Artists and Intellectuals*

1. Brenner journals, Dec. 20, 1925.
2. Brenner journals, March 7, 1927.
3. A. Azuela, *"El Machete."*
4. Amado de la Cueva, an artist who lived in Guadalajara, was killed in a motorcycle accident when he was very young. Angelina Beloff, a Russian artist, was Diego Rivera's first wife.
5. Brenner journals, April 12, 1926. *Universal* is a major daily in Mexico City. Dr. Atl (1875–1964) was an artist known for his landscapes and scenes of volcanoes. His real name was Gerardo Murillo. "Atl" is the Nahuatl word for water. The diminutive "Ortiguita" refers to Ortega, a journalist.
6. Brenner journals, Feb. 16–17, 1927.
7. Brenner journals, Mar. 4, 1926.
8. Brenner, "Orozco the Rebel" and "Mexican Prophet," 1928. The journal *L'A.B.C.* published many of Orozco's early cartoons.
9. Brenner journals, Sept. 12, 1926.
10. Brenner journals, Sept. 6, 1926.
11. Brenner journals, June 20, 1928. Frances F. Paine coordinated a special Rockefeller fund of $15,000 to promote Mexican art.
12. Alma Reed fell in love with Felipe Carrillo Puerto, the socialist governor of Yucatán, while working as a journalist. They were engaged to be married, but when she returned to the States for her trousseau, he was murdered. She never married, and she left precise instructions for her ashes to be sent to Yucatán and placed next to her lover. Needless to say, the children he had with the wife he left for Alma were not pleased.
13. Brenner journals, May 31, 1929.
14. The information in Anita's journals is confirmed in Orozco's letters to Jean Charlot. See Cardoza y Aragon and Charlot, *Jose Clemente Orozco.*
15. Brenner journals, March 15, 1926.
16. Brenner journals, March 16, 1926. See also Siqueiros, *Me Llamaban el Coronelazo,* 77.
17. Charlot, "Un precursor" and "Cien Grabados." For a complete bibliography of Charlot's writing in Mexico see Baciu, *Jean Charlot.*
18. Brenner and Charlot, "Une Renaissance Mexicaine," *La Renaissance de L'art Francais,* Feb. 1928; Brenner, "The Mexican Renaissance," 1926.
19. Brenner journals, Feb. 22, 1928.
20. Brenner journals, Nov. 26, 1926.

21. Brenner to David Glusker, Nov. 4, 1929. The title of the poem is the first two letters of the Hebrew alphabet, which also mean "alphabet." Hart Crane was in Mexico on a Guggenheim fellowship, and committed suicide on his way back to the States in 1932.

four. *Sisters, Foes, and Role Models*

1. Zurián, *Nahuí Olín*, 133–135.
2. See Cardona, "Concha Michel."
3. See Debroise, *Lola Alvarez Bravo*.
4. The novel *La Unica*, written by Guadalupe Marín, is said to be a fictionalized account of her relationship with Jorge Cuesta.
5. Zurián, *Nahuí Olín*, 133–135.
6. Weston, *Daybooks*, plate 27.
7. Brenner journals, Dec. 13, 1925.
8. Brenner journals, Dec. 27, 1925.
9. Her quota was fourteen skirts a day. I remember watching her make a lined tailored suit in two days, working without a pattern on a foot-pedal sewing machine.
10. Malvido, "Nahuí Olín," and Zurián, *Nahuí Olín*.
11. Brenner journals, April 15, 1928. She recorded these feelings while taking a psychology course at Columbia University.
12. Lowell Houser (1902–1971) was an American artist who worked for the Carnegie Institution in Yucatan.
13. List of complimentary copies of *Idols behind Altars*, Brenner Archives, unclassified.
14. Brenner journals, Feb. 3, 1926.
15. Brenner journals, Dec. 30, 1925.
16. Brenner journals, June 13, 1927.
17. Elinor Rice, taped interview by SJG in New York City, Sept. 1992.
18. Brenner journals, Feb. 23, 1927.
19. Brenner journals, March 6, 1927.
20. Brenner journals, July 13, 1926.
21. Brenner journals, July 16, 1926.
22. The period of close contact recorded in the journals was during the summer of 1926, at the onset of the *Cristero* Rebellion, an armed struggle between federal troops and Catholic partisans. The journal on July 19, 1926, explains, "To synthesize or rather illustrate the stuff in Elena, she told me—During the revolution, for some reason or another, a general shot Elena's brother in the leg. I believe he went to see him to protest about something. Elena's mother went to the general and reproached him for it. Then Elena, 16 years old—went to him and said: 'It is perfectly natural for you to shoot my brother. Being what you are and a product of the life you've led, you could not properly do otherwise.'"
23. Brenner journals, Nov. 10, 1925.

24. Brenner journals, Jan. 16, 1927.
25. Brenner journals, Feb. 17, 1927.
26. Brenner journals, Feb. 27, 1927.
27. Brenner journals, May 23, 1927.
28. Brenner journals, Aug. 16, 1927.
29. Brenner journals, Oct. 20, 1927.
30. Brenner journals, Jan. 28, 1929.
31. Ibid.
32. Brenner, "Nish Kosher," 1925.
33. Brenner journals, Oct. 14, 1926.
34. Brenner journals, March 12, 1927.
35. Brenner journals, Aug. 26, 1927.
36. See note 16, chapter 2, and Caden, *Rosalie Evans Letters from Mexico*.
37. Brenner journals, May 16, 1927.
38. Brenner journals, Aug. 31, 1927.
39. Brenner journals, May 15, 1927.
40. Brenner journals, May 16, 1927.

five. *Moving On*

1. Gruening, "Emerging Mexico 4."
2. Brenner, biographical narrative, Oct. 23, 1929, Brenner Archives, typescript, box A.
3. Dulles, *Yesterday in Mexico*, 322.
4. Brenner journals, Aug. 10, 1926. Henry was Anita's older brother and Dorothy one of her younger sisters. Anita recorded, "Long letter from Dorothy. Repents and stuff like that. Mentions, incidentally house being remodelled and redecorated. Papa must have a lot of money to spend it like that, the house did not need it. It is monstrous the money there is in the U.S. Ancient Rome must have been just like it."
5. Brenner journals, Jan. 9, 1927.

six. *Harvesting Mexican Efforts*

1. See Williams, *Covarrubias*.
2. Reed, *Orozco*, and Brenner, "Orozco the Rebel," 1928.
3. Brenner journals, Oct. 11, 1927.
4. Carleton Beals to Brenner, nd (context indicates Fall 1927), Brenner Archives, unclassified.
5. Brenner, "Idols behind Altars," *The Nation*, Oct. 20, 1926.
6. Brenner journals, Nov. 7, 1926.
7. As governor of Alaska, Gruening turned to Mexico for "technical assistance" in organizing cooperatives to produce and market popular art. See Spratling, *File on Spratling*, and Ross, *Gruening of Alaska*.
8. Brenner journals, Oct. 3, 1927.
9. Brenner, "Mexico Another Promised Land," *The Nation*, 1928.

10. Freda Kirchwey to Brenner, Feb. 7, 1934. There would be other subtle and less documented differences in the thirties, related to political sympathies. The Menorah group included liberals and radicals, a few Trotskyites, and Communist Party members. Anita participated with Herbert Solow, Elliot Cohen, Franz Boas, and others with the National Committee for the Defense of Political Prisoners. Freda Kirchwey, an editor at *The Nation*, was a party sympathizer. The problems that their political sympathies brought on in the early thirties were related to the Stalinist Communist Party's activity in Spain.

11. Brenner, untitled, *Jewish Telegraphic Agency*, Oct. 19, 1924.

seven. *An Art Critic's Career Unfolds*

1. Brenner journals, Nov. 10, 1925.
2. Brenner, "Romance and Realism," 1925. Gamio designed a system that brought artists, such as Francisco Goitia, to Teotihuacan to record the customs of the people. His style was not invasive or intrusive with questions; he simply wanted to record information that might have survived four hundred years of Spanish conquest. See Gonzalez Gamio, *Manuel Gamio*, 55.
3. Ibid.
4. Ibid.
5. Brenner, "Carlos Orozco," 1927. *Forma* was edited by Salvador Novo and Gabriel Fernández Ledesma, who were part of the group and delighted to have material.
6. Brenner, "Mexican Renascence," *Arts* 8, no. 3, Sept. 1925, 127.
7. Charlot's French version was published in *La Renaissance de Paris*.
8. Brenner journals, Dec. 5, 1925.
9. Ibid., Aug. 10, 1926.
10. Brenner, "Edward Weston," 1925. Weston had been living in Mexico with his apprentice and lover, Tina Modotti, for about three years. In 1926, when the contract came through, he was ready to return to California; however, he liked Anita's idea for both financial and professional reasons. Most of Weston's income in California and in Mexico came from portraits, which he detested, but in Mexico he had been able to exhibit and sell artistic photographs. The relationship between Weston and Modotti had deteriorated. She was interested in Xavier Guerrero, an artist who was a member of the Communist Party and who would precede Modotti to Moscow. In fact, shortly after Weston left, Modotti moved in with Guerrero. See Weston, *Daybooks*, 21.
11. Brenner journals, May 26, 1926, and Weston, *Daybooks*, 62–200.
12. Brenner journals, Aug. 27, 1926.
13. Brenner, "The Living Art of the Mexican Primitives," *L'Art Vivant*, 1926; quote from typescript, Brenner Archive box 208-136.
14. Brenner, "Painted Miracles," *The Arts*, Dec. 1928; quote from typescript, Brenner Archives box 208-136.
15. Ibid.
16. Ibid.
17. Ibid.

18. Brenner, "Street Murals of Mexico," *The Arts* 16, no. 3, Nov. 1929, 163–165; quote from typescript, April 1929, Brenner Archive box 208-136.

19. Ibid.

20. Brenner, "Une Renaissance Mexicaine," typescript, 1928.

21. Brenner, "The Mexican Renaissance," 1928.

eight. *Idols behind Altars*

1. Brenner, *Idols behind Altars*, 106–107.

2. Brenner, *Timid Ghost*, 1966.

3. My grandfather purchased the land from a priest, whose family reported that he spoke of the treasure on his deathbed. The team included Doña Carmelita Martin del Campo, the manager of the local bank, who would arrange for an armored car. My brother brought the metal detector. I was delegated to find safe storage space. My son David was small enough to crawl through the intricate network of tunnels underlying the property and the entire city of Aguascalientes. The drama went on for years. My mother made urgent long-distance phone calls with veiled indications that she was close. Alas, the roomful of gold was never found—my treasure is one of memories and friends.

4. Brenner journals, Aug. 28, 1928.

5. Brenner journals, Aug. 12, 1929.

6. Brenner journals, Sept. 2, 1929.

7. Brenner journals, Sept. 19, 1929.

8. Brenner journals, Sept. 28, 1929.

9. Brenner journals, Sept. 23, 1929.

10. Gruening, "Mexican Rhythm."

11. Beals, "Goat's Head on a Martyr," 505. Giorgio Vasari, author of *Lives of Seventy of the Most Eminent Painters, Sculptors, and Architects* (1896), was the foremost authority for art historians at that time.

12. Hansen, "First Reader." *Idols behind Altars* and *The Frescoes of Diego Rivera* were reviewed in the same article.

13. Brenner journals, April 1, 1927.

14. Brenner journals, Oct. 20, 1927.

15. Brenner journals, March 8 or 9, 1928.

16. Ibid.

17. Evans, Ernestine, untitled, *Creative Art*, Feb. 1930.

18. Rogers, "Idols behind Altars."

19. Weston to Brenner, Oct. 28, 1929, Brenner Archives, unclassified.

20. Modotti to Brenner, Oct. 9, 1929, Brenner Archives, unclassified.

21. Ibid.

22. Brenner journals, Nov. 1, 1929.

23. Brenner journals, Sept. 23, 1929.

24. Brenner, *The Boy Who Could Do Anything*, 1942; *Your Mexican Holiday*, 1932; *The Wind That Swept Mexico*, 1943.

25. Brenner journals, Feb. 28, 1930.
26. Brenner journals, Nov. 1, 1929.
27. Brenner journals, Feb. 20, 1930.

n i n e . *An Atypical Student*

1. Boas was an unusual professor, a physicist-geographer of German origin, who became interested in learning more about people while on a mission to study the Arctic. Living with the Eskimos, Boas observed that although people who lived in different climates had different lifestyles and were different physically, their feelings were similar. His first formal contract as an anthropologist was in the summer of 1888. He returned to the northwest coast to do further research for a committee of the British Association for the Advancement of Science, on the northwestern tribes of Canada, under the chairmanship of the noted English anthropologist E. B. Tyler. Boas joined Columbia's faculty in 1899 and was there until he retired in 1937. He is known both for his research and as a professor. The most important aspect of his work was an ongoing examination of misconceptions about racial inequality. His findings and his willingness to apply them to contemporary settings supported those fighting racial discrimination in courts and provided scientific support for positive government action. Boas approached the subject with physical analysis, measuring the heads of people from different races, as well as with comparative studies of people from a common background born in their country of origin and in the United States. See Herskovits, *Franz Boas.*

2. Joseph Freeman described the reaction to the firing of a professor at Columbia for openly expressing his political views, in his biographical book *American Testament.* Few faculty members supported him, and it would take in-depth research to define Boas's position at the time. Although neither Boas nor Dewey was threatened with being fired, the tone set on campus discouraged open affiliation with any given political philosophy. That may have been one of the reasons for the similarity in Boas and Dewey's ways of teaching, allowing the student total academic freedom to define a political and ethical position, as well as to sink or swim independently in course work.

3. Brenner journals, Sept. 22, 1927.
4. Brenner journals, Sept. 28, 1927.
5. Gonzalez Gamio, *Manuel Gamio,* 29. Manuel Gamio (1893–1960) was a self-taught archaeologist who studied with Franz Boas at Columbia University in New York. He created the concept and philosophy of *indigenismo* that called for valuing the indigenous people's way of life and integrating the acceptance of indigenous values into Mexico's mainstream. Gamio participated both as an archaeologist, discovering and leading the digs to unearth major sites in the Mexico City area, and as a developer of the postrevolutionary government policy to integrate indigenous peoples into the country. He is considered by many to have been the first applied anthropologist on an international level. Anita translated Gamio's work for presentation at international meetings. She was deeply influenced by his approach and contributed to making *indigenismo* known.

6. Brenner journals, Sept. 28, 1927.

7. Brenner journals, July 1926.

8. Brenner journals, Nov. 21, 1925. Tannenbaum arrived in Mexico after he had been imprisoned for leading hungry workers into a church as part of the union organizing and pacifist movement before World War I.

9. Brenner journals, April 11, 1926.

10. Freeman, who would become an editor of *New Masses* and one of the leaders of the Communist Party in the thirties, did his undergraduate work at Columbia University. Hook did graduate work in philosophy at Columbia under John Dewey and finished his degree in 1927, when Anita arrived.

11. Hook, *Out of Step*, 85. See Freeman, *American Testament*, and Herskovits, *Franz Boas*.

12. Brenner journals, Oct. 30, 1927.

13. Brenner journals, April 5, 1928.

14. Brenner journals, Oct. 27, 1927.

15. Hook, *Out of Step*, 85, and Trilling, *Beginning of the Journey*, 79–85.

16. Brenner journals, Oct. 27, 1927; Jan. 5 and 22, 1928.

17. Brenner journals, Dec. 27–31, 1927.

18. Brenner journals, Feb. 22, 1928.

19. Brenner journals, Aug. 17, 1928.

20. Brenner journals, March 10, 1929.

21. Brenner journals, May 18, 1929.

22. Brenner journals, Jan. 11, 1928.

23. Brenner journals, Jan. 22, 1928.

24. Brenner journals, April 5, 1928.

25. Ibid.

26. Maslow, *Toward a Psychology of Being*.

27. Erikson, *Identity, Youth, and Crisis*.

28. Brenner journals, Nov. 1, 1929.

29. Ibid.

30. Brenner journals, Sept. 27, 1927. On a personal level she identified as a Jew, although not a very observant one. She registered for classes at Columbia University on Rosh Hashana, the Jewish New Year, since there were fewer people on campus that day. She had celebrated the night before with the traditional dinner at a friend's home.

31. Diggins, *Rise and Fall of the American Left*, 93–138.

32. Brenner journals, Feb. 16, 1927.

ten. *Flirtations, Relationships, and Love*

1. Raul Moncada, "Historiadora de la revolución mexicana: Anita Brenner, primera amiga de México en Estados Unidos," *Hoy*, nd. SJG's translation of "Muy sencillo. Porque siendo la ciencia que trata del hombre, me parece normal que se preocupe de ella una mujer."

2. Brenner journals, Aug. 29, 1929.

3. Brenner to David Glusker, March 6, 1930, Brenner Archives box L-J.

4. Brenner, letter answering an ad for a job, Sept. 13, 1938, Brenner Archives, unclassified.

5. Carleton Beals to Brenner, nd, context indicates 1927, Brenner Archives, unclassified.

6. Brenner journals, Feb. 16, 1927.

7. Brenner journals, April 7, 1926. Amado de la Cueva invited Anita to spend the weekend with him a few days before he was killed on a motorcycle. She quarreled with him and refused a "honeymoon in Patzcuaro." "I see him in overalls working on those drawings, in smoke gray on the motorcycle, teeth gleaming. [. . .] Jumping from rock to rock and shouting, lying stomach down on the dry grass at *El Manglar*, and me telling him it was a relief to have a friend *que no se ponia pesado* [who didn't get out of line], and him telling me Mexican women could not be comrades. [. . .] As an artist he was past the potential, as a man sexually exercised. I told him the reason was I didn't want to be number 179."

8. Brenner journals, March 13, 1926. The reference is to a translation of *Castigo* written by Palavicini.

9. Brenner journals, April 11, 1926.

10. Brenner journals, Dec. 17, 1925.

11. Brenner journals, Dec. 16, 1925.

12. Brenner journals, Dec. 17, 1925.

13. Brenner journals, Dec. 27, 1925.

14. Brenner journals, Jan. 26, 1926.

15. "Cántico," ibid., June 6–8, 1928. SJG's translation from Spanish original into English.

> *Era católico él.*
> *Yo soy judía.*
> *¿Qué tiene eso de particular?*
> *Siendo que me quería.*
>
> *Yo no sabía*
> *Que se podía querer así*
> *Como él me quizo a mí.*
>
> *Y sin embargo, nunca*
> *Fuimos alegres un día.*
> *No entiendo si por que él*
> *Era católico, o yo judía.*
>
> *¡Raza mía!*
> *Madre atormentada de dolor, y de ironía.*
> *Mis bisabuelos, por miles de años,*
> *Menean las barbas entonando tu sabiduría.*
> *Magia peregrina poesía, el hálito de Dios*
> *En todas las lenguas de la apostasía.*

Por las tardes caminan mis padres
De pantufla y caftán
Con las manos en cruz en la espalda
Y a sus males ponen palabras, los llaman nostalgias
De la tierra de Isaac, y de Abrám.

Ha dicho mi padre el rey Salomón
Que es vanidad este mundo de oros y perlas.
Y yo con mis primos de todas las tierras
Pagamos la vida por verlas, y hacerlas.

Antes, cuando habían profetas,
Las mujeres todas, con sus pechos llenos de manná
Como los míos
Nutrían de tu fuerza, de tu devoción
A hijos machos, consagrados por circuncisión.

Para que engendraran en caderas anchas
Como las mías
A mis tatarabuelos que juntos haría
La unidad de Dios
Y viniera el Mesías.
Intensa raza de Israel, tu sangre es el dón
Del amor, y de la creación.

Aquel católico que me quería
Por las noches me decía
¿Por qué te atormentas tanto niña mía?

16. Brenner journals, Nov. 24, 1927.
17. Brenner journals, June 1, 1929.
18. Brenner journals, March 19, 1929.
19. Brenner journals, July 5, 1929.
20. Solomon Glusker, David's paternal grandfather, left the town of Glusk, near St. Petersburg in Russia, because he was in danger of being drafted or jailed for political activism against the czar. Like many Jewish immigrants, he sailed alone for America, where he peddled on Orchard Street in New York until he had the money to send for his family.
21. Brenner journals, July 5, 1929.
22. Brenner, more than 165 typewritten and handwritten pages of letters, Brenner Archives box L-J.
23. Brenner to David Glusker, March 23, 1930. "And we MUST manage the Mexican trip together. I am looking forward to it as a bit of savage, primitive, glorious honeymooning. It's the only place in the world where one is really alone."
24. Brenner to David Glusker, March 20, 1930, Brenner Archives, unclassified.
25. Ibid.

26. Brenner to David Glusker, Feb. 14, 1930, Brenner Archives, unclassified.

27. Waldo Frank recommended Rabbi De Sola Pool, and Anita mentioned her interview with the rabbi in her letters to David. Brenner to David Glusker, May 22, 1930, Brenner Archives, unclassified.

28. Alfred Glusker, interview by SJG, Dec. 27, 1991.

29. Brenner to David Glusker, nd, Brenner Archives, unclassified.

30. Brenner to David Glusker, March 8, 1930, Brenner Archives, unclassified.

31. Brenner, *Guerrero Imágenes de Ayer*, 1983.

32. Brenner, "Again General Calles Shows His Hand," 1932.

33. Miller, "An Interview with Anita Brenner."

eleven. *Your Mexican Holiday*

1. A. Azuela, *"El Machete,"* 82–90.

2. Eisenstein's work in Mexico became legendary. The Soviet filmmaker was financed by a group headed by Upton Sinclair and was inspired by *Idols behind Altars*. Eisenstein filmed *¡Que viva México!* without a script or schedule. Sinclair's brother-in-law, who traveled with the film crew, became more and more impatient as he watched the budget grow geometrically without a finished product. Finally the project was canceled. The raw stock was made into several movies, none satisfactory to Eisenstein, who returned to Moscow. Eisenstein's life is well documented in Seton, *Sergei M. Eisenstein*; Gedul and Gottesman, *Sergei Eisenstein and Upton Sinclair*; Eisenstein, *¡Que Viva Mexico!*; Inga Karetnikova and Leon Steinmetz, *Mexico According to Eisenstein*; and *S. M. Eisenstein: Dibujos Mexicanos Inéditos*.

3. Schmidt, "American Intellectual Discovery."

4. Spratling, *File on Spratling*, 58–66. Spratling arrived in Mexico in the early twenties to teach at the summer school of the National University. He settled in Taxco, a silver mining town, where he organized craftsmen into guilds and worked to develop designs and production. He is responsible for putting Mexico's silver and Taxco on the map. It was Spratling who introduced Diego Rivera to Ambassador Morrow and was instrumental in arranging the contract for the murals in Cuernavaca. Spratling had designed a house for Ambassador Morrow in Cuernavaca and one in Taxco for Minister of Education Moises Saenz. See Spratling, *File on Spratling*, 16–67. The Brenner Archives (box 207-28) also include the letters that Spratling wrote to Ing. Reygadas Vertiz, director of the Department of Archaeology of the Ministry of Education, in January 1931, with a list of towns and villages in Guerrero and what was in each one.

5. Letter from Nabor Ojeda to municipal presidents of several towns, 2 Feb. 1931, introducing Anita Brenner, David Glusker, and William Spratling, Brenner Archives, unclassified. Ojeda was with the Socialist Party of the State of Guerrero, within the ruling Partido Nacional Revolucionario.

6. Brenner journals, March 23, 1930.

7. Brenner, letter to Henry A. Moe at the Guggenheim Foundation, Jan. 15, 1931, Brenner Archives box 207-28. The only other record of the time they spent in Eu-

rope is a letter Anita wrote to David in the summer of 1930, asking him to give Tina Modotti an address. Anita had gone ahead to meet Franz Boas at the Americanist Congress in Hamburg. Brenner Archives, unclassified.

8. Brenner to her mother, Dec. 12, 1931, Brenner Archives box B.

9. Evans, "When You Go to Mexico."

10. Brenner, *Your Mexican Holiday*, ix.

11. Ibid., 17–18.

12. Ibid., 19–20.

13. Ibid., 109.

14. Ibid., 151.

15. Ibid., 130.

16. Ibid., 162.

17. Ibid., 145.

18. Brenner to David Glusker about apartments, nd (early 1932), Brenner Archives, unclassified.

19. Redfield, *Little Community* and *Peasant Society and Culture*. Chase, *Mexico*, 179.

20. Brenner, *Your Mexican Holiday*, 177–179.

21. Ibid., 191.

22. Ibid., 194.

23. Ibid., 202.

24. Ibid., 216.

25. Ibid., 247.

26. Ibid., 263.

27. Ibid., 306.

twelve. *Identity, Commitment, and Activism*

1. Anita mentioned not keeping a copy in a letter to David. The manuscript is discussed in correspondence with Joseph Brewer at G. P. Putnam Sons and may have been the precursor to *The Boy Who Could Do Anything*.

2. Modena, *Pasaporte de Culturas*, 57–69.

3. Krause, *Los Judíos en México*, 7–173.

4. Modena, *Pasaporte de Culturas*, 57–69.

5. Brenner, "Making Mexico Jew Conscious," 1931. Cecilia Rozovsky, National Council of Jewish Women, to Brenner, Jan. 4, 1932, with affidavits for entry permits to the United States (urges "Please no publicity"), Brenner Archives box 109. The archives also include correspondence with the *Jewish Telegraphic Agency* and individuals concerned for the safety of their relatives. See also Krause, *Los Judíos en México*, 252–263.

6. Brenner, "Race of Princes," 1925.

7. Brenner to Elliot Cohen, Dec. 4, 1929, Brenner Archives, unclassified.

8. Brenner, "Jewish Girl of Mexico," 1925.

9. Brenner, "Race of Princes," 1925.

10. These included Louis Berg, Herbert Solow, and Lionel Trilling. The archives contain short notes from all three, enclosing books for review or Spanish texts for her opinion or translation. See Wald, *New York Intellectuals*, 37–45.

11. Brenner to David Glusker, March 31, 1930, Brenner Archives, unclassified.

12. Brenner to Elliot Cohen, Dec. 4, 1929, Brenner Archives, unclassified.

13. Wald, "Herbert Solow." Trilling, *Beginning of the Journey*, 266–270. Herbert Solow was a contemporary of Anita. He attended Columbia University in the early twenties with Sidney Hook, Lionel Trilling, and Whittaker Chambers. Anita's political position is closest to that of Solow and Trilling. Trilling taught English at Hunter College and at Columbia, where he had to fight to keep his job when he was fired for being Jewish.

14. Solow to Board of Directors of Menorah Journal, Inc., Oct. 12, 1931. Herbert Solow Papers box 1, Biography Employment Record, Hoover Institution on War, Revolution, and Peace Archives, Stanford University, Palo Alto, Calif. He said that there are three classes in Jewry: that of bankers and magnates; that of suffering masses (especially East European); and that typified by himself, many Menorah governors and directors, and certain friends of his in Westchester County—small manufacturers, tradesmen, professionals, and executives with comfortable but modest incomes. He said that for each class the Jewish problem is different; for the magnates it is how to be elected to an exclusive club and marry Gentile aristocrats; for the masses it is how to keep alive despite anti-Semitic persecution; for the Westchesterites it is how to find a nice summer place, get the kiddies into college, and repair the spiritual disintegration of their lives. He said that the antagonisms between the classes lie deeper than any bonds of union. Henceforth, he said, the journal will represent the interests and voice the views only of Westchesterites and their fellows and offer them "a constructive program—Jewish education."

15. Some of the most prominent participants were Franz Boas, John Dewey, John Dos Passos, Jim Rorty, Waldo Frank, and George Novack. They appear on different mastheads.

16. Brenner, autobiographical statement, nd. May have been written during the fifties, when the McCarren Act threatened to revoke her U.S. citizenship.

17. Brenner to David Glusker, nd. Events discussed date the letter in Jan. 1932, Brenner Archives.

18. Max Gorelik to Brenner, Jan. 10, 1932, Brenner Archives box 9-B.

19. Gorelik to Brenner, Jan. 26, 1932, Brenner Archives box 9-B.

20. Brenner journals, Oct. 6, 1929.

thirteen. *Full-fledged* Menorah Journal *Radical*

1. Elliot Cohen to Brenner, Aug. 16, 1932, invitation to a meeting of the NCDPP, requesting suggestions and projects to further the work of the committee. Brenner Archives, unclassified.

2. Cohen to "Committee Members," Dec. 20, 1932, urging them to send telegrams

to the governor of Alabama to take more drastic steps to disband the armed mobs that were persecuting African Americans. Brenner Archives, unclassified.

3. Brenner, "Modern Art and William Zorach," 1929, Brenner Archives box 208-137. Anita translated for Waldo Frank, who wrote the introduction to *Tales from Argentina*, a collection of stories, and *Marcela*, a novel by Mariano Azuela.

4. Brenner Archives, unclassified, nd, typed statement attached to letter from Cohen to Anita Brenner, Aug. 16, 1932.

5. Brodsky, "For the Scottsboro Defense," 601. Seven of nine African Americans were sentenced to be executed on June 24, 1932.

6. Brenner, "Tampa's Political Prisoners," letter to *The Nation*, Dec. 28, 1932, 647.

7. O. Weintraub to Brenner, March 22, 1933, about the status of the committee's pamphlet; letter states that Comrade Paterson (ILD) was reading it and might make further changes. Brenner Archives box 204-24; the pamphlet was published with the title, "National Committee for the Defense of Political Prisoners, ILD, Tampa Defense Committee: Published by The Tampa Defense Committee, Anita Brenner Chairman."

8. An Open Letter to the Jewish People, Dec. 30, 1932. Herbert Solow Papers box 8, File "Jews in Poland," Hoover Institution.

9. Brenner to Joshua Kunitz, Secretary of NCDPP, May 1, 1933, Brenner Archives, unclassified.

10. Berg, Brenner, Novack, Trilling, Cohen, Rubin, Rice, and Solow to Joshua Kunitz, Secretary of NCDPP, May 8, 1933. Herbert Solow Papers box 8, Hoover Institution.

11. Malcolm Cowley to Brenner, Feb. 17, 1933; Grace Allen to Brenner, Feb. 10 and 17, 1933; Louise Thompson (assistant secretary) to Committee Members, Feb. 28, 1933, letter enclosing a copy of the clipping "From the N.Y. *Times*, Feb. 28, 1933," mimeographed letter about whether Will Sanders, a 16-year-old African American sentenced to death in a 77-minute trial, should be buried publicly or at the prison. Brenner Archives, unclassified. Cowley wrote inviting Anita to a reorganization meeting, in view of Cohen's resignation. A parallel letter on the same date invited Anita to join the executive committee. The documentation presents two seemingly independent currents: first, the inner organizational struggle; and second, the ongoing protest activities, such as cases involving prisoners in Peru and the conviction of a young African American in South Carolina.

12. Solow to Brenner, Feb. 3, 1933, Brenner Archives box 10-B.

13. Brenner, "Terror in Cuba," 1935. Non-Partisan Labor Defense Newsletter, Nov. 1935, Herbert Solow Papers box 10, Scottsboro Case, Hoover Institution.

14. Frank, Beals, and Brenner to the Latin American editor of the Associated Press, nd, about political prisoners, Brenner Archives, unclassified.

15. Roger Baldwin to "Friends," Feb. 4, 1933, Brenner Archives, unclassified.

16. Leon Trotsky to Brenner, Sept. 28, 1933, Brenner Archives box 10-B. Confirmation from Leon Trotsky's secretary, Nov. 3, 1933, Trotsky Papers, Houghton Library, Harvard University box 29-31.6873-7804 R16 7426-7427.

17. Trotsky, "Answers to Questions." I am especially grateful to Michael Bauman for finding and sending this material.

18. Lester Markel to Brenner, April 6, 1934, Brenner Archives box 10. Invoice for $100 for "Trotsky," May 5, 1934, Brenner Archives box 10-A.

19. Waldo Frank to Brenner, Oct. 7, 1934, Brenner Archives box 8-B.

20. Broué, *Leon Trotsky*, Dec. 1936–Feb. 1937, introduction.

21. Gall, *Trotsky en México*, 23.

22. Ibid., 23–42.

23. Broué, *Leon Trotsky*, Dec. 1936–Feb. 1937, 90 n.2.

24. Suzanne La Follette to "Dear Friend," on American Committee for the Defense of Leon Trotsky stationery, Herbert Solow Papers box 1, Hoover Institution.

25. Broué, *Leon Trotsky*, Dec. 1936–Feb. 1937, 90 n.2. Some of the others who participated were George Novack, John Dos Passos, John Dewey, and Lionel Trilling.

26. Hook, *Out of Step*, 286. The members of the American Committee for the Defense of Leon Trotsky (headed by John Dewey) who traveled to Mexico included, among others, Herbert Solow, Sidney Hook, and Carleton Beals.

27. Solow's legal statement may be a rough draft of the deposition on Whittaker Chambers, Nov. 12, 1938. There is extensive documentation in Solow's archives about Julieta Poynitz, a Communist Party member who disappeared after breaking with the party. Herbert Solow Papers box 5, Hoover Institution.

28. Wald to Brenner, Sept. 14, 1974, Brenner Archives box 202-G.

29. Trilling, *Beginning of the Journey*, 220.

30. The literature includes A. Hiss, *In the Court of Public Opinion*, T. Hiss, *Laughing Last*, and Weinstein, *Perjury*.

31. Brenner to Reuben, April 12, 1969, Brenner Archives box B.

32. For the identification of Anita within a specific group, see Gall, *Trotsky en México*, 352, and Wald, *New York Intellectuals*, 46–75. For Trotsky's identification of Anita's position, see Robert McGregor, American Consul, Mexico City, Strictly Confidential Memorandum, July 13, 1940, U.S. State Department, National Archives document RGM-1b-A-800-C-310.

33. Trotsky to Herbert Solow, Oct. 15, 1937, Trotsky Collection letter 10482. Houghton Library, Harvard University.

34. Trotsky to V. P. Calverton, Oct. 15, 1937, Brenner Archives, unclassified. Copies went to Anita, Diego Rivera, Max Eastman, Sidney Hook, James Rorty, Benjamin Stolberg, Herbert Solow, and Charles Walker. Calverton, editor of *Modern Monthly*, invited Trotsky to write for that publication. Beals's transgression was asking questions about Trotsky's activities in the twenties in Mexico, specifically about the presence of Borodin, a soviet agent. See Britton, *Carleton Beals*, 166–186.

35. Trotsky to "Comrades," Dec. 31, 1937, Trotsky Collection letter 8101, Houghton Library, Harvard University.

36. Robert McGregor, American Consul, Mexico City, Strictly Confidential Memorandum, July 13, 1940, U.S. State Department, National Archives document RGM-1b-A-800-C-310.

37. Editorial, *New Masses*, March 6, 1934. "United front from below: If a leadership obstructs the natural gravitation of the masses toward unity, there seems to be only one solution: to attempt to throw the masses together, despite the saboteurs on top."

How? Where? At demonstrations, at meetings, on the picket line, through activities which are of immediate moment to all strata of the working class. This the Communists tried to do at Madison Square Garden."

38. Freeman, *American Testament*, 342–347.

39. Stephen and Lucienne Dimitroff, interview by SJG, San Francisco, Calif., Jan. 3, 1989. Stephen noted that at that time communism was not considered the evil force that it became during the witch hunts of the McCarthy era. Although communists were not acceptable in certain circles, they had not gone underground. On the other hand, communism was also not the idealistic revolutionary force it had been in the twenties under Lenin's leadership. Stalin was in the process of increasing the party's size and power. Individual initiatives were sanctioned. The goal was to control each and every group. For example, a shift took place from unionizing workers to creating Communist Party unions. Thus, even if a factory was unionized, the new strategy looked to create a Communist union, as opposed to seeking other plants to unionize for the benefit of the workers. (Interview by SJG, San Francisco, May 16, 1989.)

40. "5,000 Reds Battle with Socialists at Garden Rally," *New York Times*, Feb. 18, 1934. The subheadings state: "20 Injured When Communist Raid Anti-Dolfuss Meeting," "Women Kicked and Beaten," "CHAIRS USED AS WEAPONS," "Leader of Invaders Is Hurled from Platform," "Speeches Drowned by Boos," "Intruders Are Ejected," "Police under Order to Keep Out, Hold Aloof until Ushers Are Overwhelmed."

41. Brenner to John Dos Passos, Feb. 20, 1934, Brenner Archives box 7.

42. Brenner, letter to the editor, *New Masses*, March 20, 1934, 21.

43. Brenner, autobiographical statement, nd, Brenner Archives, unclassified.

fourteen. *Spain*

1. Brenner to David Glusker, Aug. 28, 1933, Brenner Archives, unclassified.

2. Thomas, *Spanish Civil War*, 644–669.

3. Lester Markel, editor, *New York Times Sunday Magazine*, to Brenner, Sept. 5, 1933, responding positively to her letters. Gruening, editor, *The Nation*, to Brenner, Sept. 13, 1933, commenting on her articles and requesting a sixth article. Brenner Archives box 205-25.

4. Brenner, "Revolution from the Top," 1933.

5. Brenner, "Spain: Footnote to a Crisis," 1933.

6. Brenner, *Class War in Spain*, 1937.

7. Brenner, "Revolution in Spain," 1934, 477.

8. President Benito Juárez annulled entitlements during the Period of Reform (1855–1872) with the Constitution of 1857. Reform laws in Mexico expropriated church property and transferred birth and death records to civil authorities. Religious education, public worship, and monasteries were banned, although many stayed open in a quasi-underground fashion.

9. Brenner, "Spain Tries Democracy," *Current History*, Sept. 1933, typescript, Brenner Archives, unclassified. "Spain: Viva la Republica!" 1934, Brenner Archives box 204.

10. Brenner, "Spain: Viva la Republica!" 150–152, Brenner Archives box 204.

11. Brenner to David Glusker, Oct. 17, 1933, from Jerez de la Frontera, Brenner Archives box 205-86.

12. Brenner, manuscript, story of the end of the Spanish Civil War, nd, ca. June–July 1937, Brenner Archives box 205-85.

13. Brenner, manuscript, Aug. 1937, Brenner Archives box 205-94.

14. Brenner, *Class War in Spain*, 1937.

15. Brenner, letter to the editor, "Calling for Protest," *The Nation*, Aug. 6, 1937, Brenner Archives box 206-107. Among those arrested was Bob Smillie, grandson of the famous British mine worker leader, who died of appendicitis in jail.

16. Brenner to David Glusker, Oct. 1, 1933, Merida, Spain, Brenner Archives, unclassified.

17. Brenner, draft and notes, July 1937, Brenner Archives box 201-107. Those who signed included Liston M. Oak, James P. Cannon, Sidney Hook, and Felix Morrow. Anita did not appear on the masthead of the American Friends of Spanish Democracy, chaired by Bishop Robert L. Paddock, with John Dewey as vice chairman. Mildred Adams, Carleton Beals, John Dos Passos, Waldo Frank, Freda Kirchwey, and Oswald Garrison Villard, whom Anita knew and worked with on other political issues, were listed.

18. J. M. Escuder to Brenner, Sept. 6, 1934, Brenner Archives box 8-b. Escuder complimented Anita on her review of *The History of Spain*, by Bertrand and Petrie. He was in Tampa, resting before returning to Spain: "by Bertrand and Petrie (these names sound as a restaurant concern). In my opinion this is one of the best things [. . .] done so far. It really is demolishing and to the point. Congratulations."

19. Fenner Brockway to the International Bureau for Revolutionary Socialist Unity in London, June 21, 1937, Brenner Archives, unclassified. The group arrested also included Hugo Oehler, Charles Orr, Wolf Kupinsky (a reporter for *Modern Monthly*), and Andres Nin.

20. Skippy Escuder to Anita Brenner, Sept. 10, 1937, Brenner Archives box 205-25.

21. Jose Escuder to Brenner, telegram, June 24, 1937.

22. Gibernau, José, to Anita Brenner, Feb. 10, 1937, Brenner Archives, unclassified. The group included Herbert Solow, John Dos Passos, and Bertram Wolfe, who by this time had left the Communist Party and joined the Lovestoneites.

23. Walter Starrett to Brenner, July 8, 1937, Brenner Archives, unclassified. Anita shared the rostrum with Liston Oak (editor of *Fight*), Sam Baron (who had just returned from Spain), Carlo Tresca (an Italian anarchist who was later murdered), Bertram Wolfe, and Angelica Balabanov. T. Stamm, secretary, minutes of Revolutionary Workers League meeting, Aug. 2, 1937, Brenner Archives, unclassified. "Report by Oak: First effort on return from Spain was to get action from 'relatively large groups.' Tried primarily SP [Socialist Party], Lovestoneites and Anarchists. A weak committee was set up. Committee consisted of Thomas—chairman; Sam Baron and Hal Siegal of SP right wing; Gus Tyler of Clarity group; Tresca representing the anarchists; Wolfe of Lovestoneites; and Solow, Brenner and Oak." Brenner, "Calling for Protest," 1937. Brenner Archives document the participation of Jim Rorty, Sidney Hook, and Fenner Brockway, general secretary of the British International Labor Party,

who headed an inquiry delegation to Spain. Jim Rorty to Brenner, Aug. 21, 1937, re: editorial in *The Nation* and committee meeting. Brenner Archives box 205-101. Hook to Spain's ambassador to the United States, Fernando de los Rios, and to Solow, Aug. 21, 1937, where Hook recommends putting in "some dull passages so that it can be identified as mine." Brenner Archives box 205-107.

24. Solow to Comrade Thomas, July 22, 1937, Brenner Archives, unclassified.

25. Solow to Brenner, Aug. 7, 1937, Brenner Archives box 205-101.

26. Rosalio Negrete to Diego Rivera, Feb. 17, 1931. Bertram Wolfe papers box 115-3, Hoover Institution. Spanish text: "Están aquí O'Higgins y Plenn. Son más Stalinistas que la Chingada—especialmente Plenn."

27. Draft Statement of Purposes, Russell Negrete Blackwell Defense Committee, nd, Brenner Archives, unclassified.

28. Telegram to Secretary of State Cordell Hull, signed by Brenner, Dorothy Dunbar Bromley, V. F. Calverton, John Chamberlain, Lewis Corey, John Dewey, John Dos Passos, Max Eastman, James T. Farrell, Louis E. Hacker, Sidney Hook, Suzanne La Follette, Ludwig Lore, Eugene Lyons, A. M. Muste, Liston Oak, James O'Neal, James Rorty, Benjamin Stolberg, Norman Thomas, Carlo Tresca, Charles R. Walker, Gerry Allard, Roy E. Burt, Nov. 3, 1938. National Archives, 852.222.1 Negrete, Russell/116.

29. Unsigned letter from the Legal-Social National Committee of the CNT-AIT to Maximiliano Olay in Chicago, from Barcelona, Sept. 19, 1938. Trotsky Collection, Houghton Library, MS Rus 13804.

30. Brenner to Comrade Olay in Chicago, Nov. 2, 1938. Trotsky Collection, Houghton Library, box Y8.49, roll 25 (13804).

31. List of Members, Russell Negrete Blackwell Defense Committee, National Archives, Washington, D.C., 852.222.1 Microfilm LM74, roll 58.

32. Maximiliano Olay, Frances Heisler, Hugo Oehler, Bert Russell, Tom Stamm, and Gerry Allard, Flyer, "Welcome Home Russell Blackwell," March 1, 1939, Brenner Archives box 5. Brenner and Jim Rorty, Comparison of Two Committees, Labor Defense Policy, nd, Brenner Archives box 5.

33. Trotsky to James Steward, American consul general in Mexico, Nov. 8, 1938. National Archives, 852.222.1, roll 58, LM74.

34. Brenner, untitled typescript, nd, 28 pages, Brenner Archives box 205-85.

35. Brenner, *Class War in Spain*, 1937.

36. Brenner, "Today the Barricades," several typescript drafts, nd, Brenner Archives box 207-49.

fifteen. *Art Critic in the Thirties*

1. White, Dorothy, "Quietude of Heights Home."

2. Brenner, "Revolution in Art," 1933, 269.

3. Brenner, "Art and American Life," 1933.

4. Juliana Force to the Board of Editors of *The Nation*, Jan. 13, 1932, Brenner Archives, unclassified.

5. Brenner to the Board of Editors of *The Nation*, Jan. 18, 1933, Brenner Archives box 208-118.

6. Henry Hazlitt, editor, *The Nation*, to Brenner, Feb. 17, 1933, Brenner Archives box 10-B.

7. Peg Marshall, *The Nation*, to Brenner, March 2, 1934, Brenner Archives box 10-A.

8. Brenner, "The Races of Man," 1934, proof sheet, Brenner Archives, unclassified.

9. Lionel Reiss to Brenner, May 17, 1933, Brenner Archives box 10-B.

10. Brenner journals, July 2, 1928. See also entries for May 10, 22, and 25, 1928.

11. Brenner, "Impurity in the Modern Museum," 1934.

12. Pach to Brenner, Feb. 19, 1934, Brenner Archives box 8-B.

13. Joseph Wood Krutch to Brenner, March 8, 1934, about "Private Art and Public Interest," Brenner Archives box 10-A.

14. Krutch to Brenner, March 15, 1934, Brenner Archives box 10-A.

15. Brenner to Krutch, March 18, 1934, Brenner Archives box 10-A.

16. Brenner, "Field Day for Frankenstein," *The Nation*, nd, typescript. ["Field Day" was an earlier draft of "Private Art and Public Interest."] Brenner Archives, unclassified. Brenner, "Private Art and Public Interest," 1934.

17. Brenner, "Private Art and Public Interest," 1934.

18. Brenner, "Frontiers of Machine Art," 1934.

19. Brenner, "Art and American Life," 1933.

20. Markel to Brenner, May 12, 1933, Brenner Archives box 10-B. "This is by way of softening the shock you may encounter when you open next Sunday's paper. Your piece has been chopped virtually in half; first, because it was pretty editorial in tone and, second, because our space shrank hopelessly. [. . .] I promise to do better by your next piece."

21. Brenner, untitled typescript, submitted to *New York Times Sunday Magazine*, Jan. 1940, Brenner Archives box 208-138.

22. Brenner, "Public Inherits Princely Art," 1941. "Artistic Free-for-All," 1941.

23. Samuel Allen to Brenner, Jan. 13, 1935, Brenner Archives box 7.

24. John Beffel, Brotherhood of Utility Employees of America, to Brenner, April 1, 1935, Brenner Archives box 7.

25. Brenner, untitled typescript, submitted to *Brooklyn Daily Eagle*, nd, Brenner Archives box 208-142.

26. Brenner, "Georgio de Chirico Dreams," 1935.

27. Brenner, "Jones Is a Happy Rebel," 1936. Letter complimenting Brenner on the Siqueiros paper, March 3, 1933, and letter re: 1933–1934 courses and members of the Advisory Committee of the John Reed Club School of Art, Oct. 4, 1933, Brenner Archives box 9-B.

28. Brenner, "Artists Unite against War and Fascism," 1936.

29. Brenner, "WPA Emulates the Whitney Museum," 1937.

30. Brenner, "Spring Art Season," 1936.

31. Brenner, "About Contemporaries," 1937.

32. Brenner, "Reflections on the Art of Angna Enters," 1937.

33. Brenner, untitled typescript, nd, Brenner Archives box 208-139.

34. Brenner, "American Painters," 1935.
35. Brenner, "Muralist Lucienne Bloch," 1936.

sixteen. *A Radical Looks at Mexico*

1. A. Azuela, *"El Machete."*
2. Brenner, "Is Rivera a Counter-Revolutionary?" 1934.
3. Brenner, "Career of Rivera Marked," 1933.
4. Brenner, "Diego Rivera: Fiery Crusader," 1933.
5. Ibid.
6. Rivera, "Controversia Rockefeller."
7. Brenner, "The Rockefeller Coffin," 1933.
8. Ibid.
9. Brenner, "Tail Wags the Dog," 1933.
10. Brenner, "Rockefeller Coffin," 1933.
11. Brenner, "Diego Rivera: Fiery Crusader," 1933.
12. Ibid. See also Brenner, "Career of Rivera Marked," 1933; A. Azuela, *Diego Rivera en Detroit*, 278.
13. Rivera, list of scandals, Brenner Archives, unclassified.
14. Edwin James to Brenner, May 11, 1933, thanking her for the tip, Brenner Archives box 10-B. Henry Hurwitz to Brenner, May 11, 1933, thanking her for translating Rivera's talk, expressing interest in an article, Brenner Archives box 208-111. Brenner, "Rivera Plans to Finish," 1933. Brenner, "Career of Rivera Marked," 1933. Brenner, "Rivera's Revolution," 1933.
15. Brenner journals, April 10, 1926. See Siqueiros, "Rivera's Counter-Revolutionary Road."
16. Brenner, "Is Rivera a Counter-Revolutionary?" 1934.
17. Siqueiros to Brenner, nd [by context, 1933–1934], asking her to write article, and Siqueiros, "Rivera's Counter-Revolutionary Road."
18. David Glusker to Brenner, 1933, mentioning financial straits and the bill from Franklin Simon, Brenner Archives, unclassified.
19. Brenner, "Is Rivera a Counter-Revolutionary?" 1934.
20. Ibid.
21. Ibid.
22. Felipe Carrillo Puerto, governor of Yucatan, invited what today would be called consultants and in so doing created a nucleus of Communist Party members in Mexico, including people such as Roy and Bob Haberman. The Haberman brothers moved to Mexico City from Yucatan after Carrillo Puerto was murdered and worked at the Department of Publications of the Ministry of Education under Vasconcelos. They invited Wolfe, who was being persecuted in the United States on account of his Bolshevik organization work, to Mexico in 1921 to teach English and organize the Communist Party.
23. Brenner, "Is Rivera a Counter-Revolutionary?" 1934.
24. Ibid.

25. Ibid.

26. Brenner, editorial, 1934.

27. Brenner, writing as Jean Mendez, "Anti-Calles Drive," 1935.

28. Brenner, "Again General Calles," 1932.

29. Brenner, writing as Jean Mendez, "Anti-Calles Drive," 1935.

30. Brenner, editorial, 1935, typescript, Brenner Archives box A-4.

31. Brenner, "Old Social Struggle," 1935.

32. Brenner, Review of "Orozco: Murals with Meaning," *Creative Art*, Feb. 1933. Typescript, Jan. 9, 1933, Brenner Archives box A-4.

33. Brenner, "Orozco," *New Masses*, Feb. 28, 1933.

seventeen. *The Wind That Swept Mexico*

1. University of Texas Press brochure, 1994.

2. Brenner, "The Wind That Swept Mexico," 1942.

3. Brenner, "New Era in Mexico," 1934.

4. Brenner, "Truth about Mexico," part 1, 1934.

5. Brenner, "Truth about Mexico," part 2, 1934.

6. Ibid., but different text from previous part 2.

7. Brenner, "Truth about Mexico," part 3, 1934.

8. Horace Casselberry to Brenner, Dec. 3, 1934. See also Dec. 18, 1934, Brenner Archives unclassified; Katherine McNally Beehman to Brenner, Nov. 1934, praising articles in the *New York Post* and refuting the letter of objection from Peter Arno, editor of the *Brooklyn Tablet*, Nov. 1934, Brenner Archives unclassified. Brenner, letter to the *New York Post*, 13 Dec. 1934, Brenner Archives unclassified.

9. Brenner, letter to the *New York Post*, nd, Brenner Archives box 109.

10. Brenner, *The Wind That Swept Mexico*, caption 155, for Calles. See also "Mexican Government Dissolves Fascist Gold Shirts. Supreme Chief Nicolas Rodriguez Exiled to United States," *Mexican Labor News*, Press Department of the Workers University of Mexico (Universidad Obrera de México.), vol. 1, no. 6, Aug. 20, 1936, Brenner Archives box 208-93. See also Vicente Lombardo Toledano and Alejandro Carrillo, "Mexican President Promises Gold Shirt Suppression," ibid.

11. Brenner, "Mexico in Revolution," 1938.

12. Brenner, "Mexico: Tentative story sketch," typescript, 1934, Brenner Archives box 7.

13. Ibid.

14. Ibid.

15. Ibid.

16. Brenner to President Lazaro Cardenas, Nov. 8, 1938, Brenner Archives unclassified. See also Bokser, *Imágenes de un Encuentro*, 221, for story of boat incident. The boat was turned back from Veracruz, ultimately back to Europe.

17. Markel to Brenner, Aug. 1938 and Sept. 10, 1938, Brenner Archives box D-3.

18. Brenner, untitled drafts of article for *New York Times Sunday Magazine*, July and Aug. 1938, Brenner Archives box D-3.

19. Brenner to Markel, Nov. 22, 1938, Brenner Archives box A-4.

20. Brenner, untitled typescript of article for *New York Times Sunday Magazine*, Feb. 23, 1939, Brenner Archives box D-3.

21. John F. X. Browne, Francis G. Dempsey, Knights of Columbus, to Cass Canfield, editor of *Harper's*, June 9, 1943, six-page diatribe against *The Wind That Swept Mexico*, claiming it was not historical but a "below the belt attack on Catholics made by [a] Liberal Democrat. [. . .] We shall appreciate being informed of what steps you plan to take to remedy the injustice that has been done." Brenner Archives box Z.

22. Brenner to *Harper's*, June 10, 1943, addressing criticism of the Knights of Columbus. Brenner to George Leighton, editor at *Harper's*, establishing that the Knights of Columbus raised $1 million for a Mexican fund. Report says money was used for propaganda. Papal encyclical praises the U.S. Knights of Columbus for helping in the Mexican cause. Interview K of C and Secretary Frank Billings Kellogg, Sept. 23, 1943, Brenner Archives unclassified.

23. Prescott, "Books of the Times."

24. Brenner, letter to the *New York Times*, May 26, 1943, answering Prescott's review, Brenner Archives box Z-3.

25. "Diaz to Avila Camacho," *New York Post*, May 27, 1943; reviews of *The Wind*: Robert Molloy, "The Book of the Day," *New York Sun*, May 27, 1943; Mildred Adams, "The Swift, Violent Cycles of Revolution in Mexico," np, June 1943, Brenner Archives unclassified.

26. Lewis Gannett, "Books and Things," *New York Herald Tribune*, May 26, 1943, Brenner Archives box Z-3.

27. Katherine Anne Porter, "Mexico's Thirty Long Years of Revolution: A Story Told Simply and Effectively in Text and Photographs," *New York Herald Tribune*, May 30, 1943, Brenner Archives box Z-3.

28. Julian to Brenner, June 8, 1940, information about a coup being planned in Mexico backed by U.S. oil companies but simulated to look like Stalinists. Brenner Archives box 11.

29. Brenner, untitled typescript, June–July 1937, about the end of the Spanish Civil War; gold to Russia and jewels to Mexico. Brenner Archives box 205-85.

30. Brenner, *The Wind That Swept Mexico*, University of Texas Press, 1984, 3.

eighteen. *Epilogue*

1. Brenner, untitled manuscript, 1942, Brenner Archives unclassified.

2. "Privies para Pedro," *Time*, Nov. 22, 1943.

3. Brenner to *Saturday Evening Post*, *Ladies' Home Journal*, *Collier's*, *Redbook*, and *Harper's*; Dorothy Dunbar Bromley, editor, Sunday Women's Activities Page, *New York Herald Tribune*, to Brenner, May 2, 1944, "The most I can offer you is $25." Brenner Archives, unclassified.

4. The contract pre-dates the series of articles published in *Harper's*; the material overlapped *The Wind That Swept Mexico*, and the history of Mexico was never written.

5. Henry Brenner to Anita with news, assignments, and a check, Jan. 21, 1942. Anita

Brenner to Henry Brenner, Feb. 2, 1942, about psychological tests for employees and family news, "nervous strain." John I. H. Baur, curator of paintings and sculpture, Brooklyn Museum, to Anita Brenner, Jan. 5, 1942, regretting the lack of funds to buy the collection. Brenner Archives, unclassified.

6. Brenner to Frederick Allen at *Harper's*, Jan. 4, 1953, proposing a story about the Bolivian Revolution. One of the selling points she used was: "Dr. Victor Paz Estenssoro, who is now President of Bolivia, told me that when they were conspiring their revolution, the principal textbook was The Wind. [. . . the] problem was that they couldn't get enough copies of the book and they had to keep passing it around." Brenner Archives box Z-3.

7. Brenner, "Paricutin," 1948.

8. Brenner, "Mexico's New Deal," 1948, Brenner Archives box 208-118. A similar article, "Alemán: Mexico's Man of Promise," appeared in *United Nations World*, April 1947, Brenner Archives box 208-101.

9. Frances Pindyck to Brenner, Jan. 13, 1944, quoting the letter from the *Post* and encouraging her to "take a crack at it" since it would be "wonderful to break the Post." Brenner Archives box 207-55.

10. Brenner, "RX: A Mother," 1941.

11. Elsie Mill to Brenner, June 2, 1943, thanking her for coming to speak. "We sincerely hope that you found your son all right when you arrived home [and . . .] wish you all kinds of success with your new paper baby." Brenner Archives box Z-3.

12. "Dumb Juan and the Bandits," one of the stories in *The Boy Who Could Do Anything*, was published separately in 1957.

13. Brenner, trans., "Stalin in Spain," 1940.

14. Brenner, review of book, 1943.

15. Press release, Tresca Memorial Committee, Herbert Solow Archives box 11, Hoover Institution.

16. Solow, memorandum on the dinner of the Joint Anti-Fascist Refugee Committee, May 1944. Herbert Solow Archives, Hoover Institution.

17. Brenner to Solow, June 3, 1944. Herbert Solow Papers box 1, Hoover Institution.

18. Jose Bartoli, interview by SJG, Nov. 1992, New York, translated by SJG.

19. Mathias Goeritz, interview by SJG, May 21, 1990, Mexico City. Goeritz to SJG, postcard from Europe, nd, probably late 1957, after a visit to New York, where he opened an exhibit and invited me to come down from Bennington College. It was an unforgettable weekend, meeting Ben Shawn, David Lifshitz, and other artists at parties in Goeritz's honor.

20. Anita was frequently late picking up the school carpool. Once she forgot totally, creating great consternation among the parents of my schoolmates, as well as incurring the wrath of her daughter. She could make up for it, though. Hope Stevenson, who walked home with me that day, recalled that "she took us to the University to meet Diego Rivera and see his studio, his plans for mosaic, etc. I was very impressed by that." Stevenson to SJG, Feb. 3, 1992.

21. There are letters in her files from Waldo Frank, Sidney Hook, Elinor Rice, Herbert Solow, and Ernest Gruening.

22. Felix Morrow to Brenner, Oct. 29, 1970, Brenner Archives unclassified.

23. Elliot Cohen to Brenner, Sept. 20, 1946, Brenner Archives box 208-114.

24. Shimshon Arad, former Israeli ambassador to Mexico, to SJG, Nov. 1991.

25. Sidney Kluger to SJG, Nov. 1992. "I invited Anita to a meeting of Stella Adler, Congressman Somers, and Senator Gillette at the Union of Electricians' Auditorium condemning the Jewish leadership for not saving the Jews in Europe. A riot took place, preventing the speakers to appear. The meeting was disbanded and we went to the platform to meet Stella Adler. Anita had a letter from Waldo Frank, asking her to meet Stella Adler and her group."

26. Anita became a founding member of Beth Israel Community Center, an English-speaking Conservative synagogue, and enjoyed biblical and Talmudic study with Rabbi Everett Gendler, Paulette Ruff, and Mathias Goeritz. She pursued the study of the Cabala and urged me to search secondhand bookstores for a copy of Bachya Ibn Pakuda's *Duties of the Heart.*

27. Brenner, biographical statement, 1972, Brenner Archives box 219.

28. Wendy Holden Tolksdorff to SJG, Nov. 1992.

29. Brenner, "Art and Artists in Mexico Today," 1964.

30. Brenner to Rene D'Harnoncourt at the Museum of Modern Art, Oct. 23, 1952, enclosing samples and asking advice for distribution. Brenner Archives box 202-M.

31. Special recognition is due Earl Graham, who with loving care has been distributing back issues of *Mexico/This Month.* There are still a few available; write him at 1171 Ridge Road, South Coventry, Pottstown, PA 19465.

32. The group included Bill Richardson, head of National City Bank in Mexico, Ambassador Bill O'Dwyer, Kelso Peck and Robert LaMontagne from General Motors, and former president Miguel Aleman.

33. Joseph Freeman to Brenner, Nov. 19, 1958, Brenner Archives box 202-F.

34. Dr. John LaMontagne to SJG, Feb. 1992.

35. "Licenciado" can mean a lawyer, a person holding a B.A., or, used in an insulting tone, as it is here, a second-rate bureaucrat.

36. Bartoli to SJG, Nov. 1992. Translation by SJG. The art department at that time included the Russian refugee Vlady and two Spanish refugees: German Horacio, from Galicia, known in Spanish as a Gallego, and Bartoli, a Catalan.

37. Virginia McMillan to Brenner, April 30, 1965, about the crisis. "The printer won't print without money and the government subsidy agency, Nacional Financiera, will not pay without a magazine." Brenner Archives box B.

38. Friedeberg, interview by SJG, Feb. 16, 1995, Mexico City.

39. Bartoli to SJG.

40. Myra Landau, for example, wrote a long letter thanking Anita for recommending her for a Guggenheim fellowship, even though Myra thought they were not communicating at that point. Brenner Archives unclassified.

41. Dr. Pablo Weisz Carrington, personal interview by SJG, Feb. 16, 1995.

anita brenner bibliography

The following documents and manuscripts are found in Anita Brenner's files and, along with 900 pages of her journals from 1925 to 1930, were used as the primary sources to document her life and ideas. All untitled documents are manuscripts.

1923

Unfinished autobiographical novel. Manuscript, 1923. Brenner Archives box 207-38.

1924

"The Jew in Mexico." *The Nation*, Aug. 27, 1924.

Untitled. *Jewish Telegraphic Agency*, Oct. 18, 1924. Immigration of Jewish refugees to Mexico increasing. Difficult to settle 400 a month. Need for funding for Jews to go into agriculture.

Untitled. *Jewish Telegraphic Agency*, Oct. 19, 1924. Obituary of Francisco Rivas Puigcerver.

Untitled. *Jewish Telegraphic Agency*, Oct. 28, 1924. Five cousins travel from Odessa to Constantinople, reach port two days after quota to U.S. closed. Arrive in Veracruz a year later.

Untitled. *Jewish Telegraphic Agency*, Nov. 8, 1924. Settling Jewish immigrants. Influx increased, President-elect Calles invitation.

Untitled. *Jewish Telegraphic Agency*, Nov. 9, 1924. Arrival of Jewish immigrants at Regis Hotel. Identification of notables such as Haberman, Boder, and Rivas.

Untitled. *Jewish Telegraphic Agency*, Nov. 18, 1924. Difficulties for unmarried women immigrants.

Untitled. *Jewish Telegraphic Agency*, Dec. 1, 1924. Report on B'nai B'rith meeting to consider Mexico for Jewish farmers.

Untitled. *Jewish Telegraphic Agency*, Dec. 10, 1924. Joseph Schlossberg, head of Amalgamated Clothing Workers of America and also a member of the relief committee, states that Jews who immigrated to the U.S. had a much harder time. Encourages immigration to Mexico.

"Race and Religion in Mexico." *Jewish Woman*, Dec. 1924.

"Song of the Indians." *Mexican Folkways* 1, no. 4 (Dec.–Jan. 1925): 8. Poem in Spanish that Brenner recorded from an indigenous dancer at the Festival of Guadalupe celebrations on Dec. 12, 1924.

1925

"Ave Maria." Manuscript, 1925.

"Edward Weston nos muestra nuevas modalidades de su talento." *Revista de Revistas* (Mexico D.F.), Oct. 4, 1925.

"An Inventory." *Jewish Morning Journal*, 1925. Manuscript.

"Helping Wanderers Help Themselves." *Jewish Morning Journal*, 1925. Manuscript.

"The B'nai B'rith in Mexico." *Jewish Morning Journal*, 1925. Manuscript.

"Assimilation in Mexico." *Jewish Morning Journal*, 1925. Manuscript.

Untitled. *Jewish Telegraphic Agency*, Jan. 1, 1925. Difficult economic situation for immigrant Jews. Some returning to Russia. Trouble with unions, foreign capital fearful of investing in small industries due to revolution of 1910. Manuscript.

"A Race of Princes." *Jewish Daily Forward*, May 1925.

"A Jewish Girl of Mexico." Unidentified clipping, similar to "A Race of Princes," nd. Brenner Archives box D.

Untitled. *Jewish Telegraphic Agency*, June 17, 1925. Demonstration and demands from Hexter for help in farming. Manuscript.

Untitled. *Jewish Telegraphic Agency*, July 23, 1925. Successful dairy. Also sent to *Jewish Morning Journal* under title "A Samovar Scheme and How It Works: Some Jewish Farmers in Mexico." Manuscript.

Untitled. *Jewish Telegraphic Agency*, July 23, 1925. Description of new Zionist organization. Manuscript.

Untitled. *Jewish Telegraphic Agency*, July 23, 1925. Description of the Jewish agricultural colony structure and system. Manuscript.

Untitled. *Jewish Telegraphic Agency*, July 28, 1925. Profile of Louis Schapiro, a former journalist and professor who raises hogs successfully. Manuscript.

Untitled. *Jewish Telegraphic Agency*, July 1925. From New York. Demonstration against Hexter. Manuscript.

"The Petate: A National Symbol." *Mexican Folkways* 1, no. 1 (June–July 1925): 14–15.

"Romance and Realism in a Modern Aztec Theatre." *Art and Archaeology*, Aug. 1925, 67–69. Manuscript.

Untitled. *Jewish Telegraphic Agency*, Aug. 2, 1925. Description of YMHA, manuscript. Published in *Jewish Morning Journal*, Sept. 1925, as "Where the Young People Go."

Untitled. *Jewish Telegraphic Agency*, Aug. 11, 1925. Frank Tannenbaum's lecture series on prisons. Tannenbaum will do research on the Mexican agrarian situation, sponsored by the Washington Institute of Economics of the Brookings Institution.

Untitled. *Jewish Telegraphic Agency*, Aug. 11, 1925. Medical dispensary opened by B'nai B'rith. Manuscript.

Untitled. *Jewish Telegraphic Agency*, Aug. 17, 1925. YMHA opens play "Die Puste Kretscome," by Hirschbein.

Untitled. *Jewish Telegraphic Agency*, Aug. 17, 1925. Article refuting article in *New York World* stating that Jews starve on park benches. Manuscript.

Untitled. *Jewish Telegraphic Agency*, Aug. 18, 1925. Rosenberg and three officers win lottery and donate 15 percent to the Zionists. Manuscript.

Untitled. *Jewish Telegraphic Agency*, Aug. 18, 1925. Five thousand Czechoslovakians ask for immigration visas to Mexico. Restrictive policies. Not possible to ascertain how many are Jews. Manuscript.

Untitled. *Jewish Telegraphic Agency*, Sept. 1925. Increase of immigrants and the controversy of using Mexico and Mexican citizenship to immigrate to United States. Manuscript.

Untitled. *Jewish Telegraphic Agency*, Sept. 6, 1925. Need for a savings and loan association. Small loans, low interest. No funds to start. Manuscript.

Untitled. *Jewish Telegraphic Agency*, Sept. 6, 1925. Illegal immigration of Jews to United States. Manuscript.

Untitled. *Jewish Telegraphic Agency*, Sept. 12, 1925. Review of anti-Semitic book. Intellectualized Ford. Manuscript.

Untitled. *Jewish Telegraphic Agency*, Sept. 23, 1925. Review of book by Dr. Alphonse Goldschmidt, German economist and writer, illustrated by Diego Rivera. Manuscript.

Untitled. *Jewish Telegraphic Agency*, Sept. 24, 1925. Denial of white slave trade of Jewish immigrant women. Manuscript.

"Park Benches." *Jewish Morning Journal*, Sept. 24, 1925. Manuscript.

"Bread, Butter, and Cake." *Jewish Morning Journal*, Sept. 1925. Manuscript.

"The Very Young Jew in Mexico." *Jewish Morning Journal*, Sept. 1925. Manuscript.

"Where the Young People Go: The YMHA of Mexico." *Jewish Morning Journal*, Sept. 1925. Manuscript.

"Mexico: Another Promised Land." *Jewish Morning Journal*, Sept. 1925. Manuscript.

"Mexico to Jerusalem." *Jewish Morning Journal*, Sept. 1925. Manuscript.

"A Mexican Renascence." *The Arts* 8, no. 3 (Sept. 1925), 127.

Untitled. *Jewish Telegraphic Agency*, Oct. 16, 1925. Issues of whether the community needs a rabbi or a union delegate. Manuscript.

"An Investigation Is Being Conducted." Oct. 1925. Manuscript.

Untitled. *Jewish Telegraphic Agency*, Oct. 16, 1925. Conflict between public school and Talmud Torah schedules. Issues of Sephardic-Ashkenazi schools. Manuscript.

Untitled. *Jewish Telegraphic Agency*, Nov. 6, 1925. Cantor Samuel Molovsky comes to visit brothers and a sister. Sings for community. Manuscript.

"Death and the Dog Markets of San Agustin de Acolman." Translation of the story by Dominguez Assaiayn. *Mexican Folkways* 1, no. 3 (Oct.–Nov. 1925): 28.

"Retablos." Translation of the story by Diego Rivera. *Mexican Folkways* 1, no. 3 (Oct.–Nov. 1925): 7.

"The Sephardim: Our 'Latin' Brothers." *Jewish Morning Journal*, Dec. 1925. Manuscript.

"Nish Kosher." *Jewish Morning Journal*, Dec. 1925. Manuscript.

"Revolution and the Jews." *Jewish Morning Journal*, Dec. 1925. Manuscript.

1926

"The Living Art of the Mexican Primitives." 5-page manuscript for *L'Art Vivant*, 1926.

Untitled. *Jewish Telegraphic Agency*, Jan. 25, 1926. Jewish community raises $5000 for Palestine. Scholarship for a girl to study agriculture in Haifa. Positive statement from Minister of Foreign Affairs. Manuscript.

"Francisco Goitia." Jan. 9, 1926. Manuscript.

"Carlos Merida: A Painter from the Land of the Mayas." *International Studio*, April–May 1926.

"Día de Muertos." 6-page manuscript for ballet project, May 1926.

"Mexico's Stand for Autonomy." Manuscript sent to *Jewish Morning Journal* and *Jewish Tribune*, Aug. 1926.

"Persecution of the Faithless." *Jewish Morning Journal*, 1926. Manuscript.

"Idols behind Altars." *The Nation*, Oct. 20, 1926.

1927

"Carlos Orozco como retratista." *Forma, Revista de Artes Plásticas* 1, no. 3 (1927): 4–5.

"Saint Judas." *Jewish Morning Journal*, April 1927. Manuscript.

"Saint Judas." *Vanguard* 1, no. 1 (April 1927).

"The Madonna of a Jew." 3-page manuscript for *Jewish Morning Journal*, April 1927.

"New Hats and Miracles." 7-page manuscript for *Jewish Morning Journal*. April 1927.

"The Command upon Us." 6-page manuscript for *Jewish Morning Journal*. April 1927.

"A Country of White Towers." 8-page manuscript for *Jewish Morning Journal*. May 1927.

"Chichen-Itza, the City of the Sacred Well." From the diary of a wandering Jew's daughter. For the *Jewish Morning Journal*, May 1927. Manuscript.

"Yankele's Kaleh." *Menorah Journal*, Aug. 1927. Manuscript.

"A Mexican Rebel." *The Arts*, Oct. 1927, 201–207.

"Weeping the Bone." *The Nation*, Nov. 16, 1927.

1928

"Afternoons of a Patriarch." *Menorah Journal*, Jan. 1928. Manuscript.

"The Mexican Renaissance." (With Jean Charlot.) 4-page typescript for *New York World*, Jan. 1928.

"Une Renaissance Mexicaine." (With Jean Charlot.) *La Renaissance de L'Art Francais et Des Industries de Luxe* (Paris), Feb. 1928.

"Orozco the Rebel." *New Masses*, Jan.–Feb. 1928.

"The Mexican Primitives." *The Nation*, no. 3265 (Feb. 1, 1928): 129–130.

"A Scientist Turns to Art." *The Nation*, no. 3276 (April 18, 1928).

"Mexico Another Promised Land." *Menorah Journal*, April 1928. Manuscript.

"Mexico Another Promised Land." *The Nation*, 1928.

"A Sympathetic Exploration." *The Arts*, June 1928. Manuscript.

"A Mexican Prophet." *The Arts*, July 1928. Manuscript.

"The Death of Betci." Translation of the story by Samuel Glusberg, in *La Levita Gris*. *Menorah Journal*, Aug. 1928. Manuscript.

"Mexican Messiah." *The Nation*, Sept. 19, 1928. Manuscript.

Editorial paragraph. *The Nation* 127, no. 3299 (1928).

"Mexico's Great Trial." *The Nation* 127, no. 3307.

Review of "Red Mexico." *New York Evening Post*, Dec. 1928.

Review of "Mexican Architecture in the Vice-Regal Period," by Walter Kilham. Dec. 1928 [letter thanking her].

"Student Rebels in Latin America." *The Nation* 127, no. 3310 (Dec. 12, 1928).

"The Man Who Cheats." Review of *Ananias, or The False Artist*, by Walter Pach. *The Nation*, Dec. 19, 1928.

"Sculpture and Latin America." *Encyclopedia Britannica*, 1928. Manuscript.

1929

"Cavaliers and Martyrs." *Menorah Journal*, Jan. 1929. Manuscript.

"Painted Miracles." *The Arts* 15, no. 1 (Jan. 1929), 11.

"Modern Art and William Zorach." *Menorah Journal*, Feb. 1929. Manuscript.

"Mexico's Uprising." *The Nation* 128, no. 3323 (March 13, 1929).

"The Mysterious Aborigine." Review of *Old Civilizations of the New World*, by A. Hyatt Verrill. Manuscript, June 1929, for *The Nation*, Aug. 7, 1929.

"Peace-loving Mexico." *The Nation* 128, no. 3333 (May 22, 1929).

Untitled. Editorial. *The Nation* 129, no. 3339, 3 July 1929.

"Gomez Still Rules." *The Nation*, Aug. 29, 1929. Manuscript.

Idols behind Altars. New York: Payson & Clark, 1929.

"Cántico." *Vida Literaria* (Buenos Aires), Oct. 1929.

"Street Murals of Mexico." *The Arts* 16, no. 3 (Nov. 1929), 163–165.

1930

Catalog for "Jean Charlot: Exhibition of Mexican Paintings." Art Students League, New York City, Jan. 1930.

1931

The Influence of Technique on the Decorative Style in the Domestic Pottery of Culhuacan. New York: Columbia University Press, 1931.

"Making Mexico Jew Conscious." *The Nation*, Sept. 9, 1931.

1932

Your Mexican Holiday. New York: G. P. Putnam Sons, 1932.

"Again General Calles Shows His Hand." *New York Times Sunday Magazine*, Sept. 18, 1932.

"On Going Native in Mexico." *The Arts*, Oct. 1932. Manuscript.

"Drama of Mexico's Church Struggle." *New York Times Sunday Magazine*, Oct. 23, 1932.

"Tampa's Reign of Terror." *The Nation* 135, no. 3518 (Dec. 7, 1932): 555–557.

"The World Over the Stars Now Blaze." *New York Times Sunday Magazine*, Dec. 25, 1932.

"Christmas." *New York Times Sunday Magazine*, Dec. 31, 1932.

1933

"Art and Big Business." *The Nation* 136, no. 3522.

"Art and American Life." *The Nation* 136, no. 3524 (Jan. 18, 1933).

"The Decade of Illusion." *The Nation*, Jan. 19, 1933.

"Orozco: Murals with Meaning." *Creative Art*, Feb. 26, 1933.

"Orozco." *New Masses*, Feb. 28, 1933.

"Revolution in Art." *The Nation* 136, no. 3531 (March 8, 1933).

"Diego Rivera: Fiery Crusader of the Paint Brush." *New York Times Sunday Magazine*, April 2, 1933.

"Life Beating the Door In." *The Nation*, April 19, 1933.

"The Rockefeller Coffin." 3-page manuscript for *The Nation*, May 11, 1933. Brenner Archives box 208-118.

"Rivera Plans to Finish Barred Mural." *New York Herald Tribune*, May 11, 1933. Manuscript.

"Career of Rivera Marked by Strife." *New York Times Sunday Magazine*, May 14, 1933.

"The Clinical Eye." *The Nation* 136, no. 3541 (May 17, 1933).

"Rivera's Revolution." *The Nation* 136, no. 3542 (May 24, 1933).

"The Tail Wags the Dog." *The Nation* 136, no. 3547 (June 28, 1933).

"The Trends and Tides of Modern Education." *New York Times Sunday Magazine*, June 1933.

"A Skeptical Mood Found in Colleges." *New York Times Sunday Magazine*, June 1933.

"Riddle of the Ancient World of America." *New York Times Sunday Magazine*, July 11, 1933.

"Three Provinces against Castile." *The Nation*, Aug. 1933. Manuscript.

"Revolution from the Top." *The Nation*, Aug. 1933. Manuscript.

"Spain in Crisis." *The Nation*, Aug. 1933. Manuscript.

"Spain: Footnote to a Crisis." *The Nation*, Sept. 1933. Manuscript.

Untitled. Manuscript for *New York Times Sunday Magazine*, Sept. 10, 1933.

"A Letter from Spain." *Saturday Review of Literature*, Sept. 16, 1933. Manuscript.

"Republic." *New York Times Sunday Magazine*, Sept. 16, 1933. Manuscript.

"Whither? Is Uneasy Spain's Question." *New York Times Sunday Magazine*, Sept. 24, 1933. Manuscript.

"Spain's Stage Set for the Second Act." *New York Times Sunday Magazine*, Oct. 8, 1933. Manuscript.

"Battle for Possession." *New York Times Sunday Magazine*, Oct. 14, 1933. Manuscript.

Untitled. Manuscript for *New York Times Sunday Magazine*, Nov. 1933.

"Spain Strides into the New Age." *New York Times Sunday Magazine*, Nov. 19, 1933. Manuscript.

"Spanish Letter." *Opinion: A Journal of Jewish Life and Letters*, Nov. 1933, 20–22. Manuscript.

"Spain Tries Democracy." *New York Sun*, Dec. 9, 1933. Announcement that Anita Brenner will deliver an address on "Spain Tries Democracy."

"Spain, Her Republic Failing, Girds for a Bitter Conflict." *New York Times Sunday Magazine*, Dec. 17, 1933.

Untitled. Manuscript for *New York Times Sunday Magazine*, Dec. 1933.

Invoice for "Spanish Republic." *New York Times Sunday Magazine*, Dec. 23, 1933 [date of invoice].

"Spain's Venture in Democracy." *Current History*, Dec. 1933.

Untitled. Manuscript for *New York Times Sunday Magazine*, Dec. 1933. Manuscript.

1934

"Is Rivera a Counter-Revolutionary?" Review of *Portrait of America*, by Bertram Wolfe and Diego Rivera. Manuscript for *New International* 1934. Brenner Archives, unclassified.

"Impurity in the Modern Museum." *The Nation* 138, no. 3580 (Jan. 1934).

"El Sacristán." *Fight*, Jan. 1934. [*Fight* was a new magazine published by the American League against War and Fascism.]

Untitled. Manuscript for *New York Times Sunday Magazine*, Feb. 1934.

"The Rise of a Fascist." *Fight*, Feb. 1934.

"The Races of Man in Sentiment." *The Nation*, Feb. 1934.

"Spain: Viva la Republica!" *The Nation* 138, no. 3579 (Feb. 7, 1934).

"Arts Storied Debate Renewed." *New York Times Sunday Magazine*, Feb. 25, 1934.

"Private Art and Public Interest." Typescript submitted to *The Nation*, March 8, 1934. Brenner Archives, unclassified.

Letter to the editor. *New Masses* (March 20, 1934): 21.

"Frontiers of Machine Art." *The Nation* 138, no. 3586 (March 28, 1934).

"Life Crashes the Art Salons." *The Nation*, May 2, 1934.

"Trotsky vs Stalin." *New York Times Sunday Magazine*, May 5, 1934.

"While Spain Starves." *The Nation* 138, no. 3292 (May 9, 1934).

"Arthur Warner." Letter to the Editors. *The Nation* 138, no. 3597 (June 13, 1934): 675.

Untitled. Manuscript for *The Nation*, June 1934. (James Rorty to Brenner, June 6, 1934: "We used your Spanish paragraph this week." Brenner Archives.)

"American Folkways." *The Nation* 138, no. 3597 (June 1934).

Editorial (about Calles's expulsion from Mexico). *The Nation*, June 1934. Manuscript.

"Morocco." *New York Times Sunday Magazine*, June 16, 1934.

"Aesthetics and Agitation." *The Nation* 138, no. 3599 (June 27, 1934): 737–738.

"Matador." *New York Times Sunday Magazine*, June 30, 1934.

"The Art of Mexico or Mexican Art Monographs." *New Republic*, June 30, 1934.

"The Health Insurance Issue Stirs Doctors to New Debate." *New York Times Sunday Magazine*, July 15, 1934.

Untitled. Manuscript for *Militant*, July 1934.

"Spanish Literature since the Republic." *The Nation*, Aug. 1934.

"Algiers." *New York Times Sunday Magazine*, Aug. 18, 1934.

"Riveting in Art." *New York Times Sunday Magazine*, Aug. 25, 1934.

"Twelve Hundred Years of Spanish History." Review of *The History of Spain*, by Louis Bertrand and Charles Petrie. *New York Times Sunday Magazine*, Sept. 1, 1934.

"Some Artists Lose Some Chains." Manuscript for *The Nation*, Oct. 1934.

Untitled. 5-page manuscript (contrasting Catalans and Madrid) for *New York Times Sunday Magazine*, Oct. 1934.

"The Revolution in Spain: Act Three." *The Nation* 139, no. 3616 (Oct. 24, 1934).

"The Truth about Mexico," part 1. 5-page manuscript for *New York Post*, Nov. 1934. Brenner Archives.

"The Truth about Mexico," part 2. 5-page manuscript for *New York Post*, Nov. 1934. Brenner Archives.

"The Truth about Mexico," part 3. Manuscript for *New York Post*, Nov. 1934. Brenner Archives.

"Centuries Clash in Many-Sided Mexico." *New York Times Sunday Magazine*, Nov. 11, 1934.

"The Triple Revolution in Spain." *Current History*, Nov. 1934.

"The New Era in Mexico." 8-page manuscript for WEVD Radio, Dec. 14, 1934. Brenner Archives.

"The New Era in Mexico," second program. 8-page manuscript for WEVD Radio, Dec. 14, 1934.

"The New Era in Mexico," third program. 9-page manuscript for WEVD Radio, Dec. 1934.

[Jean Mendez, pseud.] Untitled. 6-page manuscript, 1934.

1935

"Calles Again Opposes Cardenas." *New York Times Sunday Magazine* (Times Wide World and European), undated clipping.

Review of Carlos Merida show. *Brooklyn Daily Eagle*, nd. Manuscript.

Article about WPA regulations. *Brooklyn Daily Eagle*, nd. Manuscript.

Review of the German show at Brooklyn Museum. *Brooklyn Daily Eagle*, nd. Manuscript.

Review of American Artists' Congress. *Brooklyn Daily Eagle*, nd. Manuscript.

Review of Dada show at Museum of Modern Art. *Brooklyn Daily Eagle*, nd. Manuscript.

Review of [?] Houmere exhibit at the Pierre Matisse. *Brooklyn Daily Eagle*, nd. Manuscript.

Review of Gauguin show. *Brooklyn Daily Eagle*, nd. Manuscript.

Invoice for "Florida." *New York Times*, Feb. 25, 1935.

"The Labor Duel." *New York Times Sunday Magazine*, April 1, 1935.

Editorial. *New Republic*, July 1935.

"Silver Changes Mexico's Pattern." *New York Times Sunday Magazine*, July 28, 1935.

[Jean Mendez, pseud.] "The Anti-Calles Drive in Mexico." *New International*, Aug. 1935.

"Portes Gil Emerges in Mexican 'Revolt.'" *New York Times Sunday Magazine*, Aug. 6, 1935.

"Old Mexico Changed by a New Highway." *New York Times Sunday Magazine*, Aug. 18, 1935.

Untitled. 8-page manuscript (about Ethiopia and Italy) for *New York Times Sunday Magazine*, Sept. 1935.

"Giant in Silver." 7-page manuscript for *American Spectator*, Sept. 1935.

Review of Henri Matisse show at Brooklyn Museum. *Brooklyn Daily Eagle*, Oct. 1935.

"Terror in Cuba." Letter to the Editors. *The Nation*. Oct. 23, 1935.

"Surrealism and Proletarianism." *Brooklyn Daily Eagle*, Nov. 1935. Manuscript.

Review of automobile show. *Brooklyn Daily Eagle*, Nov. 1935. Manuscript.

"Vincent Van Gogh and the Artist's Life." *Brooklyn Daily Eagle*, Nov. 10, 1935.

"Georgio de Chirico Dreams of Destruction." *Brooklyn Daily Eagle*, Nov. 24, 1935.

"Old Social Struggle Is Renewed in Mexico." *New York Times Sunday Magazine*, clipping dated only 1935. Brenner Archives box D-3.

Untitled. 7-page manuscript (about dog walkers) for *Brooklyn Daily Eagle*, Nov. 1935. Manuscript.

Review of photography exhibits. *Brooklyn Daily Eagle*, Dec. 1935. Manuscript.

"American Painters and the 'Art of the State.'" *Brooklyn Daily Eagle*, Dec. 1, 1935.

Review of *Trailing Cortez through Mexico*, by Harry Franck. *Brooklyn Daily Eagle*, Dec. 15, 1935.

1936

"Jones Is a Happy Rebel." *Brooklyn Daily Eagle*, Jan. 5, 1936.

"We Finally Have a Municipal Gallery." *Brooklyn Daily Eagle*, Jan. 12, 1936.

Editorial. *The Nation*, Feb. 1936.

Review of Georgia O'Keeffe exhibit. 5-page manuscript for *Brooklyn Daily Eagle*, Feb. 1936.

Review of Kandinsky and Calder shows. 3-page manuscript for *Brooklyn Daily Eagle*, Feb. 1936.

"Muralist Lucienne Bloch: Product of the WPA." *Brooklyn Daily Eagle*, Feb. 2, 1936.

"Backwardness of the Modern Craftsman." *Brooklyn Daily Eagle*, Feb. 9, 1936.

"Affair of Honor." Undated manuscript.

Untitled. Manuscript for *New York Times Sunday Magazine*, Feb. 1936.

"The Architectural League and the Housing Problem." *Brooklyn Daily Eagle*, March 1, 1936.

"Carlos Chavez to Conduct Philadelphia Orchestra." *Brooklyn Daily Eagle*, March 1, 1936.

"An Important Survey of Non-Pictorial Art." *Brooklyn Daily Eagle*, March 8, 1936.

"Art of the Lens at the Brooklyn Museum." *Brooklyn Daily Eagle*, March 15, 1936.

"The World of Art in Facsimile Reproduction." *Brooklyn Daily Eagle*, March 22, 1936.

"Fresco and the Social Content of Art Forms." *Brooklyn Daily Eagle*, April 5, 1936.

"Student Art Work in Brooklyn." *Brooklyn Daily Eagle*, April 12, 1936.

"Forain and the Fashionable World." *Brooklyn Daily Eagle*, April 19, 1936.

"Artists Unite against War and Fascism." *Brooklyn Daily Eagle*, April 26, 1936.

"Spain Mobilizes for Revolution." *The Nation* (April 29, 1936): 546–548.

"Corner of Sicily in New York." *Travel*, May 1936.

"The Spring Art Season Draws to a Close." *Brooklyn Daily Eagle*, May 10, 1936.

"False Witness." Review of *Mexican Martyrdom*, by Wilfrid Parsons. July 1936. Manuscript.

"Inhumanity: Page Gil Robles." Undated manuscript for *The Nation*.

"Spain's Proud, Stormy People." *New York Times Sunday Magazine*, Aug. 16, 1936.

"Who's Who in Spain." *The Nation*, Aug. 15, 1936.

"New Horizons in American Art." *New York Times Sunday Magazine*, Sept. 13, 1936.

"Spain in Revolt." *The Nation*, Oct. 17, 1936[?].

"An American Resume." *The Nation*, 1936, 311–312.

"Pablo Picasso: He Is the Man of His Time." *Brooklyn Daily Eagle*, Nov. 8, 1936.

"Younger Generation at Whitney Museum: A Mood of Self-Confidence Dominates the Current Biennial." *Brooklyn Daily Eagle*, Nov. 15, 1936.

"The Sculptor in the Machine Age." *Brooklyn Daily Eagle*, Nov. 22, 1936.

1937

"Today the Barricades." Undated manuscript.

"Blueprint of Mexico." Review of *Portrait of Mexico*, by Bertram Wolfe. *The Nation*, 1937.

Review of exhibits at Radio City and Westermann (Louis Corinth), and the Mexican movie *The Wave*. 5-page manuscript for *Brooklyn Daily Eagle*. [Dated by event.]

Review of WPA easel work at Whitney. 5-page manuscript for *Brooklyn Daily Eagle*. [Dated by event.]

"Reflections on the Art of Angna Enters." *Brooklyn Daily Eagle*, Jan. 3, 1937.

"A Masterly Show at the Pierre Matisse Gallery." *Brooklyn Daily Eagle*, Jan. 10, 1937.

"The Artist and His Relation to His Public." *Brooklyn Daily Eagle*. Jan. 31, 1937.

"Academician, Author, in One-Man Shows." *Brooklyn Daily Eagle*, Feb. 7, 1937.

"Painters and English Architects: Dust Gathers at the Whitney Museum." *Brooklyn Daily Eagle*, Feb. 14, 1937.

"The Sand Paintings of the Navajos." *Brooklyn Daily Eagle*, Feb. 21, 1937.

"The WPA Emulates the Whitney Museum." *Brooklyn Daily Eagle*, Feb. 28, 1937.

"About Contemporaries, American and German." *Brooklyn Daily Eagle*, March 7, 1937.

"Prints and Paintings of Today." *Brooklyn Daily Eagle*, March 14, 1937.

"Some Notes on the Art of Facsimile Printing." *Brooklyn Daily Eagle*, March 21, 1937.

"Manet and Bourgeois Tradition." *Brooklyn Daily Eagle*, March 28, 1937.

"Designs for Living: Accomplished and Projected." *Brooklyn Daily Eagle*, April 4, 1937.

"Decorative and Factual Styles in Photography: Annual Camera Show at Brooklyn Museum." *Brooklyn Daily Eagle*, April 11, 1937.

"American Artists' Congress Holds First Exhibit." *Brooklyn Daily Eagle*, April 25, 1937.

"The Spanish Anarchists and the Government." Letter to the editor. *The Nation*, July 3, 1937.

"Calling for Protest." Letter to the editor. *The Nation*, Aug. 6, 1937.

"Facts about Spain: Class War in Republican Spain." *Modern Monthly*, Sept. 1937.

"Modern Housing, Mainly Low-cost." *The Nation*, Nov. 1937.

Review of *The New Architecture in Mexico*, by Esther Born, and *Contemporary Mexican Artists*, by Agustin Velazquez Chavez. 3-page manuscript for *The Nation*, Nov. 1937.

"The City Child Paints Life as He Sees It." *New York Times Sunday Magazine*, Dec. 19, 1937.

Class War in Spain: An Exposure of Fascism, Stalinism, etc. Booklet. Sydney: Socialist Labor Party. Dec. 1937.

1938

"America Creates American Murals." *New York Times Sunday Magazine*, April 10, 1938.

Mexico oil expropriation. Nine manuscripts between July 1938 and Feb. 23, 1939.

[Unsigned.] "Mexico in Revolution." *Fortune* 18, no. 4 (Oct. 1938).

1939

"Mexico in Transition." *New York Times Sunday Magazine*, Jan. 15, 1939.

"As New York Views Two Exhibitions the Question Merits Various Answers, from Artists and Public." *New York Times Sunday Magazine*, Feb. 5, 1939.

"And Now There's Talk of Murals for Straphangers." *New York Times Sunday Magazine*, Feb. 26, 1939.

"Diego Rivera: His Life and Times." Review of *Diego Rivera: His Life and Times*, by Bertram Wolfe. 5-page manuscript for *New York Times Sunday Magazine*, April 1939.

"City Host at Many Museums." *New York Times Sunday Magazine*, July 16, 1939.

"City Proud of Its Art." *New York Times Sunday Magazine*, July 23, 1939.

"Profile of Louis Michel Eilshemius." 7-page manuscript for *New York Times Sunday Magazine*, Oct. 1939.

"Picasso versus Picasso." *New York Times Sunday Magazine*, Nov. 1939. Manuscript[?].

1940

"Can Both Be Art?" *New York Times Sunday Magazine*, Jan. 28, 1940.

"Fabulous Pageant of Persian Art." *New York Times Sunday Magazine*, April 21, 1940.

"Stalin in Spain." Translator and introduction to the article by Indalecio Prieto. *American Mercury*, 1940. Manuscript.

"Living Art of Mexico." *New York Times Sunday Magazine*, May 12, 1940.

"Twenty Centuries of Mexican Art." Review of *Twenty Centuries of Mexican Art. New York Herald Tribune*, July 1940. Manuscript.

"Modern Art: What? Why?" *New York Times Sunday Magazine*, Dec. 8, 1940.

1941

"Mexican Renaissance." *Harper's*, Jan. 1941.

"American Art." 12-page manuscript for *New York Times Sunday Magazine*, Oct. 1941.

"Life below the Rio Grande." *Independent Woman*, Feb. 1941.

"The Public Inherits Princely Art." *New York Times Sunday Magazine*, March 9, 1941.

"American Primitives." *New York Times Sunday Magazine*, April 6, 1941.

"Artistic Free-for-All." *New York Times Sunday Magazine*, April 13, 1941.

"What Is a Dodger Fan?" *New York Times Sunday Magazine*, May 11, 1941.

"Mexico on Wheels." *Woman's Home Companion*, Aug. 1941.

"Whirlaway: Problem Horse." *New York Times Sunday Magazine,* Aug. 10, 1941.

"Boy with a Baton." *New York Times Sunday Magazine,* Aug. 17, 1941, 5.

"High School Youth, Not Flaming but Realistic." *New York Times Sunday Magazine,* Oct. 26, 1941. Also published in *Scholastic,* Nov. 1941.

"Is There an American Art." *New York Times Sunday Magazine,* Nov. 23, 1941.

"RX: A Mother." Typescript, 1941. Brenner Archives box 208-128.

1942

The Boy Who Could Do Anything. New York: Young Scott Books. 1942.

"Americanos All." *New York Times Sunday Magazine,* Feb. 1, 1942, 6.

"Women in White." *New York Times Sunday Magazine,* Aug. 30, 1942.

"Museum Run for and by Children." *New York Times Sunday Magazine,* Oct. 4, 1942.

"The Political Battleground in Mexico." *New York Times Book Review,* Nov. 22, 1942: 9.

"The Wind That Swept Mexico." *Harper's,* Nov. 1942.

1943

"A Latin American Speaks." *New York Times Sunday Magazine,* ca. Feb. 13, 1943.

Review of book that describes pro-Nazi Argentina. 5-page manuscript for *New York Times Sunday Magazine,* April 1943, Brenner Archives.

Letter. (Answer to Prescott's review of *The Wind That Swept Mexico.*) *New York Times,* May 26, 1943.

"Portrait." *Saturday Review of Literature,* May 29, 1943.

"What Can I Do to Help with the War?" *New York Times Sunday Magazine,* June 7, 1943.

The Wind That Swept Mexico. New York: Harper's, 1943.

I Want to Fly. New York: Young Scott Books, 1943.

1946–1974

"Mexico: Ballots without Bullets." *The Nation* (Aug. 3, 1946): 124–127.

"Mexican Fact and Fiction." *Holiday,* Feb.–March 1947.

"Paricutin." *Holiday*, May 1948. Manuscript.

"Mexico's New Deal Two Years After." *New York Times Sunday Magazine*, Nov. 28, 1948.

"Love." Typescript, 1948. Brenner Archives box 208-14.

"The Mexicans Rediscover Tradition." *Art News*, Summer 1951.

Untitled. 3-page manuscript for *Art News*, May 1953. Brenner Archives box 208-150.

A Hero by Mistake. New York: Young Scott Books, 1953. (Winner of New York Herald Tribune Honor Medal.)

"Baseball? A Thousand Years Ago." *This Week*, Jan. 27, 1955.

Person to Person. Monthly column for *Mexico/This Month*, 1955–1972.

Untitled. Manuscript for *Art News*, May 1955. Brenner Archives box 207-55.

Dumb Juan and the Bandits. New York: Young Scott Books. 1957.

"Art and Artists in Mexico Today." *Atlantic*, Spring 1964.

The Timid Ghost, or What Would You Do with a Sackful of Gold? New York: Young Scott Books, 1966. (Britannica Prize.)

Idols behind Altars. Reprint, new introduction. Boston: Beacon Press, 1970.

The Wind That Swept Mexico. Reprint. Austin: University of Texas Press, 1971.

Guerrero Imágenes de Ayer. Mexico D.F.: Taller Libre de Arte José Clemente Orozco, Universidad Autónoma de Guerrero, Sedue, 1983.

published translations

Frank, Waldo. *Tales from Argentina*, np, 1932.

Azuela, Mariano. *Marcela.* New York: Farrar & Reinhart, 1932.

Magdaleno, Mauricio. *Sunburst* [*Resplandor*]. New York: Viking Press, 1944.

Lopez y Fuentes, Gregorio. *El Indio.* New York: Bobbs Merril Co., 1937.

undated manuscripts

"His First Adventure."

"Witches and Wings of Straw." 7 pages.

"On Horseback to Paradise." 5 pages.

"A Blue Rebozo." 3 pages.

"We Got the Works." 8 pages, unfinished.

Review of *Texas and Southwestern Lore,* edited by J. Frank Dobie. Texas Folk-Lore Society, no. 6.

"The Question of Jewish Art." Review of book by Aaron Spivak.

"Good Influence." [1925?]

"The Miracle." [1925?]

"The Devil in Business." 3 pages. [1925?]

"Mazel." [1925?]

"How the World Was Made." 5 pages.

"The Mexican Messiah." 6 pages on Quetzalcoatl. [1925?]

"A Mexican Tragedy." 9-page story of Hernandez Galvan, using pseudonym Manuel Fernandez Margain. [1926?]

"Mexican Indian Art in the Colonial Period." *Creative Art,* before 1928.

"Mexican Pottery," *Creative Art,* before 1928.

"Mexican Children's Art Schools," *Creative Art,* before 1928.

"Mexican Indian Interpretation of Spanish Church Art," *Creative Art,* before 1928.

Introduction to catalogue of Caroline Durieux exhibit, Mexico City. In Spanish. [1931–1932?]

"Spain in Transit." 10 pages.

"A Mind of Your Own." *Mademoiselle.* [1935?]

"Field Day for Frankenstein." [1936?]

"Spain at Her Great Decision." *Digest and Review.* Reprint of the *New York Times* article. [title and date not specified]

Review of Picasso, for *Brooklyn Daily Eagle.* [1937?]

"The Serpent in Andorra."

"Letter from Mexico." 10 pages. [1944?]

general bibliography

Aguayo, Sergio. "An Essay on the Evolution of World Views and Ideologies in the United States: Mexico as Reflected in the *New York Times*, 1946–1979." Ph.D. diss., Johns Hopkins School of Advanced International Studies, 1984.

Albers, Patricia. "Dear Vocio," exhibit catalogue. San Diego: University of California, 1997.

Azuela, Alicia. *Diego Rivera en Detroit*. Mexico D.F.: UNAM, Instituto de Investigaciones Estéticas, 1985.

―――. "*El Machete* and Frente a Frente: Art Committed to Social Justice in Mexico." *Art Journal*, Political Journals, Guest Editor Virginia Hagelstein Marquardt, College Art Association 52, no. 1 (Spring 1993): 82–90.

―――. "Public Art: Meyer Schapiro and Mexican Muralism." *Oxford Art Journal* 17, no. 1 (1994): 55–60.

―――. "La Vanguardia Mexicana en la Revista Contemporáneos." Paper presented at Sixteenth International Latin American Studies Association meetings, Sept. 21–23, 1989, New Orleans.

Azuela, Mariano. *Marcela*. Introduced by Waldo Frank and translated by Anita Brenner. New York: Farrar & Rinehart, 1932.

Baciu, Stefan. *Jean Charlot estridentista silencioso*. México D.F.: Editorial "El Café de Nadie," 1981.

Bateson, Mary Catherine. *With a Daughter's Eye*. New York: Washington Square Press, 1984.

―――. *Composing a Life*. New York: Plume Books, 1989.

Beals, Carleton. *Mexico: An Interpretation*. New York: E. W. Huebsch, 1923.

―――. "Tina Modotti." *Creative Art*, Feb. 1923.

―――. "Goat's Head on a Martyr." *Saturday Review of Literature*, Dec. 7, 1929.

————. *Mexican Maze*. Philadelphia: J. B. Lippincott Co., 1931.

————. *Porfirio Díaz*. México: Editorial Domés, 1982.

Beloff, Angelina. *Memorias*. Mexico: UNAM/SEP, 1986.

Blair, Kathryn S. *A la sombra del ángel*. México: Alianza Editorial, 1995.

Bokser, Jehudit. *Imágenes de un encuentro: La presencia judía en México durante la primer mitad del siglo XX*. México: UNAM, Tribuna Israelita, Comité Central Israelita de México, Multibanco Mercantil Probursa, 1993.

Bradu, Fabienne. *Antonieta, 1900–1931*. México D.F.: Fondo de Cultura Económica, 1991.

Brenner, Anita. See Anita Brenner Bibliography, above.

Brenner, Anita, and Louis Berg. "Doctor in Petticoats." Undated typescript from the late forties. Brenner Archives box 207-14.

Brenner, Anita, and Jean Charlot. "Une Renaissance Mexicaine." *La Renaissance de L'Art Francais et Des Industries de Luxe* (Paris), Feb. 1928.

Britton, John. *Carleton Beals: A Radical Journalist in Latin America*. Albuquerque: University of New Mexico Press, 1987.

Brodsky, Joseph. "For the Scottsboro Defense." *The Nation*, May 25, 1932.

Broué, Pierre, ed. *Leon Trotsky: Oeuvres, Aout–Decembre 1936*. Paris: EDI, 1982.

————. *Leon Trotsky: Oeuvres, Decembre 1936–Fevrier 1937*. Paris: EDI, 1982.

————. *Leon Trotsky: Oeuvres, Janvier–Fevrier 1937*. Paris: EDI, 1982.

Bush, Wendell T., et al. Letter to John D. Rockefeller, May 12, 1933. Brenner Archives box 247-49A.

————. Letter to John D. Rockefeller, May 15, 1933. Brenner Archives box 247-49A.

Cacucci, Pino. *Tina Modotti*. Barcelona: Circe, 1995.

Caden Pettus, Daisy. *The Rosalie Evans Letters from Mexico*. Bobbs-Merrill Co., 1926.

Cardona, Patricia. "Concha Michel." *Fem* 9, no. 42 (Oct.–Nov. 1985): 24–25.

Cardoza y Aragón, Luis, and Jean Charlot. *José Clemente Orozco: El artista en Nueva York*. México: Siglo Veintiuno Editores, S.A., 1971.

Charlot, Jean. "Un precursor del movimiento de arte mexicano: El Grabador Posada." *Revista de Revistas*, no. 25 (Aug. 30, 1925).

————. "Cien grabados en madera por José Guadalupe Posada." Prologue to a folio of 100 woodcuts. México: Arsacio Vanegas Arroyo, 1945. English translation published in 1947.

————. *The Mexican Mural Renaissance*. New Haven: Yale University Press, 1963.

————. *An Artist on Art: Collected Essays of Jean Charlot*. Honolulu: University Press of Hawaii, 1972.

Chase, Stuart. *Mexico: A Study of Two Americas*. New York: Macmillan Co., 1931.

Constantine, Mildred. *Tina Modotti: A Fragile Life*. New York: Paddington Press, 1975.

D'Chumacero, Rosalia. *Perfil y pensamiento de la mujer mexicana*. México: Asociación de Escritoras y Periodistas de México, 1961.

Debroise, Olivier. *Lola Alvarez Bravo: In Her Own Light*. Tucson: Center for Creative Photography, University of Arizona, 1994.

Diggins, John Patrick. *The Rise and Fall of the American Left*. New York: W. W. Norton & Co., 1973.

Dulles, John W. F. *Yesterday in Mexico: A Chronicle of the Revolution, 1919–1936*. Austin: University of Texas Press, 1961.

Eisenstein, S. M. *¡Que Viva México!* México D.F.: Ediciones Era, S.A., 1964.

S. M. Eisenstein dibujos mexicanos inéditos. México D.F.: Dirección de Cinematografía de la Dirección General de Radio, Televisión y Cine, 1978.

Elmendorf, Mary L. *La mujer maya y el cambio*. México D.F.: SEP, 1972.

————. "Mexico." In *Village Women: Their Changing Lives and Fertility*. Washington, D.C.: American Association for the Advancement of Science, 1977.

————. *Women: Roles and Status in Eight Countries*. New York: John Wiley & Sons, 1977.

Erikson, Erik H. *Identity, Youth, and Crisis*. New York: Norton, 1968.

————. *Young Man Luther*. New York: Norton, 1958.

————. *Gandhi's Truth*. New York: Norton, 1969.

Evans, Ernestine. "When You Go to Mexico." *New York Herald Tribune*, June 26, 1932.

————. Untitled. *Creative Art*, Feb. 1930.

Fernández Vilchis, Octavio. "Como se obtuvo el derecho de asilo para Trotsky en México." *La Prensa*, April 20, 1956.

Fischer, Louis. Editorial. "Uprising in Catalonia." *The Nation*, May 15, 1937.

Frank, Waldo. *Tales from Argentina*. Translated by Anita Brenner. Np, 1932.

Freeman, Joseph. *An American Testament*. New York: Farrar & Rinehart, 1936.

Gall, Olivia. *Trotsky en México*. México: Ediciones Era, 1991.

Gamio, Manuel. *Forjando Patria*. México: Porrua, 1916.

Gannett, Lewis. "Books and Things." *New York Herald Tribune*, May 26, 1943.

Gedul, Harry M., and Ronald Gottesman, editors. *Sergei Eisenstein and Upton Sinclair: The Making and Unmaking of Que Viva Mexico!* Bloomington: Indiana University Press, 1970.

Gibson, Ian. *Federico García Lorca: A life*. New York: Pantheon Books, 1989.

Gómez Arias, Alejandro. *Un testimonio sobre Frida Kahlo*. Mexico: Instituto Nacional de Bellas Artes, 1977.

González Gamio, Angeles. *Manuel Gamio: Una lucha sin final*. México: Universidad Nacional Autónoma de México, 1987.

Gonzalez, Luis. "El liberalismo triunfante." *Historia general de México*. México: Colegio de México, 1987.

Gruening, Ernest. "Emerging Mexico: 1. The Heritage." *The Nation* 120, no. 3127 (June 10, 1925): 649–650.

———. "Emerging Mexico: 2. Education." *The Nation* 120, no. 3128 (June 17, 1925): 683–684.

———. "Emerging Mexico: 3. Land and Labor." *The Nation* 120, no. 3129 (June 24, 1925): 713–714.

———. "Emerging Mexico: 4. Democracy." *The Nation* 121, no. 3130 (July 1, 1925): 28–32.

———. *Mexico and Its Heritage*. New York: Century Co., 1928.

———. "The Mexican Rhythm." *Portland News*, Oct. 1, 1929.

Hale, Charles. "Frank Tannenbaum and the Mexican Revolution." Paper presented at Latin American Studies Association Meeting, Atlanta, Ga., March 1994.

Hansen, Harry. "The First Reader." *New York World*, nd., 1929.

Hart, John Mason. *Revolutionary Mexico*. Berkeley: University of California Press, 1987.

Herberg, Will. "What Happened to American Socialism?" *Commentary*, Oct. 1951.

Herrera, Hayden. *Frida: A Biography of Frida Kahlo*. New York: Harper & Row, 1983.

Herring, Hubert, and Herbert Weinstock, eds. *Renascent Mexico*. New York: Covici, Friede Publishers, 1935.

Herskovits, Melville J. *Franz Boas: The Science of Man in the Making*. New York: Charles Scribners Sons, 1953.

Hexter, Maurice. "The Jews in Mexico." *Separata*. American Jewish Congress, 1926.

Hiss, Alger. *In the Court of Public Opinion*. New York: Harper Colophon Books, 1957.

Hiss, Tony. *Laughing Last: Alger Hiss by Tony Hiss*. Boston: Houghton Mifflin Co., 1977.

Hook, Sidney. *Out of Step: An Unquiet Life in the Twentieth Century.* New York: Harper & Row, 1987.

Hooks, Margaret. *Tina Modotti: Photographer and Revolutionary.* London: Pandora, 1993.

Inman, Henry. Review of Feb. issue of *Creative Art*, "Orozco: Murals with Meaning." *New York Times*, Feb. 26, 1933.

Jamis, Rauda. *Frida Kahlo.* México: Edivisión, 1987.

Kahan, Solomon. "The Jewish Community in Mexico." *Contemporary Jewish Record* 1 (1940).

Karetnikova, Inga, and Leon Steinmetz. *Mexico According to Eisenstein.* Albuquerque: University of New Mexico Press, 1991.

Katz, Friederich. *The Secret War in Mexico.* Chicago: University of Chicago Press, 1981.

Krause, Corinne. *Los judíos en México.* México: Universidad Iberoamericana, Departamento de Historia, 1987.

Laikin Elkin, Judith. *Jews of the Latin American Republics.* Chapel Hill: University of North Carolina Press, 1980.

———, ed. *Resources for Latin American Jewish Studies.* Proceedings of the first research conference of the Latin American Jewish Studies Association. Ann Arbor, Mich.: LAJSA, 1982.

Lowe, Sarah. *Frida Kahlo.* New York: Universe Publishing, 1991.

———. *Tina Modotti Photographs.* Philadelphia Museum of Art, Harry N. Abrams, 1995.

Madero, Francisco I. *La sucesión presidencial.* San Pedro, Coahuila: El Partido Nacional Democrático, 1908.

Malvido, Adriana. "Nahuí Olín: Una vida." *La Jornada Semanal.* México, D.F. March 22, 1992.

Marín, Guadalupe. *La única.* México: Editorial Jalisco, 1938.

Maslow, Abraham. *Motivation and Personality.* New York: Harper's, 1954.

———. *Toward a Psychology of Being.* Princeton: Von Nostrand, 1968.

Mexico Labor News. "Mexican Government Dissolves Fascist Gold Shirts. Supreme Chief Nicolas Rodriguez Exiled to United States." Press Department of the Workers University of Mexico (Universidad Obrera de México.) vol. 1, no. 6, Aug. 20, 1936. Brenner Archives box 208-93.

Miller, Beth. Transcript and tape of interview of Anita Brenner, Jan. 1974. Brenner Archives unclassified.

————. "An Interview with Anita Brenner." *Bilingual Review* (York College and CCNYU) 4 (Jan.–Aug. 1977).

Miller, Beth, and Alfonso González. *26 autoras del México actual*. México: Costa-Amic, 1978.

Modena, Maria Eugenia. *Pasaporte de culturas: Viaje por la vida de un judío ruso en México*. México D.F.: Instituto Nacional de Antropología e Historia, Colección Científica, Etnología, 1982.

Moncada, Raúl. "Historiadora de la Revolución Mexicana: Anita Brenner, Primera Amiga de México en Estados Unidos." México D.F., nd.

New Masses (New York), editorial. March 6, 1934.

Orozco, José Clemente. *Cartas a Margarita, 1921–1949*. Edited by Tatiana Herrero Orozco. México: Ediciones Era, 1987.

Oulahan, Dick. Story proposal for *Time Magazine*. Memorandum, 1958. Brenner Archives box B.

Pandolfi, Sylvia. *Frida Kahlo—Tina Modotti*. México: Museo Nacional de Arte, 1983.

Plenn, Abel. *Wind in the Olive Trees*. New York: Boni & Gaer, 1946.

Poniatowska, Elena. *Tinísima*. México: Ediciones Era, 1992.

Poniatowska, Elena, and Carla Stellweg. *Frida Kahlo: The Camera Seduced*. London: Chatto & Windus, 1992.

Prescott, Orville. "Books of the Times." *New York Times*, May 28, 1943.

Reed, Alma. *Orozco*. 1955. México: Fondo de Cultura Económica, 1983.

Redfield, Robert. *A Village That Chose Progress*. Chicago: University of Chicago, 1962.

————. *The Primitive World and Its Transformations*. Ithaca, N.Y.: Great Seal Books, 1953.

————. *The Little Community* and *Peasant Society and Culture*. Chicago: Phoenix Books, University of Chicago Press, 1956 & 1963.

Rice, Elinor. *Mirror, Mirror*. New York: Duell, Sloan & Pearce, 1946.

Rivas Mercado, Antonieta. *La campaña de Vasconcelos*. México: Editorial Oasis, 1985.

————. *87 cartas de amor y otros papeles*. Veracruz: Biblioteca Universidad Veracruzana, 1980.

Rivera, Diego. "Controversia Rockefeller." Manuscript, nd [1933]. Brenner Archives box 207-44 A.

Robles, Martha. *La sombra fugitiva: Escritoras en la cultura nacional*. México: Editorial Diana, 1989.

Rogers, J. W. *"Idols behind Altars* Throws New Light on Mexican Ideas of Art." *Dallas Times Herald,* Nov. 3, 1929.

Rojas, Beatriz. *La destrucción de la hacienda en Aguascalientes, 1910–1931.* Michoacán, Mex.: El Colegio de Michoacán, 1981.

Ross, Sherwood. *Gruening of Alaska.* New York: Best Book, 1968.

Saborit, Antonio. *Una mujer sin país.* México: Cal y Arena, 1992.

Salas, Elizabeth. *Soldaderas in the Mexican Military: Myth and History.* Austin: University of Texas Press, 1990.

Schmidt, Henry C. "The American Intellectual Discovery of Mexico in the Twenties." *South Atlantic Quarterly* 77 (Summer 1978): 335–351.

Seligson, Sylvia. "Los judíos en México: Un estudio preliminar." Tesis licenciatura, Escuela Nacional de Antropología e Historia, México, Nov. 1975.

Seton, Marie. *Sergei M. Eisenstein.* London: Bodley Head, 1952.

Simpson, Lesley Bird. *Many Mexicos.* University of California Press, 1966.

Siqueiros, David Alfaro. *Me llamaban el Coronelazo.* Mexico: Grijalbo, 1977.

———. "Rivera's Counter-Revolutionary Road." *New Masses,* May 29, 1934.

Smith, H. Allen. *Pig in the Barber Shop.* New York: Little, Brown, 1958.

Spratling, William. *File on Spratling.* 1932. Boston: Little, Brown, 1967.

———. *Little Mexico.* New York: Jonathan Cape & Harrison Smith, 1932.

Steffens, Lincoln. *The Autobiography of Lincoln Steffens,* vol. 2. New York: Harcourt, Brace & World, 1931.

Tannenbaum, Frank. "The Mexican Art Invasion." *Current Opinion* 76, no. 3 (March 1924) [New York: Current Literature Publishing House].

———. "The Anvil of American Foreign Policy." *Political Science Quarterly* 63, no. 4 (Dec. 1948).

———. *Mexico: The Struggle for Peace and Bread.* New York: Alfred A. Knopf, 1950.

Thomas, Hugh. *The Spanish Civil War.* New York: Harper Colophon Books, 1961.

Tibol, Raquel. *Frida Kahlo: Una vida abierta.* México D.F.: Editorial Oasis, 1983.

Toledano, Vicente Lombardo, and Alejandro Carrillo. "Mexican President Promises Gold Shirt Suppression," *Mexico Labor News.* Press Department of the Workers University of Mexico (Universidad Obrera de México), vol. 1, no. 6, Aug. 20, 1936. Brenner Archives box 208-93.

Toor, Frances. *A Treasury of Mexican Folkways.* New York: Crown Publisher, 1947.

Trilling, Diana. *The Beginning of the Journey: The Marriage of Diana and Lionel Trilling*. New York: Harcourt Brace, 1993.

Trotsky, Leon. "Answers to Questions by Anita Brenner." In *Writings of Leon Trotsky, 1933–1934,* edited by George Breitman and Bev Scott, 142–144. New York: Pathfinder Press, 1972.

Turner, John Kenneth. *México Bárbaro*. México: Costa Amic Editores, S.A., 1995. (Originally published in 1909.)

Unger, Irwin, and Debi Unger. *Twentieth-Century America*. New York: St. Martin's Press, 1990.

Wald, Alan. *The New York Intellectuals: The Rise and Decline of the Anti-Stalinist Left from the Thirties to the Eighties*. Chapel Hill: University of North Carolina Press, 1987.

———. "The *Menorah Journal* Moves Left." Undated manuscript, Herbert Solow Papers box 12. Hoover Institution on War, Revolution, and Peace, Stanford University, Palo Alto, Calif.

———. "Herbert Solow: Portrait of a New York Intellectual." Undated manuscript, Herbert Solow Papers box 1. Hoover Institution on War, Revolution, and Peace, Stanford University, Palo Alto, Calif.

Walsh, Thomas. *Katherine Anne Porter and Mexico: The Illusion of Eden*. Austin: University of Texas Press, 1992.

Weinstein, Allen. *Perjury: The Hiss-Chambers Case*. New York: Alfred A. Knopf, 1978.

Weston, Edward. *The Daybooks of Edward Weston*, Vol. 1. Edited by Nancy Newhall. Rochester, N.Y.: George Eastman House, 1961.

White, Dorothy. "Quietude of Heights Home Thrills Anita Brenner, Youthful Authoress, after Exciting Adventures Afield." *Brooklyn Citizen*, April 3, 1933.

Williams, Adriana. *Covarrubias*. Austin: University of Texas Press, 1994.

Wise, Ruth R. "The New York Jewish Intellectuals." *Commentary*, Nov. 1987.

Wolfe, Bertram D. *Diego Rivera: His Life and Times*. New York: Knopf, 1939.

———. Letter to the Editor. "The Struggle in Catalonia." *The Nation*, June 5, 1937, 657.

———. *Portrait of Mexico*. New York: Covici, Friede, 1937.

———. *A Life in Two Centuries*. New York: Stein & Day, 1981.

Woods, Richard. "Anita Brenner: Cultural Mediator of Mexico." *Studies in Latin American Popular Culture* 9 (1990): 209–222.

Zárate Miguel, Guadalupe. *México y la diáspora judía*. México D.F.: Instituto Nacional de Antropología e Historia, Colección Divulgación, 1986.

Zigrosser, Carl. *Caroline Durieux*. Louisiana State University Press, 1949.

Zurián, Tomás. *Nahuí Olín: Una mujer de los tiempos modernos*. México: Consejo Nacional para la Cultura y las Artes, Instituto Nacional de Bellas Artes, and Museo Estudio Diego Rivera, 1992.

index